Mao's Cultural Army

Charting their training, travels, and performances, this innovative study explores the role of the artists that roamed the Chinese countryside in support of Mao Zedong's communist revolution. DeMare traces the development of Mao's "cultural army" from its genesis in Red Army propaganda teams to its full development as a largely civilian force composed of amateur and professional drama troupes in the early years of the PRC. Drawing from memoirs, artistic handbooks, and rare archival sources, *Mao's Cultural Army* uncovers the arduous and complex process of creating revolutionary dramas that would appeal to China's all-important rural audiences. The Communists strived for a disciplined cultural army to promote party policies, but audiences often shunned modern and didactic shows, and instead clamored for traditional works. DeMare illustrates how drama troupes, caught between the party and their audiences, did their best to resist the ever-growing reach of the PRC state.

BRIAN JAMES DEMARE is an Assistant Professor at the Department of History, Tulane University, were he teaches courses on modern Chinese history.

Cambridge Studies in the History of the People's Republic of China

Series Editors

Jeremy Brown, Jacob Eyferth, Daniel Leese, Michael Schoenhals

Cambridge Studies in the History of the People's Republic of China is a major series of ambitious works in the social, political, and cultural history of socialist China. Aided by a wealth of new sources, recent research pays close attention to regional differences, to perspectives from the social and geographical margins, and to the unintended consequences of Communist Party rule. Books in the series contribute to this historical re-evaluation by presenting the most stimulating and rigorously researched works in the field to a broad audience. The series invites submissions from a variety of disciplines and approaches, based on written, material, or oral sources. Particularly welcome are those works that bridge the 1949 and 1978 divides, and those which seek to understand China in an international or global context.

Mao's Cultural Army

Drama Troupes in China's Rural Revolution

Brian James DeMare

Tulane University

CAMBRIDGE
UNIVERSITY PRESS

CAMBRIDGE
UNIVERSITY PRESS

University Printing House, Cambridge CB2 8BS, United Kingdom

One Liberty Plaza, 20th Floor, New York, NY 10006, USA

477 Williamstown Road, Port Melbourne, VIC 3207, Australia

4843/24, 2nd Floor, Ansari Road, Daryaganj, Delhi - 110002, India

79 Anson Road, #06-04/06, Singapore 079906

Cambridge University Press is part of the University of Cambridge.

It furthers the University's mission by disseminating knowledge in the pursuit of education, learning and research at the highest international levels of excellence.

www.cambridge.org
Information on this title: www.cambridge.org/9781107432222

© Brian James DeMare 2015

First published 2015
First paperback edition 2017

A catalogue record for this publication is available from the British Library

Library of Congress Cataloging in Publication data
DeMare, Brian James.
Mao's cultural army: drama troupes in China's rural revolution / Brian James DeMare, Tulane University.
    pages cm. – (Cambridge studies in the history of the People's Republic of China)
ISBN 978-1-107-07632-7 (Hardback)
1. Theater–China–History–20th century.   2. Amateur theater–China–History–20th century.   3. Theater–Political aspects–China–History–20th century.
4. Theater and society–China.   I. Title.
PN2874.D47 2015
792.0951´0904–dc23   2014042748

ISBN 978-1-107-07632-7 Hardback
ISBN 978-1-107-43222-2 Paperback

Contents

Illustrations

Preface and acknowledgements

Nearly a decade later, I can still recall with the utmost clarity the endless bus rides, freezing cold showers, uncomfortable beds, and bureaucratic red tape. Nothing can quite compare to conducting research in rural China. It was the summer of 2005, and I had joined up with two fellow UCLA graduate students to venture out into the North China countryside. Having spent the past few years in Beijing crafting my dissertation on rural political culture during land reform, I was determined to investigate what had emerged as the most intriguing yet elusive aspect of my research: revolutionary drama in the countryside.

Working in tandem to make the most of our time in the countryside, the three of us dined with local academics, interviewed villagers, and did our best to charm suspicious archivists. The trip was grueling, but to borrow an oft-used phrase from the land reform era, the harvest from our time in the countryside was indeed bountiful. We befriended new colleagues and unearthed surprising finds in sweltering archives. Most vivid are the memories of the many times we were welcomed into the homes of villagers to hear their stories of rural life in Mao's China.

The stories and documents I discovered on that 2005 trip inspired return visits and ultimately this book. Meeting with amateur and professional dramatists, musicians, and actors, I encountered a vibrant cultural scene that was a comfortable mixture of the traditional and the modern. In Ding County, drinking fizzy warm beer and listening to what can only described as an evening roadside jam session, I recognized Yan'an era revolutionary classics. In the Changzhi countryside, I took in an open-air performance by a professional rural drama troupe. The show, which stretched on for well over three hours, was a traditional number featuring scholars and maidens. Yet the troupe also put on modern and didactic works, and in private conversations, older actors even waxed nostalgic for the good old days, when their revolutionary works were often the only shows around. These experiences inspired me to get past scripts and capture the performances of these dramas during the formative stages of Mao's rise to power. It was time to put the spotlight on drama troupes and question their role in the revolution, as well as what their shows meant for the nature of the Communists' great enterprise.

A trip to the countryside inspired this book, but that trip only took place because I was lucky enough to study history with Philip Huang. His belief in the importance of rural culture to the Chinese revolution inspired the direction of my research, and his careful reading of my work pushed me to become a better scholar. Kathryn Bernhardt held up the other half of the sky at UCLA. Her nuanced approach to the issue of gender in Chinese history has profoundly influenced my teaching and research. I also had the great fortune to study with Lynn Hunt, and my determination to investigate rural China from a cultural perspective owes much to her guidance. Fred Notehelfer's infectious joy for studying Japanese history, meanwhile, provided the final essential piece to my education at UCLA.

Professors Huang and Bernhardt trained several generations of talented historians at UCLA, and I am very proud to count myself as a member of their final cohort of students. Four of my UCLA classmates warrant special mention. Thomas Dubois helped me navigate the minefield of early career academia with equal parts wit and wisdom. Zhang Jiayan generously offered his understanding of rural China as he read through this entire manuscript. Byungil Ahn has proven a capable research partner and done much to make my time in the countryside both productive and enjoyable. Norm Apter, whose untimely passing we are still mourning, kept me closely tied to the UCLA program even when I found myself in the farthest reaches of China.

As years of research slowly grew into this manuscript, many gifted scholars have read and commented on my work. Neil Diamant, Yang Kuisong, Julia Strauss, Li Huaiyin, Jacob Eyerth, and Carma Hinton all commented on various conference papers. Zhang Xiaojun provided much inspiration as we chatted over pumpkin cakes and dark beer at Qinghua University. Many other scholars have contributed to this work, and even if they were not aware they were providing help, Marc Matten, Margherita Zanasi, Felix Wemheuer, and Hauke Neddermann were among the many that shaped this project along the way. Matthew Johnson, who has been a friend and colleague for over a dozen years, generously provided his insightful comments into every chapter of this book.

I offer sincere thanks to the scholars at the Chinese Social History Research Center run by Professor Xing Long. Xing Long and his students at Shanxi University, most importantly Ma Weiqiang and Deng Hongqin, were instrumental in helping me access the Shanxi countryside, as well as the province's notoriously bureaucratic archives. Han Yanke, Shen Maqun, Zhang Fuqing, Wei Bao'en, and Han Tiansheng all helped introduce me to a vibrant rural cultural scene. And a most heartfelt thanks goes out to Wang Jinhong, longtime village leader of Longbow Village, where William Hinton researched his study of land reform in rural Shanxi. "Secretary Wang" welcomed me into his home and provided me with contacts, introductions, and so many bowls of noodles that I feared for my life. Wang, referencing his good friend from the West, even called me "the next Hinton." While I suspect I am only one of many to receive this title, I count it among my most treasured accomplishments.

Research and writing were supported by a Fulbright-Hays Doctoral Dissertation Research Award and a National Security Education Program David L. Boren Fellowship. Additional funds were provided by a Peking University Harvard-Yenching Fellowship, a UCLA Center for Chinese Studies Grant, and multiple Foreign Language and Area Studies fellowships. Tulane University has also generously supported my work by providing funds and an indispensable network of colleagues. Deepest thanks to everyone in my department, including George Bernstein, Jana Lipman, Thomas Luongo, Elisabeth McMahon, Linda Pollock, Patrice Downs, Samuel Ramer, Randy Sparks, Karissa Haugeberg, and Donna Denneen. My students have been a great source of inspiration, and special thanks goes to those students who braved their way through this book to offer an undergraduate perspective: Spencer Karr, Jane Hayashi, Travis Tessnow, and Anna Gaca.

Further thanks are due to the teachers and directors at the Inter-University Program based out of Qinghua University, where I spent two years studying Chinese. My classmates and friends from these years remain incredibly dear to my heart. Keefer Douglas, Robert Hoppens, Matt Furchen, Brent Haas, Salena Chow, Jenifer Bubel, Bryan Withall, and John Furman all went through the crucible of IUP with me, honing our language skills with late night cram sessions at the Hidden Tree. Cao Jian, A Jian, Li Ailing, Scott Harold, and Bradley Murg also helped make Beijing special.

Seeing this book published through Cambridge University Press has brought me immense satisfaction. The support of Lucy Rhymer, my editor, proved essential for this first time author. Thanks are also due to Joanna Breeze, Amanda George, Trevor Matthews, and Anne Valentine for their help in moving this book into production. And I would be remiss if I did not express my debts to the editors of the Cambridge Studies in the History of the People's Republic of China, especially Jeremey Brown and Michael Schoenhals, who both read and commented on the manuscript. I am thrilled that my book is the first in this new series and look forward to future publications.

My son Miles came into this world just as I was finishing this book, greatly complicating my life in a most wonderful way and reminding me of the importance of family. This book would not exist without the love and support I received from my wife Nina. Nor would I be the person I am today without my three older siblings. Pamela provided my early music education and the important lesson that feminism is cool. Jeffery served as my role model, for better or worse but mostly better. Tracey never forgot to be a friend as well as a sister.

In closing, I must admit that I was not always the most filial of sons. Confucius would have surely disapproved of my decision to spend so many years on the other side of the globe. But I have always deeply appreciated the affection and wisdom my parents, Paul and Maggie, have given me over the years. This book is dedicated to them.

Abbreviations for archives, serials, and collections

BLZK   *Balujun lao zhanshi koushu shilu* [Oral history records from old Eighth Route Army soldiers]. Zhang Junfeng, ed. Beijing: Zhongyang wenxian chubanshe, 2005.

HBTX   *Hubei wenhua tongxun* [Hubei cultural newsletter]: Hubei: Hubei sheng renmin zhengfu suo wenhua shiye guanli ju.

HBWY   *Hubei wenyi* [Hubei literature and arts]. Wuhan: Hubei sheng wenlian.

HJSQ   *Zhongguo renmin jiefangjun wenyi shiliao xuanbian: hongjun shiqi* [PLA literature and arts historical materials: Red Army era]. 2 vols. Beijing: Jiefangjun chubanshe, 1986.

HPA   Hubei provincial archives (Wuhan).

JCJX   *Jin-Cha-Ji cun jutuan juben xuan* [Selected plays from Jin-Cha-Ji village drama troupes]. Zhang Xuexin, ed. Jin-Cha-Ji wenyi yanjiu hui: 2002.

JZSQ   *Zhongguo renmin jiefangjun wenyi shiliao xuanbian: jiefang zhanzheng shiqi* [PLA literature and arts historical materials: War of Liberation era]. 2 vols. Beijing: Jiefangjun chubanshe, 1989.

LCA   Lucheng County archives (Lucheng, Shanxi).

THFY   *Taihang fengyu: Taihangshan jutuan tuanshi* [The storms of Taihang: troupe history of the Taihang Mountains Drama Troupe]. Zhao Luofang, ed. Taiyuan: Shanxi renmin chubanshe, 2001.

SGWZ   *Shanxi geming genjudi wenyi ziliao* [Literature and arts historical materials from the Shanxi Revolutionary Base Area]. Two vols. Taiyuan: Beiyue wenyi chuban she, 1987.

SPA   Shanxi provincial archive (Taiyuan).

SXWY   Shanxi wenyi [Shanxi literature and arts]. Taiyuan: Shanxi sheng wenlian.

WZCT   *Wenyi gongzuozhe zenyang canjia tugai* [How cultural workers should take part in land reform]. Hunan wenlian chou wei hui bian. Hunan: Xinhua shudian, 1950.

ZWGD   *Zhonghua quanguo wenxue yishu gongzuozhe daibiao dahui wenji* [Collected literature from the All-China Literature and Arts Worker Representative Congress]. Beijing: Xinhua shudian, 1950.

Introduction
Performing Mao's revolution

In the spring of 1947, the Combat Dramatic Society premiered its latest creation, a tragic drama laden with revolutionary concepts closely related to the two all-encompassing campaigns then shaking the Chinese countryside. The first, a military campaign, was the Chinese Civil War, a brutal conflict that pitted soldiers under the direction of the Chinese Communist Party against the forces of its longtime rival the Guomindang. When not performing for war-weary soldiers, the Combat Dramatic Society toured in support of the second campaign, land reform, which promised to tear down and transform rural China through the introduction of class labels, violent class struggle, and the subsequent redistribution of village property. Like most of the cultural performance units then under Communist direction, the Combat Dramatic Society was a motley mixture of urban intellectuals and rural artists brought together to inspire revolutionary action among soldiers and citizens alike. The troubadours of the revolution and the centerpiece of Mao Zedong's "cultural army," drama troupes represented the vanguard of revolutionary culture, yet were often held in suspicion by the military and political leaders whose causes they ceaselessly promoted.

On one particular spring night in 1947, the Combat Dramatic Society staged what would quickly become its most famous creation, a "land reform opera" that the troupe hoped would inspire audiences to dramatic acts of violence against the agents of counter-revolution, be they landlords or Guomindang soldiers. The troupe named its "true life" show *Liu Hulan* after the story's heroine, a young peasant woman who devoted her short life to supporting the Communists and their armed forces, only recently renamed the People's Liberation Army (PLA). In *Liu Hulan*, the titular character's ties to the Communists and her participation in land reform enraged her village landlord, who conspired with enemy soldiers under the notorious "Big Beard" to capture and terrorize Liu, eventually beheading the peasant girl on the village threshing grounds. The Combat Dramatic Society staged this cruel tale of class struggle with the intention of mobilizing soldiers to strike at the enemy,

1

but the audience instead attacked the troupe's own actors. During the scene depicting the execution of Liu Hulan, the dénouement of the show, the audience grew incensed. The result, according to one local gazetteer, was a near-murderous scene:

> During the first performance, many cadres and soldiers were so touched that tears streamed down their faces. Some soldiers were so moved they forgot they were watching a drama and started throwing rocks and firing their guns at [the villainous and evil bandit] "Big Beard."[1]

During future performances of *Liu Hulan*, the Combat Dramatic Society banned live ammunition and required soldiers to sit on their bags instead of on rocks, which could be used as lethal weapons. Furthermore, three squads were to patrol the crowd to maintain order and ensure the safety of actors, lest the audience once again confuse on-stage drama for off-stage revolution.

Five years later, the Liucao Village Drama Troupe similarly took to the stage to bring the revolution to its audience, and once again the lines between reality and performance blurred in unexpected ways. While this drama troupe was staffed by amateur actors and mostly performed in its native Hubei village, the outfit had striking commonalities with the Combat Dramatic Society. Grassroots soldiers in Mao's cultural army, the troupe was a mixture of diverse artists brought on stage to present the perceived truths of the revolution to a crowd that was expected to internalize this vision before bringing rural revolution to fruition. As had been the case with professional PLA troupes, the professed importance of these amateur actors to the revolution lay in sharp contrast to the limited support they received from their leaders. But much had changed. Formed after the successful establishment of the People's Republic of China (PRC), which allowed the Communist Party unfettered access to villages throughout Mao's "New China," amateur troupes were composed of an uneasy alliance of poor peasant activists, rural schoolteachers, and local artists. As amateurs, they often clashed with PRC cultural policies, especially when actors put entertainment and opportunities for profit before the political and economic priorities of the young state.

The competing agendas of amateur actors and the state could thus become touchstones for political conflict, a problem evident in the incident surrounding the Liucao Village Drama Troupe and its original production, *New People*. Created and staged during the height of land reform in Hubei, *New People* offered what might be seen as a refreshing

---

[1] *Shanxi tongzhi di sishi juan: wenhua yishu zhi* [Shanxi General Gazetteer #40: Culture and Art Gazetteer] (Beijing: Zhonghua shuju, 1996), 157.

take on the problem of class division. According to the show's narrative, the arrival of the PLA in Liucao provided an unexpected solution to class conflict. As performed on its village stage, the magnanimous nature of the PLA had transformed the landlords of Liucao into loyal citizens, ready to stand with the peasant masses. Land reform, the drama further explained, could conclude without violent class struggle and the ritualistic humiliation of "class enemies," who were now in fact the "new people" of the show's title. Tellingly, the Liucao Village Drama Troupe entered the historical record as one of many troupes criticized by Hubei's cultural authorities for falling under the sway of landlords and other class enemies, who used their mastery of culture to take over village troupes. Once in charge of cultural production, critics charged, these "class enemies" forced peasants to act out counterrevolutionary scripts, with the goal of using the power of the stage to whitewash their crimes against the masses. For provincial cultural authorities, *New People* was "sheer nonsense,"[2] but the show's rejection of party policy was no laughing matter.

The performances of *Liu Hulan* and *New People* are just two instances of the staging of revolutionary drama in the Chinese countryside, where Mao's revolution took root and grew to fruition.[3] With Mao repeatedly insisting on drama as the most effective way to disseminate policy, instigate political action, and transform the Chinese people, the staging and reception of these works in the countryside offer true insight into the culture of Maoist revolution and state-building. Scholars have long recognized that the success of the Chinese Communists must be in part due to their distinctive approach to culture. Most recently, Elizabeth Perry has argued that Mao and other top leaders' use of symbolic resources ("religion, ritual, rhetoric, dress, drama, art, and so on") allowed mass acceptance of the revolution.[4] While Perry is certainly right to highlight the role of culture in the Chinese revolution, her focus on a handful of top political leaders in a single mining town demonstrates the need to broaden the scale of inquiry and capture the wide range of cultural interactions that occurred across rural China during the course of the

---

[2] "Nongcun jutuan yao xuanchuan Mao Zedong sixiang, jianjue fandui fengjian sixiang" [Rural drama troupes must propagate Mao Zedong ideology, resolutely oppose feudal ideology] HBWY #13 (1952), 4–5.

[3] Recent scholarship has reconfirmed the primacy of the countryside in understanding the rise of the Chinese Communists to power. Odd Westad, for example, has argued that deft and numerous compromises with rural populations gave the party a decisive edge over its rivals. See Odd Westad, *Decisive Encounters: The Chinese Civil War, 1946–1950* (Stanford, CA: Stanford University Press, 2003), 107.

[4] Elizabeth. J. Perry, *Anyuan: Mining China's Revolutionary Tradition* (Berkeley, CA: University of California Press, 2012), 4.

Communist revolution. Any attempt to understand what Maoist culture meant for the revolution and everyday life under Communist rule must fully engage the Chinese countryside, where the vast majority of Chinese citizens lived during the tumultuous twentieth century.

Investigation into the drama troupes and propaganda teams of Mao's cultural army over the long course of the revolution reveals China's rural revolution as a participatory political performance highly informed by the cultural performances staged by Communist directed actors. After the arrival of Communist power, villagers had to actively take part in rural revolution, which meant imbibing and performing Maoist political culture. For most rural Chinese, this was a process that included taking on the identity of "peasant" (*nongmin*), a new concept in the country-side.[5] Less fortunate villagers were forced to accept class identities that would mark them as enemies of the people, most commonly "landlord" (*dizhu*), a role the Communists would force unlucky village households to play for generations. Frank Dikkötter, emphasizing the novelty of the term, has gone as far as to suggest that the idea of China having a "dominant class" of landlords was pure fiction.[6] Dikkötter's claim is part of his recasting of Communist "liberation" as "tragedy," and while this approach may overshadow the real class inequalities that existed in parts of rural China, his rhetorical choices also reveal how the theatricality of China's revolution had real consequences for political participants.

Rural audiences saw powerful examples of new class identities on Communist stages, but they did not passively accept the messages and ideas imbedded in revolutionary dramas – as noted in recent studies of Chinese culture during the revolution, audience reception is difficult to gauge, especially in light of the autonomous power of audiences to reject or interpret cultural productions.[7] But even when rural audiences did not become Maoist true believers, they learned new skills essential for life

---

[5] The term *nongmin* was a Japanese creation based on classical Chinese, where it meant "country folk." For classical examples, see Luo Zhufeng, ed., *Hanyu Da Cidian* [Comprehensive Chinese dictionary] (Shanghai: Hanyu da cidian chubanshe, 1997), 5919. For more on the modern creation of the Chinese peasant, see Myron Cohen, "Cultural and Political Inventions in Modern China: The Case of the Chinese Peasant," *Daedalus* 122, No. 2 (1993).

[6] Frank Dikotter, *The Tragedy of Liberation: A History of the Chinese Revolution, 1945–1957* (New York: Bloomsbury Press, 2013), 70. Dikötter's claim is partly based on the discussion of class labels found in my dissertation. See Brian James DeMare, "Turning Bodies and Turning Minds: Land Reform and Chinese Political Culture, 1946–1952" (doctoral dissertation, University of California, Los Angles, 2007), 152–153.

[7] For example, see Paul Clark, *The Chinese Cultural Revolution: A History* (Cambridge: Cambridge University Press, 2008), 3. Also Barbara Mittler, *A Continuous Revolution: Making Sense of Cultural Revolution Culture* (Cambridge, MA: Harvard University Asia Center, 2013), 12–13.

under Communist rule. For these newly created peasants, performing Maoist political culture was the true meaning of the revolution on an experiential level. Drama troupes served as the mainstay of Mao's cultural army because their staging of the revolution could be re-performed by rural audiences during mass campaigns and in their everyday lives under Communist rule.

This was particularly true during the land reform era of 1945–1952, roughly bookended by the performances of the Combat Dramatic Society and the Liucao Village Drama Troupe. The combination of all-out warfare, radical agrarian revolution, and intensive state-building between 1946 and 1952 enabled the full development of new dramatic organizations and new forms of cultural performance. Mobilized on an ever-greater scale, propaganda teams and drama troupes continually brought land reform operas, charged with a radical political culture built around Maoist rhetoric and ritual, ever deeper into the countryside. The Combat Dramatic Society represented one of the finest examples of the professional revolutionary drama troupe, a highly mobile unit staging powerful shows that drew their power from their "real-life" backgrounds, deft use of gender tropes, and malleable folk forms that could be adapted by troupes throughout the Chinese countryside. The Liucao Village Drama Troupe, meanwhile, demonstrates the full flowering of revolutionary drama made possible by land reform and other state-building campaigns in the early PRC era. In a few short years, the PRC state mobilized tens of thousands of amateur drama troupes throughout rural China, performing in popular local styles while directing land reform and related mass campaigns at the local level. At no other time would Mao's cultural army have such a direct impact on the course of the Communist revolution.

The experiences of these two divergent troupes, however, also suggest the limits of revolutionary drama as staged by professional and amateur performers. As Paul Clark has noted, live performances, unlike film, must rely on distant and thus difficult-to-control performers as intermediaries between producers and viewers, greatly complicating the dissemination of party messages.[8] Adapting to local cultural tastes, meanwhile, was a lengthy and difficult process. The Combat Dramatic Society, for example, only created its signature drama after troupe members spent years searching for the right mixture of traditional culture and revolutionary politics. Even at the height of their fame, these actors struggled for the respect and pay given to their peers working outside

---

[8] Paul Clark, *Chinese Cinema: Culture and Politics since 1949* (Cambridge: Cambridge University Press, 1988), 2.

of the cultural realm. And while performances of *Liu Hulan* evoked passionate responses from audiences, villagers were often equally passionate in rejecting revolutionary works and demanding traditional operas. In an environment where the stage became an accepted voice for party policy and a mirror for village society, controlling cultural performances assumed critical importance.

This was still true after the Communists turned from military conquest to state-building in the 1950s. Traversing the 1949 divide, this study explores the staging of revolutionary drama in the PRC countryside and finds a rich assortment of drama troupes caught between audience expectations and the directives of the young state. With Maoist political culture in continual need of reinforcement, the Communists assigned their cultural army the difficult task of promoting mass campaigns and creating socialist peasants. But drama troupes, now mostly operating outside of the military structures that had informed the early development of Mao's cultural army, could scarcely ignore the fact that rural audiences, free from decades of endemic warfare, were eager to get politics off stage and demanded a return to traditional opera. The resulting and seemingly endless series of interventions by the PRC state into the dramatic realm never overcame audience preference for traditional opera. Despite their usefulness as performers of Maoist political culture, drama troupes were never an easy fit with the Communist Party or the PRC state, and their need to please audiences ensured the PRC dramatic world was a contested realm. Frustration with the inability to control troupes would eventually culminate in the failed attempt by Jiang Qing and like-minded cultural critics to finally and fully tame drama during the Cultural Revolution.[9]

The constant campaigns to control drama troupes serve as important reminders that, while always an unruly force, the importance of these troupes in performing political culture during mass campaigns and in everyday life ensured the continued prominence of Mao's cultural army. The dramatic quality of Maoist revolution, furthermore, had a powerful legacy for the PRC era, ensuring that political life in Mao's China was profoundly theatrical. From the parading of landlords donning dunce caps in land reform, to the public denunciations of "rightists" during the 1950s, and peaking in the highly staged "struggle" sessions (from the Chinese *douzhenghui*, a gathering to denounce class enemies or other hostile elements), political life in Mao's China can be characterized as a unique mode of mass participatory theater. As Barbara Mittler has

---

[9] Even the most paradigmatic Cultural Revolution dramas could not overcome the tensions inherent in the dramatic world. See Clark, *The Chinese Cultural Revolution*, 108.

recently argued for the Cultural Revolution, propaganda art was "not just received and reacted to, but was formed and enacted by its audience."[10] While most identified with mass campaigns during the Cultural Revolution, the performance of politics has outlived Mao. One of the most influential interpretations of the 1989 Tian'anmen Square protests, for example, classified the event as an instance of political street theater.[11] Politically charged acting was an essential facet of life even before the founding of the PRC, and drama troupes paved the way in turning all Chinese citizens into political actors. During the early stages of the revolution, long before film and radio were ubiquitous, drama troupes provided essential models of cultural and political performances.

The analysis of drama troupes during the Chinese revolution requires the mobilization of a diverse set of sources in order to access the daily lives of drama troupe members and recreate their unique mode of revolutionary practice, but these sources present unique challenges to historians. Dramatist memoirs, typically created in the aftermath of the Cultural Revolution, reveal the mundane details of staging revolutionary dramas, even as their authors used discursive strategies to reclaim the mantle of revolutionary culture from Jiang Qing and her radical allies. Contemporary documents issued by the Communist Party and the PRC state explicate official policy, but often overstate the power and reach of the Communist cultural infrastructure. First-hand reports by educated artists and other intellectuals contain a wealth of information concerning the successes and failures of cultural work in the countryside, although this information is often colored by the ulterior motives of authors, particularly when these documents were attempts to lay claim to revolutionary authority.

Contemporary accounts penned by Western observers contain a rare combination of criticism of the Communists and the drive to record details of dramatic performances that often seemed commonplace to Chinese audiences. These outsiders tended to accept the basic assumptions of their Communist hosts, including the inevitability of class struggle in rural society. Cultural handbooks and literary journals bring to light the workings of mass cultural campaigns at the local level, but while they were often forthcoming with the difficulties of rural cultural work, these authors shared their own set of preconceived truths regarding the power of culture and the correctness of the revolution. Provincial and

[10] Mittler, *A Continuous Revolution*, 14.
[11] Joseph Esherick and Jeffery Wasserstrom, "Acting out Democracy: Political Theater in Modern China," *The Journal of Asian Studies*, Vol. 49, No. 4 (November 1990).

county archival sources offer insights into the tensions between the state and the dramatic realm, yet tend to present artists as either loyal cultural workers or deviant hooligans. Even revolutionary drama scripts, subject to revision over time and space as they were performed by successive drama troupes in an ever-diversifying set of local styles, must be used with caution.

When deployed carefully and in tandem, these sources reveal revolutionary drama – which Mao Zedong promoted as the most effective propaganda weapon in the arsenal of the Communists' cultural army – as a decidedly difficult weapon to wield. Communist-directed drama troupes spent decades searching for the correct formula for drawing rural audiences, only finding success after making significant concessions to local cultural traditions. During the early years of revolutionary drama, troupes struggled to provide a meaningful role beyond entertaining party leaders and providing some measure of relaxation and motivation to weary soldiers. And while the Anti-Japanese War is often seen as the golden age of revolutionary drama, it was not until the land reform era that cultural work truly came into its own. Drama troupes staged land reform operas to inculcate audiences in the radical political culture that informed the Civil War, agrarian reform, and early PRC mass campaigns. To be sure, village audiences never forgot their deep preference for traditional opera, but the arrival of land reform gave modern shows a unique relevancy in the countryside. Adapting traditional cultural forms to help draw audiences, actors staged performances using new rhetoric and new ritual, teaching audiences the very political culture that was needed to navigate life under Communist rule. Recent scholarship has highlighted the importance of political culture in the Chinese revolution, and this study further demonstrates that the symbolic power of Maoist language and politically charged behaviors, the core of drama troupe performances, were the defining characteristics of the Chinese revolution.[12]

---

[12] James Gao, for example, has explored how the Communist Party used "cultural weapons" to consolidate the PRC regime in urban areas, arguing that the party excelled at embedding meaningful symbols in ritual performances, especially the political meeting. Daniel Leese has similarly argued for the importance of rhetoric and ritual for the development of the Maoist cult during the Cultural Revolution. Chang-tai Hung, meanwhile, has noted that the "creation of a series of novel political-cultural forms" in the 1950s helped consolidate the PRC regime and inculcate a socialist culture in China. See James. Z. Gao, *The Communist Takeover of Hangzhou: The Transformation of City and Cadre, 1949–1954* (Honolulu: University of Hawaii Press, 2004), 3; Daniel Leese, *Mao Cult: Rhetoric and Ritual in China's Cultural Revolution* (New York: Cambridge University Press, 2011); Chang-tai Hung, *Mao's New World: Political Culture in the Early People's Republic* (Ithaca, NY: Cornell University Press, 2010), 2.

Politics and drama in Mao's revolution

This study situates Mao's cultural army within the context of the long ties between political and cultural performances in China. Reformers and revolutionaries consistently used drama to promote social change and national issues throughout the twentieth century. In this regard, Chinese dramatists and political leaders, as well as historians interested in Chinese drama, accept a direct correlation between dramatic acting and political action. May Fourth iconoclast and pioneering Chinese Marxist Chen Duxiu succinctly summed up the revolutionary implications of drama *vis-à-vis* literature in 1904:

Some are promoting social reform by writing new novels or publishing their own newspapers, but they have no impact on the illiterate. Only the theater, through reform, can excite and change the whole society – the deaf can see it, and the blind can hear it. There is no better vehicle for social reform than the theater.[13]

Qu Qiubai would succeed Chen as the leader of the Communist Party, only to take the blame for the party's subsequent failures and be pushed into cultural work. But in this capacity, Qu firmly established the concept of drama as the preeminent form of Communist propaganda. After helping to found the Communists' first drama academy in 1934, he insisted on sending units to tour villages and the frontlines.[14] By the land reform era, political activists accepted drama as a powerful medium that could not only mobilize audiences for political action, but fundamentally transform the audiences' views as well. Thus, at the outset of Hubei's land reform, one literary journal announced that drama was the primary component of the literature and arts propaganda "weapon" that would enlighten and mobilize the peasantry for the campaigns.[15] It was not just cultural elites positing a firm connection between viewing dramas and personal transformation. One village leader, noting that his wife was fed up with his activism to the point of halting her housework and threatening him with violence, pleaded for a cultural work team to come to his village so that it might "perform shows and help change the thinking of such people."[16]

---

[13] Chen Duxiu, "On Theater," in *Chinese Theories of Theater and Performance from Confucius to the Present*, ed. Faye Chunfang Fei (Ann Arbor, MI: The University of Michigan Press, 1999), 120.

[14] Chen Baichen and Dong Jian, eds., *Zhongguo xiandai xiju shigao: 1899–1949*. [Chinese modern drama draft history: 1899–1949] (Beijing: Zhongguo xiju chubanshe, 2008), 451.

[15] "Yingjie di er ge fanshen nian" [Welcoming the second year of fanshen] HBWY 3.1 (1951), 11.

[16] "Nongmin daibiao tan wenyi" [Peasant representatives discuss literature and arts] HBWY 1.5 (1950), 9.

Historians, following the lead of artists and political activists, have also believed in the power of drama to influence Chinese audiences.[17] While this is particularly true for historians working within the PRC, Western historians have expanded the linkages between theater and politics, arguing that Chinese drama has promoted political and religious messages since at least the Yuan dynasty, with later dynasties practicing censorship while also hoping to influence audiences through drama. This perspective was initially popularized by Colin Mackerras, a pioneer in the academic study of Chinese drama, who argued that drama played a decisive role in the downfall of the imperial system as well as the rise of the Communists to power.[18] More recent studies have confirmed Mackerras's conviction that politicized dramas provided one of the keys to Communist success. Chang-tai Hung stressed how the Communists' mastery of popular culture, including the party's development of new dramatic forms, helped ensure its victory over the Guomindang.[19] Investigating the formation of these new dramatic forms, David Holm similarly argued that during the Civil War:

the drama movement was undoubtedly one of the most powerful propaganda weapons in the Communists' arsenal, and one which gave them a considerable advantage with their rivals when it came to communicating with the civilian peasant population and with their own troops.[20]

Exploring theater in the Cultural Revolution era, Xiaomei Chen suggested that even when far removed from times of war, drama still held immense power over its audiences, shaping personal and national identities.[21]

---

[17] For example, see Deng Bangyu, ed., *Jiefangjun xiju shi* [A history of PLA drama] (Beijing: Zhongguo xiju chubanshe, 2004), 5; Chen Baichen and Dong Jian, eds., *Zhongguo xiandai xiju shigao: 1899–1949*, 449.

[18] Looking at the Qing dynasty, Mackerras emphasized the strong link between politics and the theater; according to Mackerras the politicization of drama, the best way to reach the masses, helped bring about the downfall of the dynasty as well as the imperial model. Turning to the revolutionary era, Mackerras argued that theater was driven ever closer to the masses as activists performed propaganda that was simple and direct, and thus effective. Just as politicized theater had contributed to the downfall of the Qing state, so too does Mackerras suggest that the Communist Party's ability to use theater as a "political weapon" was one factor leading to its victory" over the Guomindang. See Colin Mackerras, "The Drama of the Qing Dynasty," in *Chinese Theater: From its Origins to the Present Day*, ed. Colin Mackerras (Honolulu, University of Hawaii Press, 1983), 114. Colin Mackerras, "Theater and the Masses," in *Chinese Theater: From its Origins to the Present Day*, ed. Colin Mackerras (Honolulu: University of Hawaii Press, 1983), 159.

[19] Chang-tai Hung, *War and Popular Culture: Resistance in Modern China, 1937–1945* (Berkeley, CA: University of California Press, 1994), 271.

[20] David Holm, *Art and Ideology in Revolutionary China* (New York: Oxford University Press, 1991), 319.

[21] Xiaomei Chen, *Acting the Right Part: Political Theater and Popular Drama in Contemporary China* (Honolulu: University of Hawaii Press, 2002), 74.

Staging the revolution: modern Chinese drama

The belief that the performances of Mao's cultural army played a key role in the triumphs of the Communist Party is thus widely accepted, even among scholars whose focus is not explicitly cultural.[22] As of yet, however, historians have not explored why propaganda teams and drama troupes were so important during the Communists' efforts to resist Japanese invasion, their victory in the Civil War, and their attempts at state-building and regime consolidation in the early years of the PRC. Investigations into modern Chinese drama have typically ignored the "crude" forms of drama Mao's cultural army staged for the rural audiences that won his revolution. Instead, scholars focused on Western influenced spoken dramas (*huaju*) and elite forms of traditional opera (*xiqu*), especially Peking opera (*Jingju*), often called China's "national drama" (*guoju*).[23] This general scholastic trend has created a "lacuna" in research concerning Chinese theater. As Mackerras noted in the mid-1990s, the "vast bulk of research carried out so far and published has been about several of China's major cities, especially Beijing, Shanghai, Guangzhou, Chengdu, and Nanjing."[24]

In sync with Mackerras's call for drama produced and performed in the "margins" of China to be moved to center stage, scholars have increasingly investigated the Communist Party's use of dramatic forms during its long, rurally based rise to power after the shattering of the First United Front in 1927. Ellen Judd, for example, provided a rare look into rural performances in the Jiangxi Soviet, finding the development of new hybrid forms of drama and new cultural organizations.[25] These early developments were of great importance for artistic policy in the 1940s,

---

[22] In his wide-ranging account of the Civil War, to cite one example, Odd Westad largely focuses on military and political reasons behind the Communist victory but still notes that the Communists' "local successes were … dependent on their propaganda skills." Westad, *Decisive Encounters*, 10.

[23] Hung has thus explored how Xiong Foxi and other proponents of rural reconstruction hoped to use spoken dramas as a force for change in Ding County. See Hung, *War and Popular Culture*, Chapter 2. More recently, Joshua Goldstein has explained how the "invented tradition" of Peking Opera became a forum for the promotion of views on a proper national culture. Goldstein's study is indicative of mainstream scholarship into Chinese drama, as he investigates China's most advanced artistic forms as produced by elite artists and performed for urban audiences in Beijing and Shanghai. See Josh Goldstein, *Drama Kings: Players and Publics in the Re-creation of Peking Opera, 1870–1937* (Berkeley, CA: University of California Press, 2007).

[24] Colin Mackerras, "What about Those at the Margins?: A Lacuna in Chinese Theatre Research," *Asian Theatre Journal*, Vol. 11, No. 1 (1994), 92.

[25] Ellen. R. Judd, "Revolutionary Drama and Song in the Jiangxi Soviet," *Modern China*, Vol. 9, No. 1 (January, 1983), 125–127.

an era explored by Paul Clark and David Holm. In his examination of the clash between the Yan'an and Shanghai visions of film, Clark emphasized the connections in Yan'an between filmmaking and spoken drama, which was created for and performed by "a narrow, Western-educated intelligentsia."[26] Holm, meanwhile, traced the debates over proper art forms that raged in and around the Yan'an capital. As Holm argues, the emphasis on folk art popular with rural audiences led to the creation of the hybrid *yangge* form, which was then popularized by the means of a well-orchestrated mass campaign.[27]

These studies have opened up the countryside as a realm for the study of drama and shed light on the connections between cultural performance and political mobilization, yet their topics of inquiry remain limited. Holm, for example, has a tight focus on Yan'an, the base of operations for the Communist Party and its cultural organizations. As a result, Holm details the debates over proper cultural forms, but his exploration of the campaign to promote *yangge* is primarily focused on "Luyi," the Lu Xun Academy of Art. The dramatists, actors, and musicians grouped at Luyi played an essential role in the development of *yangge*, while the drama movement they helped oversee helped promote Communist Party policies throughout the base areas. But Luyi artists were essentially a small group of elite intellectuals living and working in the center of Communist power. How exactly were Luyi's unique cultural forms and concepts inculcated throughout the vast Chinese countryside? The Communists' drama movement was designed to be brought to full fruition by a cultural army composed of hundreds of thousands of artists, mostly of the amateur variety. These "marginal" actors, not elite cultural theorists, need to be brought to center stage.

This is especially true in light of the long-standing belief that local drama troupes were an essential propaganda force, in part responsible for both the rise of the Communist Party to power as well as its ability to spur mass mobilization in support of PRC-era policies. With most scholarship directed at the formation of artistic policy and the activities of elite troupes, the actual implementation of artistic policy at the local level, including amateur artists, has yet to be fully investigated.[28] Scholars have noted the thousands of drama troupes the Communists claimed to

---

[26] Clark, *Chinese Cinema*, 6.   [27] Holm, *Art and Ideology in Revolutionary China*.

[28] In her overview of PRC drama, for example, Constantine Tung notes the mass development of village drama troupes, but does not say exactly how these troupes were formed, nor can she say how they functioned as artistic or political units. Constantine Tung, "Introduction: Tradition and Experience of the Drama of the PRC," in *Drama in the People's Republic of China*, Constantine Tung and Colin Mackerras, eds. (Albany, NY: State University of New York Press, 1987), 2.

organize, but it is essential to go beyond broad party declarations and investigate the actual formation and deployment of Mao's cultural army, from elite cultural leaders in Beijing to peasant actors in remote villages.[29]

This study is primarily concerned with dramatic performance as an expression of political culture as opposed to its artistic or aesthetic qualities. Judging these works from an artistic perspective is difficult, for as Perry Link has argued for literature produced under the Communist Party, the quality of these works is intrinsically tied to their ability to influence audiences.[30] But in exploring drama troupe performances, it is still necessary to consider artistic elements. In part, this is because of the simple fact that in order to find an audience, dramatic performances had to be entertaining. Here a comparison to literature is instructive, for while the Communists believed that literature was a means of engineering a better citizen, Link uncovered a variety of "unofficial" uses of literature, most prominently entertainment. Because party directed drama troupes directly competed with traditional opera, staging an entertaining revolutionary drama required a fair amount of talent, especially from local musicians.

An entertaining drama also needed a powerful narrative to draw and hold audience attention, a fact significant in light of scholarship emphasizing the power of narratives to help organize identities and guide political behavior. David Apter and Tony Saich, for example, have explored the importance of narrative and discourse in the rise of Mao Zedong to a position of supreme authority, arguing that the "narrative reconstruction of reality," accomplished through study and self-confession, made true believers out of members of the Yan'an discourse community.[31] Ann Anagnost, meanwhile, has looked at the role of narrative in the revolutionary ritual of "speaking bitterness," or *suku*. In her analysis, *suku* becomes a narrative structure useful for promoting the revolution, providing "a new frame for the reworking of consciousness in which the speaker comes to recognize himself or herself as a victim of an immoral system rather than a bearer of bad fate or personal shortcoming."[32] The process of speaking bitterness made abstract concepts such as class and economic exploitation real through the narrative

---

[29] Colin Mackerras, *The Chinese Theatre in Modern Times: From 1840 to the Present Day* (Amherst, MA: University of Massachusetts Press, 1975), 187.

[30] Perry Link, *The Uses of Literature: Life in the Socialist Chinese Literary System* (Princeton, NJ: Princeton University Press, 2000), 332.

[31] David. E. Apter and Tony Saich, *Revolutionary Discourse in Mao's Republic* (Cambridge, MA: Harvard University Press, 1998), 13.

[32] Ann Anagnost, *National Past-Times: Narrative, Representation, and Power in Modern China* (Durham, NC: Duke University Press, 1997), 29.

and the person of speaker. This performative aspect of *suku* made this ritual particularly potent, as speakers would publically weep while they exposed their sufferings: "Indeed, it was precisely the evocation of sorrow and loss that made these narratives so powerful in eliciting an identification among class peers."[33] And as Xiaomei Chen has argued in her exploration of model works during the Cultural Revolution, narratives, when performed as drama, could reshape identities and consciousness.[34] Using entertaining and powerful narratives to draw audiences and make Maoist political culture both meaningful and understandable, drama troupes provided essential models for political performance in Mao's China.

Revolutionary drama and Maoist political culture

This study investigates the connections between cultural and political performances by directly exploring the role of drama troupes and their revolutionary dramas over the long course of the Chinese revolution. The Chinese revolution is an opportune forum for investigation into the relationship between drama and politics, as propaganda teams and drama troupes staged dramas from the late 1920s to the Cultural Revolution and beyond in the hope of influencing their audiences. But the most critical moment for revolutionary drama lay in mid-century China, during the epic land reform campaigns that engulfed the country from 1946 to 1952. Following the view of historian Philip Huang, this study holds land reform, the start of widespread structural change in the Chinese countryside, to be of much greater "revolutionary" significance than the Communist Party's military rise to power.[35] These six years of land reform dramatically altered the countryside, a change some scholars have understood in economic terms.[36] While these economic shifts were of great importance, a purely economic understanding of land reform obscures the broader significance of these campaigns. For as some Hunan peasants wondered in 1951, if the point of land reform was to help the poor by giving them more land, "why doesn't Chairman Mao

---

[33] Ibid., 32.   [34] Chen, *Acting the Right Part*, 40.

[35] Philip C.C. Huang, "Rural Class Struggle in the Chinese Revolution," *Modern China*, Vol. 21, No. 1 (January , 1995), 105–143.

[36] This emphasis on economic transformation is understandable given the vast quantities of property involved: 43% of land was redistributed, and over ten million landlords expropriated. For an overview of the economic changes wrought by land reform, see John Wong, *Land Reform in the People's Republic of China: Institutional Transformation in Agriculture* (New York: Praeger Publishers, 1973), Chapter 6.

just print some banknotes, buy the land from the landlords, and then give us our share?"[37]

What these Hunan tenants failed to realize was that for their Chairman Mao, the transfer of land was meaningless if not accompanied by radical cultural change. Beyond the redistribution of property, land reform was an attempt to create a new and highly politicized rural culture that characterized life in Mao's "New China." Because mere economic change was not enough, the Communist Party consistently emphasized the primacy of a political and cultural transformation; as one popular saying held, "if you want to turn the body (*fanshen*, a metaphor for economic transformation), you have to turn the mind (*fanxin*), turn from the head and the feet will follow."[38] This emphasis on "turning minds" had dramatic implications for the campaigns. As one 1946 Communist Party report on land reform explained in colloquial terms, "digging out the poor roots to spit out bitter water and settle accounts is the key to turning minds."[39] In other words, viewing class struggle as the key to peasant *fanshen*, the Communist Party insisted that organizing the poor to ritualistically and publicly denounce traditional village leaders was the only way to ensure the cultural transformation of village China.

In recent years, the importance of politics and culture in land reform has at times been downplayed as the Communist Party increasingly finds legitimacy through its economic reforms in the post-revolutionary era.[40] Overall, however, the centralities of culture and politics in the campaigns are readily accepted within the PRC. As land reform leader turned scholar of rural policy, Du Runsheng, has argued: "Land reform was not only a profound economic transformation, but a profound political transformation as well, a prelude to the establishment and construction

---

[37] Xiao Gan, "Cong Li Aijie de yi sheng kan Hunan nongmin de fanshen" [Viewing the fanshen of Hunan peasants from the life of Granny Li], *Renmin ribao* [The People's Daily], March 20, 1951, 2.

[38] *Guizhou shengzhi: wenhua zhi* [Guizhou Provincial Gazetteer: Culture Gazetteer] (Guiyang: Guizhou renmin chubanshe, 1999), 61.

[39] Quoted in Luo Pinghan, *Tudi gaige yundong shi* [A history of the land reform movement] (Fuzhou: Fujian renmin chubanshe, 2005), 45.

[40] Zhou Zhiqiang, *Zhongguo gongchandang yu zhongguo nongye fazhan daolu* [The Chinese Communist Party and the path of Chinese agricultural development] (Beijing: Zhonggongdang shi chubanshe, 2003), 69–84. In this study, published by the Chinese Communist Party History Press, Zhou Zhiqiang posits that the particular form of feudalism that appeared in China stunted economic growth, and once coupled with Western imperialism, blocked modernization. Because of the Guomindang's reliance on "capitalist-feudal power," Zhou Zhiqiang argues that only the Communists could destroy feudalism and thus set the stage for later economic transformation.

of a New China."[41] Land reform was not simply about creating a more equitable division of land. These campaigns recreated the village as a social and political unit more amiable to the new government and its policies. And as Du Runsheng strongly reminded his readers, to one-sidedly judge land reform "by how much land was distributed" can only result in a "neglect of the tremendous achievements in the political and social realms."[42]

Land reform thus was not merely an economic program, but a campaign to inculcate a new political culture. Lynn Hunt, who has explored how political culture provided the logic for political action during the French Revolution, has usefully defined political culture as the "values, expectations, and implicit rules that expressed and shaped collective intentions and actions."[43] Best investigated through symbolic practices such as rhetoric and ritual, a focus on political culture reveals the meaning of rural revolution on a lived and experiential level. Spotlighting these symbolic practices, moreover, helps explain how the Chinese countryside was introduced to the new rhetorical and ritualistic performances that would profoundly mark everyday life in Mao's "New China." Land reform, as the first national rural mass movement, was the crucible of the revolution, the moment when the Communists attempted to fundamentally and permanently transform village life.[44]

In terms of rhetoric, the land reform era saw a new vocabulary enter the countryside, but no neologism was more closely linked to the campaign then *fanshen*. Literally meaning "to turn the body," *fanshen* quickly became a metaphor for socialist-led awakening. As William Hinton explained in his account of land reform in Longbow Village, *fanshen* was a complex concept:

It meant to throw off superstition and study science, to abolish "word blindness" and learn to read, to cease considering women as chattels, and establish equality

---

[41] Du Runsheng, ed., *Zhongguo de tudigaige* [China's land reform] (Beijing: Dangdai zhongguo chubanshe, 1996), 2.

[42] Ibid., 4.

[43] Lynn Hunt, *Politics, Culture, and Class in the French Revolution* (Berkeley, CA: University of California Press, 1984), 10.

[44] Here a comparison with Chang-tai Hung's study of the dissemination of Maoist culture during the 1950s is telling. Hung is certainly correct in his claim that the Communist Party used culture as a propaganda tool to instill "political values" through "a system of indoctrination and of control." Yet as he notes in his conclusion, his study is a collection of investigations into selected topics in a few localities, "mainly Beijing and key cities such as Shanghai." Thus, while Hung's discussions on the symbolic power of Tiananmen Square, for example, are enlightening, relatively few peasants ever had to the chance to visit Beijing. Hung, *Mao's New World*, 6, 267.

between the sexes, to do away with appointed village magistrates and replace them with elected councils. It meant to enter a new world.[45]

Long before Hinton introduced this concept to Western audiences, *fanshen* was synonymous with the land reform process. But it was far from the only neologism introduced into the countryside during the campaigns. Aside from the previously mentioned "peasant" and "landlord," other new terms such as class (*jieji*) and "struggle" (*douzheng*) were needed for the campaign to function. Older concepts such as bitterness (*ku*), revenge (*baochou*), local despot (*eba*), and settling accounts (*qingsuan* or *suanzhang*) were also re-purposed during the campaigns. Villagers, now classed as "peasants," had to master these neologisms, not just for land reform, but for everyday life under Communist rule as well.

Drama was not the only transmitter of rhetoric that marked the new political culture that took over rural China during the land reform era. Mao's cultural army had many weapons. One of the most innovative tools for spreading Communist rhetoric at the local level, for example, was the blackboard-news (*heibanbao*), a new phenomenon in the country-side, where literacy rates remained low.[46] Cheap and easy to set up, the blackboard-news was an incredibly cost-effective propaganda tool. The public nature of this medium, meanwhile, allowed literate villagers to explain the content of the blackboard-news to their fellow villagers. The blackboard-news thus served as the focal point for information con-cerning current events that the Communist Party wished to disseminate within any given village.[47]

Cultural worker Lin Yinpin's 1950 handbook *How to Run the Village Blackboard-News* provides a number of articles that had appeared on a Shandong village blackboard-news, including this piece criticizing Qian Xiuying. Far from a generalized attack on sloth, the article, written in the rhyming *kuaiban* "wooden clapper" style, is both personal and vindictive:

> Let's not beat around the bush,
> this village has a lazy wife.
> Her name is Xiuying,

[45] William Hinton, *Fanshen: A Documentary of Revolution in a Chinese Village* (Berkeley, CA: University of California Press, 1997), vii.

[46] Despite the promotion of winter schools during land reform, literacy rates in rural China were low and remained so after the 1950 decision by the Ministry of Education that literacy classes should await the end of land reform in any given village, so as to not distract peasants from the all-important campaigns. Glen Peterson, "State Literacy Ideologies and the Transformation of Rural China," *Australian Journal of Chinese Affairs*, No. 32 (July 1994), 104.

[47] Lin Yinpin, ed., *Zenyang banhao nongcun heibanbao* [How to run the village blackboard-news] (Jinan: Xinhua shudian Shandong zong fendian, 1950), 3–4.

her natal family's surname is Qian, her husband's surname is Huang.
This year Xiuying is twenty years old,
she eats well but does not work.
Her in-laws and husband all despise her,
they all say she is rubbish.
But she still does not understand,
and continues to eat and drink.
Even though she is a hooligan,
it seems she feels no shame.
If she does not change her ways,
Her reputation will spread to other villages.[48]

While this attack was introduced as an example of what not to do, the article demonstrates the ability of the blackboard-news to criticize and shame villagers, as well as its ability to use powerful rhetoric, here seen in the casting of Qian Xiuying as a "hooligan," to further Communist Party interests. But while there were benefits to spreading rhetoric through the blackboard-news, there were also significant problems with this medium, especially in its reliance on literate members of the community to read the text to their neighbors. As cultural leaders were well aware, drama provided the ideal medium to teach rhetoric to villagers. Audiences flocked to shows for entertainment and were introduced to new terms through politically charged narrative performances that gave these neologisms real meaning. In the case of *Liu Hulan*, to cite one example, audiences not only learned what a "landlord" was, but they were also given an emotionally charged example of an evil and cruel landlord worthy of hatred.

Turning to ritual, there were a number of rituals that villagers had to participate in to bring the land reform process to completion. Anthropologist Clifford Geertz has noted how religious, artistic, and political rituals can all be usefully conceptualized as cultural performances that intend to provide a transformative experience. As Geertz argued in "Religion as a Cultural System": "In a ritual, the world as lived and the world as imagined, fused under the agency of a single set of symbolic forms, turn out to be the same world, producing that idiosyncratic transformation in one's sense of reality."[49] This transformation of reality closely corresponds with the Communist Party's own understanding of the unique rituals of land reform, which were to play a pivotal role in the total and irrevocable transformation of village society. No ritual, however, proved more critical to the campaigns than the "struggle" meeting.

---

[48] Ibid., 31–32.
[49] Clifford Geertz, "Religion as a Cultural Symbol," in *The Interpretation of Cultures* (New York: Basic Books, 1973), 112.

During "struggle" meetings, newly labeled peasants publicly and ritualistically humiliated newly labeled class enemies. The insistence on the use of "struggle" in land reform was first and foremost based on the belief that confrontational struggle, by allowing the public venting of past crimes and humiliations, would lead to class hatred and thus class consciousness. The Communists also saw class struggle as the only truly effective mechanism for altering power relations landlord class that would never relinquish its power unless faced with a fierce class "struggle."

The model for the "struggle" meeting came from Mao Zedong's highly influential "Report on an Investigation of the Peasant Movement in Hunan," where he famously postulated on the certainty of an eventual hurricane-like rising of the peasantry. Mao carefully described how organized groups of peasants ritualistically and publicly humiliated village elites with methods that would eventually be recognized as typical elements of "struggle" meetings. During "major demonstrations" (*da shiwei*), for example, peasants rallied together and marched to the house of a landlord or local tyrant, slaughtering the household's pigs and consuming their grain as well. Another highly ritualistic political attack was to forcibly parade a class enemy wearing a dunce cap (*gao maozi*) through the village for further ridicule. Mao, noting that "this sort of thing is very common," outlined the proper method of ritualized humiliation and its expected results:

A tall paper-hat is stuck on the head of one of the local tyrants or evil gentry, bearing the words "Local tyrant so-and-so" or "So-and-so of the evil gentry." He is led by a rope and escorted with big crowds in front and behind. Sometimes brass gongs are beaten and flags waved to attract people's attention. This form of punishment more than any other makes the local tyrants and evil gentry tremble. Anyone who has once been crowned with a tall paper-hat loses face altogether and can never again hold up his head.[50]

As Mao emphasized in his "Report," ritualistic and public humiliation coupled with economic expropriation were the most effective methods of striking against class enemies.

By the mid-1940s, the party had a template for the "struggle" ritual that would define rural revolution, but for newly classed peasants, participating in a "struggle" meeting was a new and difficult experience. This was a public ritual that demanded the poorest members of the community to take to the stage and denounce their wealthiest neighbors for numerous and specific acts of class exploitation. Taking part in a

[50] Mao Zedong, *Selected Works of Mao Zedong, Volume I* (Beijing: Foreign Languages Press, 1965), 37.

"struggle" meeting was a public and theatrical performance, using a script filled with unfamiliar terms and concepts. Beyond the rhetorical challenge, participants also had to use physical actions, often including violence, to humiliate and punish their "struggle objects." The difficulties of performing the confrontational and theatrical political culture of rural revolution are clear in Hinton's description of a failed "struggle" meeting in Longbow. As activists rain down blows on an ousted village head, the audience "waited fascinated, as if watching a play. They did not realize that in order for the plot to unfold, they themselves had to mount the stage and speak out what was on their minds."[51] Just as narrative based performances gave meaning to new rhetoric, so too did drama make the rituals of land reform understandable to village audiences. The visual nature of the dramatic medium made drama the perfect teacher of violent forms of land reform "struggle." At a time when film was still extremely rare in the countryside, land reform rituals were primarily visually represented through the dramatic arts.[52] Even after the establishment of the PRC state, the Communists continued to push cultural performance as the most effective means of creating proper socialist peasants. The centrality of drama for rural entertainment, in conjunction with the strong connective tissues binding cultural and political performances, would ensure the continued importance of drama troupe performance long after the completion of land reform.

Overview of the study

Starting from impromptu variety shows hosted by Red Army officers for their soldiers in the late 1920s, this study follows the long effort by Communist cultural leaders to create and stage revolutionary dramas, the primary weapons for the party's cultural army. Chapter 1 explores the era of "Red Drama," when the Communist Party's first cohort of cultural workers experimented with cultural performance as propaganda. Drawing on artist memoirs, this chapter reveals the sharp juxtaposition between Mao Zedong's insistence on the importance of dramatic

---

[51] Hinton, *Fanshen*, 114.

[52] In his study of Communist propaganda, Franklin Houn noted that the Communists began to use film to spread ideas as early as 1938. During land reform, films such as *The Northern Shanxi Shepherd*, *The Cheerful Peasant Family*, and a production of the land reform opera *The White-Haired Girl* were deployed to indoctrinate peasants. As Houn admits, the impact of these films was limited by the ability of the Communist Party to get the movies to the villages; in 1950, there were only 100 mobile projection units in China. Franklin. W. Houn, *To Change A Nation: Propaganda and Indoctrination in Communist China* (New York: Crowell-Collier Publishing Co., 1961), 199–201.

performance and the actual experiences of cultural workers, who were mostly uneducated children led by intellectuals pushed "down" into cultural work. As explored in Chapter 1, the Communists' nascent cultural army focused on performing for Red Army soldiers defending the base areas, but at this early stage revolutionary drama was little more than an ineffective weapon of war. Yet the Communist Party continued to place great faith in the power of drama, channeling resources and personnel to drama troupes and propaganda teams even as the Jiangxi Soviet collapsed and the Red Armies undertook the costly Long March. Once sanctioned by Mao, dramatic performance became an essential element of Chinese Communism. For feuding Communist leaders, patronage of "Red Drama" was part of their own performances as revolutionaries.

Chapter 2 turns to the era of Japanese invasion, an important formative phase for Chinese revolutionary drama. Moving beyond the study of elite intellectuals working in Yan'an, the Communists' wartime capital, this chapter investigates the deployment of propaganda teams and drama troupes throughout the North China countryside. Of particular interest is the Taihang Mountains Drama Troupe, active in what eventually grew into the Jin-Ji-Lu-Yu[53] Border Region. Ignored in studies of revolutionary drama as well as the larger historiography of the revolution because of its "marginal" position far from Yan'an, this Taihang troupe toured extensively, established its own training school, and created its own branch troupes. Despite significant gains during this era, the spread of revolutionary drama was severely limited by wartime considerations. In particular, the Communists' cultural army of amateur drama troupes, often said to provide an invaluable propaganda function in the war against Japan, is shown to be of little value, with troupes distributed unevenly and performing erratically.

Not until the launch of all-out land reform during the Civil War did the Communist Party finally find the winning formula for linking cultural and political performances by bringing drama into the actual process of rural revolution. With propaganda teams attached to military units and compliance from professional drama troupes in base areas, the Communist Party fielded a cultural army capable of promoting land reform policies and mobilizing soldiers to fight enemy forces. This era is covered in Chapter 3, which considers revolutionary drama during the Civil War and the first half of the Communists' lengthy implementation of land reform. As detailed in this chapter, PLA propaganda teams and drama

---

[53] Shanxi-Hebei-Shandong-Henan.

troupes played key roles in civil war, land reform, and the ensuing urban takeover as the war came to a close. Troupes supported the war effort by engaging in political work and motivating soldiers, but their most important assignment was teaching Maoist performance to the massive numbers of enemy soldiers captured by the PLA during the conflict. In land reform, drama troupes staged shows to inspire class hatred and spread the political culture needed to complete the campaigns, but actors also served on land reform work teams, using their highly valued political skills to oversee these complex and violent campaigns. During the urban takeover, finally, cultural workers brought land reform operas to new audiences. Urban crowds, anxious to learn about the Communists, flocked to these shows in huge numbers. Audiences, however, were often hostile to newly arrived cultural workers, and some rural artists found difficulty handling the culture clash that urban work represented.

When cultural workers in the late 1940s performed to mobilize soldiers for war and peasants for land reform, they did so with a single set of shows. The "land reform operas" produced during this era were protean creations, able to generate anger and hatred against enemy soldiers and class enemies alike. The power of these shows was largely due to the ability of party cultural workers to master the hybrid form of cultural performance called *geju*. This form of drama, best translated as "new folk opera," was a mixture of various folk songs, local operatic traditions, and Western drama. Chapter 4 offers close readings of the three most important "land reform operas" of the era: *The White-Haired Girl* (Bai mao nü), *Liu Hulan*, and *Red Leaf River* (Chi ye he). In some regards, the term "land reform opera" is a misnomer, as some of these operas do not directly discuss land reform, but all share a common desire to use the dramatic form to push audiences towards specific goals while spreading the rhetoric and ritual that was to characterize life under Communist rule. All of these works, furthermore, insisted on a "realism" firmly based in the Maoist conception of village society. This chapter's focus on creation is balanced by an exploration of the problems faced by one professional drama troupe in its attempt to find a receptive audience for *Red Leaf River* and other modern shows. As revealed in archival reports, despite the great effort by party dramatists to create dramas with mass appeal, only government intervention could ensure that modern shows had a chance of competing with traditional operas for demanding and sophisticated rural audiences.

Investigating the establishment of the PRC as a break with past efforts to stage revolutionary drama while emphasizing continuities on both side of the 1949 divide, Chapter 5 traces the Communists' attempt to establish a new cultural order after their victory in the Civil War.

This investigation starts with analysis of the first All-China Literature and Arts Worker Representative Congress, held in Beijing during the summer of 1949.[54] During this event of great discursive significance, cultural leaders deployed a divisive rhetorical style that privileged their revolutionary experience but only served to complicate future mass work. This chapter then considers the issues facing regional cultural workers as they headed out to the countryside as newly created agents of the PRC state. The world of amateur dramatists and actors, finally, is examined to better understand how state culture was to be staged for village audiences. Although the newly established PRC state aimed for an integrated and directed cultural network to serve its propaganda needs, this chapter highlights the contradictions and complications that marked the emerging cultural order. These contradictions were many, from confusing directives over the depiction of "struggle" in creative works to the problem of funding rural dramatic production. No contradiction, however, would prove more troubling than the essential divide between elite cultural workers and village artists.

The deployment of revolutionary drama by Mao's cultural army reached its zenith as the new PRC state conducted land reform and other mass campaigns to solidify the new regime in the early 1950s. Performances of rural revolution reached new highs during the Civil War era, but the persuasive power of land reform opera was restricted by the number of trained actors and musicians available for mobilization by the Communist Party. Such limitations largely fell by the wayside with the establishment of the PRC. After the successful conclusion of the Civil War, the PLA reduced its commitment to dramatic production, and while military propaganda teams continued to perform for soldiers, in the countryside they were quickly overshadowed by the emergence of newly created professional troupes and a vast network of amateur village troupes. Thus, during the second half of the land reform campaigns, the Communists' cultural army largely relied on civilian drama troupes to spearhead propaganda efforts. Chapter 6 traces this shift by focusing on the province of Hubei, where the Communists organized civilian cultural work teams to promote land reform and other party programs. But because this civilian cultural army was insufficient for the vast Hubei countryside, the Communists also assigned work teams the task of creating amateur drama troupes at the village level. This necessitated deep collaboration with local artists and newly emerging local activists, but as explored in Chapter 6, the local focus created new problems for cultural

---

[54] At the time, the city was still called Beiping.

leaders. Most notably, the Communist Party's decision to rely on amateur performers gave considerable agency to local actors, whose personal career goals were often at odds with the political dictates of the state.

Chapter 7 concludes this study by exploring the role of Shanxi's professional drama troupes in the early PRC era. Having completed land reform during the height of the Civil War, the Shanxi countryside did not see a sustained drive to develop amateur troupes, as had been the case in Hubei. Without a campaign to mobilize amateurs in large numbers, Shanxi rural audiences largely relied on traveling private drama troupes for their entertainment. As would eventually be the case for all professional troupes, professional artists in Shanxi found themselves vexed by opposing forces. On one hand, with decades of warfare finally over, audiences were keen to get politics off stage and called for a return to traditional opera. But the state, insistent on using dramatic performance to fully inculcate Maoist political culture in the countryside, increasingly pushed Shanxi's professional troupes to stage modern and didactic works. As explained in Chapter 7, while the new state was able to successfully influence professional drama troupes through repeated "rectification" campaigns, it was helpless when facing the autonomous power of audience preference for traditional operas, resulting in a confused dramatic realm that would vex cultural leaders throughout the revolutionary era.

1 The revolution will be dramatized
Red Drama troupes

In the late 1920s, Wang Jichu, a young intellectual from Henan's Shangcheng County, decided to start his own drama troupe. While he later gained a reputation as a fiery revolutionary dramatist, Wang's new troupe was a traditional *xibanzi* opera outfit, performing for entertainment and profit. A progressive with a deep passion for Peking opera, Wang eschewed the usual all-male troupe and staffed his troupe with young female actors and male musicians, making him part of a national theatrical elite experimenting with China's most prestigious operatic form.[1] Despite his best efforts to train and promote his players, the troupe failed to turn a profit. Much to the displeasure of his gentry family, Wang sold off his landholdings to support his interests in the arts. When the December 1929 Shangcheng Uprising unexpectedly brought his hometown under Communist rule as part of the emerging E-Yu-Wan[2] Base Area, however, Wang Jichu's fortunes took a dramatic turn.

The Communists initially locked up Wang as a landlord, only to free him and welcome the young troupe leader into world of "Red Drama."[3] Once released Wang dedicated his talents to promoting the Communist cause, giving his troupe the properly revolutionary name of the Red Sun Drama Troupe and even rechristening his female actors with names containing a character meaning red (*chi*). Now a "party run drama troupe" (*dang ban jutuan*), Wang's players performed for Red Army forces under Zhang Guotao, a powerful Communist leader. While the troupe's rich assortment of musical instruments and talented Peking opera performers revealed its traditional *xibanzi* background, the Red Sun Drama Troupe now functioned as a Red Army propaganda team.[4] A gifted composer, Wang Jichu is mostly remembered for his song

---

[1] Goldstein, *Drama Kings*. See Chapter 7 for a discussion of issues that emerged as female actors were brought onto Peking opera stages.

[2] Hubei-Henan-Anhui.

[3] Hua Zhuang, "Bayue guihua biandi kai de zuozhe Wang Jichu" [Author of August Osmanthus Flowers Blooming Everywhere Wang Jichu] HJSQ (1984), 345–347.

[4] Wu Shushen, "Hongri jutuan" [Red Sun Drama Troupe] HJSQ (ca. 1980s), 336–338.

"August Osmanthus Flowers Blooming Everywhere" (Bayue guihua biandi kai). As the E-Yu-Wan Base Area collapsed in 1932, the Red Sun Drama Troupe accompanied its Red Army patrons into Sichuan, and while Wang Jichu did not survive the journey, his song did, eventually becoming a popular ditty in the Sichuan countryside.[5]

The experiences of Wang Jichu and his Red Sun Drama Troupe attest to the essentially military nature of early Communist Party revolutionary drama, typically called "Red Drama" (hongse xiju). Wang Jichu started out as an idealistic dramatist, but he died on a forced march alongside his Red Army comrades. Because early Communist propaganda teams and drama troupes operated under difficult wartime conditions and left little paper trail, save a handful of glowing reports from base area newspapers, understanding the dynamics of Red Drama presents a challenge for historians. And in anticipation of the "national forms" (minzu xingshi) debates of the Yan'an era, most studies of Red Drama have tended to focus on the development of artistic forms in the Jiangxi base areas.[6] This chapter draws on dramatist memoirs to delve into Red Army drama troupes and propaganda teams in order to investigate the cultural army's rank and file in the first Communist base areas and on the subsequent Long March to the far Northwest.

These memoirs cannot be used uncritically. Red Drama veterans, writing in the aftermath of the Cultural Revolution, attempted to reclaim the mantle of revolutionary drama from Jiang Qing and her "model works." Publishing in the PRC, furthermore, meant their accounts never dared to directly criticize or even question the Communist Party. Memoir writers constantly praised patrons, emphasized hardships, and insisted on having always privileged local cultural forms. The most common point of agreement in these accounts – that cultural work was universally successful in mobilizing the masses – is also the greatest sign of caution in seeking to understand the connections between dramatic and political performances. But given the wealth of information contained in memoirs concerning daily life inside early drama troupes, this essential resource cannot be ignored. Luckily, dozens of dramatists

---

[5] Liu Ruilong, "Hong si fangmian jun wenyi gongzuo luetan" [A brief discussion Red Fourth Front Army literature and arts work] HJSQ (ca. 1980s), 355.

[6] Ellen Judd, one of the few scholars to examine Red Drama, thus examined this era as a time of experimentation that served as a prelude to the Yan'an era. As Judd notes, this era created a legacy for the Yan'an era through its "hierarchical structure of literary and artistic organizations with an urban and professional centre and a wide network of amateur groups." Judd argues that the failure of this center to adapt to the countryside led to the Yan'an creation debates. Judd, "Revolutionary Drama and Song in the Jiangxi Soviet," 155.

and actors penned their experiences, providing a multiplicity of perspectives on this foundational era of revolutionary drama. Furthermore, the rhetorical choices made by memoirists are often quite revealing. For example, Red Drama veterans disagree on the name of one important Long March drama troupe. While the troupe was technically called the Forward Drama Troupe, many former members deny this name in their memoirs, choosing instead to anachronistically call the troupe the Worker-Peasant Dramatic Society. As discussed in this chapter, by attempting to elide the true name of the troupe, these artists have actually revealed their embarrassing ties to Zhang Guotao, a "traitorous" Communist leader.

This chapter first traces the creation of Red Army propaganda teams and the establishment of drama troupes and cultural education centers in the Jiangxi Soviet, an era that saw a flood of dramatic creation with over 150 works produced, mostly *huaju* spoken dramas popular with intellectuals.[7] The second half of this chapter investigates the experiences of three drama troupes as they fled their respective base areas and made a circuitous journey to the far Northwest during the Long March. The centrality of military mobilization in the era of Red Drama, best seen in Long March "agitation stations," underlines the fact that in its early days, drama was little more than a weapon of war. Red Drama owed its growth and development to the military needs of the Red Army, yet the military nature of Red Drama was ultimately limiting. As one early dramatist noted, Red Drama existed not for entertainment or art, but to serve the dictates of base area political and mass work needs, which meant above all else military survival in the face of a series of "encirclement campaigns" launched by the Guomindang.[8] Even as the revolution seemed to be in its death throes, Mao and the Communist Party continued to believe in the power of drama. For Red Army leaders, cultural patronage was part of their performances as revolutionary leaders, and despite a reputation for factional infighting, Red Army leaders displayed striking continuity in cultural practice.[9]

---

[7] Deng Bangyu, ed., *Jiefangjun xiju shi*, 58.

[8] Zhao Pinsan, "Guanyu zhongyang geming genjudi huaju gongzuo de huiyi" [Regarding spoken drama work in the Central Revolutionary Base Area] HJSQ (1957), 39.

[9] Elizabeth Perry has already noted the importance of cultural patronage for top Communist leaders. Perry is primarily concerned with how these leaders crafted ties to the historically important city of Anyuan to bolster their political authority. My usage of "cultural patronage" emphasizes the financial and other forms of support that tied Communist leaders to their respective drama troupes. Just as had been the case with Anyuan, cultural patronage of drama troupes offered a way to raise the profile of party leaders. See Perry, *Anyuan*, 11–13.

The first stage: dramatic performances
in the Jiangxi Soviet

Shortly after the initial formation of the Red Army during the Nanchang Uprising of 1927, talented individuals were already staging dramas for soldiers. As the newly founded and freshly defeated Red Army marched towards Guangdong, several officers staged an impromptu performance of *Old Grandmother Recites the Diamond Sutra* (Lao zumu nian jingang jing). This performance of a *huaju* spoken drama to motivate soldiers certainly had precedent in the Northern Expedition.[10] But thanks to Mao Zedong's insistence that the Communist Party maintain firm ideological control over its armed forces, drama would become a hallmark of the Red Army as well as its eventual successors, the Eighth Route Army and the People's Liberation Army; no revolutionary army was complete, and no revolutionary leader was legitimate, without a drama troupe.

Mao first stressed the importance of cultural performance during the October 1927 "Sanwan Reorganization."[11] This reorganization, which aimed at increasing party control over the Red Army, represented the first step in the establishment of revolutionary drama troupes as the bulwark of Mao's emerging cultural army. After the Sanwan Reorganization, each Red Army company organized a party branch, which in turn organized an Officers and Soldiers Committee to lead cultural entertainment and recreational activities.[12] Even at this early date, female performance proved a popular component of Red Drama performances. At the very first evening celebration (*wanhui*) held in the Jinggangshan Base Area, a female cadre named Tong Luo performed a Peking opera number for Red Army soldiers.[13] Yet Tong Luo was a rare figure: the Communists' revolutionary enterprise was a decidedly male undertaking, and early propaganda teams largely lacked female members.

These propaganda teams were first organized in January 1928, when Luo Ronghuan divided his soldiers into "propaganda teams" (*xuanchuan dui*) to carry out mass work in the countryside. Luo's temporary teams only pasted Communist slogans and delivered speeches, but the "propaganda team"

---

[10] If not much earlier: in terms of a direct link between drama and political mobilization, Colin Mackerras has suggested that during the Taiping Rebellion, Hong Xiuquan's armies, seemingly anticipating Red Army practice, mobilized drama troupes to entertain soldiers and villagers. Colin Mackerras, "Theater and the Taipings," *Modern China*, Vol. 3, No. 4 (October, 1976), 484.

[11] The name comes from the location of the 1927 meeting that produced the reorganization, Sanwan Village in Jiangxi Province, Yongxin County.

[12] Deng Bangyu, ed., *Jiefangjun xiju shi*, 28–29.

[13] Zou Gengsheng, "Hongjun wenyi de chumeng" [Sprouts of Red Army literature and arts] HJSQ (ca. 1980s), 36.

would prove a permanent part of Red Army organization. The team system was formalized by mid-1928, with orders for propaganda teams at the army, division, and regiment levels as well as "propaganda units" (*xuanchuan zu*) at the battalion and company levels. Exempted from military service, propagandists were expected to focus on their craft, especially by improving performances through the addition of music and costumed dramas. In theory, dramatic performance was now a staple of the Red Army's political work, although at this early stage teams used simple dramatic forms, especially the new "living newspaper drama" (*huobaoju*). These shows were essentially lectures that combined elements of dance, song, or impromptu acting in the Western dramatic style. Built around simple narratives, early *huobaoju* such as *No Road for the Despotic Gentry* (Hao shen mei lu) and *Beat the Local Tyrant* (Da tuhao) represented early attempts at rhetorically charged drama.[14]

Despite finding some success with these early experimental works, the forced departure from the Jinggangshan Base Area in January 1929 and the exigencies of war devastated Red Army propaganda teams. During the December 1929 Gutian Conference, Mao Zedong characterized Red Army propagandists as "captured soldiers, cooks and grooms, opium users, those disarmed and made propagandists because they were suspected of desertion, those that failed in their jobs as clerks and were sent to propaganda teams, and those that were crippled and not wanted by other working bodies."[15] Mao lambasted the work done by this sorry lot, which mainly consisted of painting slogans on walls and handing out leaflets. Most troubling for Mao, these teams had yet to stage any costumed propaganda (*huazhuang xuanchuan*). As Mao now demanded, propaganda teams were to be attached to Red Army detachments, bringing cultural work to ever-smaller military units in order to educate soldiers and peasants.[16] And while Mao envisioned his cultural army deploying a wide variety of propaganda forms, he singled out drama, "the most specific and effective form of propaganda," as the most important weapon in a propaganda team's arsenal.[17]

As evidenced by Mao Zedong's harsh criticism of his cultural army, there was a clear contradiction between the oft-stated importance of

---

[14] Deng Bangyu, ed., *Jiefangjun xiju shi*, 29–30.

[15] Mao Zedong, "Hongjun xuanchuan gongzuo wenti" [Red Army propaganda work problems] HJSQ (1929), 10.

[16] "Resolutions from the Gutian Conference" further dictated that each propaganda team would have one chair, one vice-chair, one porter, two non-combatants, and sixteen regular members; each unit would be under its respective political commissar, while elite army-level teams would be directly under the Political Department's Propaganda Section. Deng Bangyu, ed., *Jiefangjun xiju shi*, 38.

[17] Mao Zedong, "Hongjun xuanchuan gongzuo wenti," 7.

Figure 1 Li Bozhao, aged eighteen in Moscow

propaganda and the quality of actual propagandists. Because of the existential threat of war, the able bodied and capable were needed as soldiers or leaders in the military and political realms. While never explicitly stated as policy, the Communist Party solved this staffing problem by relying on female cadres to take leading roles in propaganda teams, drama troupes, and cultural education centers. As one woman would later explain, female cadres "did propaganda because it was light work."[18] While there were many important female dramatists during the Jiangxi Soviet era, the two most important figures were Li Bozhao and Wei Gongzhi. Of the two, Li was the more natural choice to take to the stage, having studied the theater in Moscow. But Li and Zhao were intelligent, talented, and conveniently married to leading Communist figures, making them obvious leaders in the world of Red Drama.[19]

Both women would have long careers working in the Communists' cultural realm. Li Bozhao would play a leading role in a string of seminal Jiangxi Soviet cultural units, culminating in the Worker-Peasant Dramatic Society, the most important drama troupe in the Jiangxi Soviet. While most of its members did not survive the final Guomindang encirclement campaign, Li Bozhao would find herself at the head of a new drama troupe on the Long March. Wei Gongzhi helped launch Red Drama with the Red Army Academy Social Club, and would similarly join the Long March. After arriving in Northwest China, she led the prestigious People's Drama Troupe, which regularly performed for top Communist Party leaders. Despite falling under political suspicion, both women had successful careers as dramatists, yet most of their fellow drama troupe comrades met unfortunate fates. In this regard, the Red Sun Drama Troupe leader Wang Jichu, killed during a forced march fleeing a collapsing base area, is a far more representative figure.

The Red Army Academy Social Club

Mao Zedong's imagined cultural army would need talented individuals. Thus, in and around the Soviet capital in Ruijin, educational centers

---

[18] Helen Praeger Young, *Choosing Revolution: Chinese Women Soldiers on the Long March* (Chicago and Urbana, IL: University of Illinois Press, 2007), 35.

[19] Li, a Sichuan native, had begun acting in her progressive middle school, where she took to Marxism before eventually joining the Communist Youth League and traveling to Moscow. In Moscow, she studied politics and drama at Sun Yat-sen University, providing her with a highly prized revolutionary education. Hailing from Henan, Wei Gongzhi's path to the stage was decidedly circuitous, as she had actually been trained in military affairs at the Wuhan branch of the Whampoa Academy before also studying in Moscow. Despite her background in military matters, Wei would be shunted off into the cultural sphere, even before she ran afoul of the Communist Party in 1931. Li was married to Yang Shangkun, a highly educated Red Army leader. Despite being labeled as one of the "28 Bolsheviks" Yang would have a long and successful career, eventually becoming president of the PRC in 1988. Wei, meanwhile, wed Ye Jianying, another Red Army leader who would play a key role over the long course of the twentieth century. Brief overviews of both women can be found in Lily Xiao Hong Lee, ed., *Biographical Dictionary of Chinese Women: The Twentieth Century* (New York: M.E. Sharpe, 2003).

sprung up to train aspiring artists, starting with the Red Army Academy. Founded in the winter of 1930, this academy was by definition a military school, but after Li Bozhao and Wei Gongzhi joined the faculty as political instructors in 1931, the school's Social Club (*julebu*) began hosting weekend variety shows for students and Red Army officers. Audiences might be treated to songs, harmonica solos, or perhaps a violin performance from the newly arrived musician Cui Yinbo. Audiences, however, particularly favored the modern performances of the three "red dancing stars": Li Bozhao, Shi Lianxing, and Liu Yuehua. Traditionally, dancing had always been combined with singing and dramatic elements, as was the case with Jiangxi's local "tea pickers' opera" (*caichaju*).[20] But Li Bozhao, having studied dance in the USSR, performed and taught foreign dances, including works created by the progressive American dancer Isadora Duncan.[21]

The Red Army Academy Social Club started entertaining on a larger scale with the First Worker-Peasant Representative Meeting, held in November 1931.[22] Establishing an important pattern of actors entertaining top leaders, Li Bozhao, Qian Zhuangfei, Hu Di, and other figures tied to the club organized performances for the meeting. Qian and Hu were newcomers to the Jiangxi Soviet, having fled to the base areas after Gu Shunzhang, a magician and Moscow-trained Communist spy, defected to the Guomindang and helped decimate the party underground.[23] Working with these recent arrivals from the "White Areas," Li Bozhao set up a surprisingly grand entertainment program, including a torch parade, a bonfire, and dance performances from the three "red dancing stars." The program was highlighted by two dramas, both of which had a leading role for Li Bozhao.[24] The first show, Qian's *Last Supper* (Zuihou de wancan), dramatized a painter's quest to create a portrait of a dinner scene featuring the world's most beautiful person as well as its most ugly person. As depicted in the drama, the artist first finds a model for his beautiful person in a laboring woodcutter, and later finds his "ugliest man," a bone-thin and debased thief. Yet the two models are revealed to be the same man, his degradation a symbol of how fighting between warlords had brought the common people to

---

[20] Ouyang Ya and Wang Mulan, "Kai zai hongse turang shang de yishu zhi hua: suqu wudao" [Artistic flowers open on red soil: Jiangxi Soviet dance] HJSQ (ca. 1980s), 117.

[21] Guo Bing, ed., *Hongse ruijin* [Red ruijin] (Beijing: Zhongyang wenxian chubanshe, 2010), 473.

[22] Also called the "Yi Su Da" meeting for short.

[23] Li Bozhao, "Suiyue mobuqu de huiyi" [Unforgettable recollections] HJSQ (ca. 1980s), 60.

[24] Guo Bing, *Hongse ruijin*, 474–475.

ruin.[25] The second show was Li Bozhao's interpretation of *Uncle Tom's Cabin*.[26] While Red Army artists unanimously lauded these two shows as powerful and moving, they were a far cry from the highly focused political performances that would later find their way to Communist stages.

Drama troupes in the Jiangxi Soviet

While the Red Army Social Club would continue to entertain officers and students, the center of base area cultural activities shifted after the formation of the August 1 Drama Troupe (*Bayi jutuan*). Formed in Ruijin in the spring of 1932 under the leadership of Li Bozhao and Wei Gongzhi, the troupe essentially took their old weekend variety shows off campus.[27] In the aftermath of the Ningdu Uprising, for example, Mao Zedong personally instructed Li Bozhao to organize performances for the large numbers of former Guomindang soldiers that had joined the Red Army. According to Li, Mao claimed that because many of the soldiers were from the north, they were unaccustomed to eating rice and were suffering from diarrhea. More importantly, these unhappy soldiers needed to be educated and taught "who they were fighting for and who they were sacrificing themselves for." In accordance with his instructions, the troupe created *Who We Fight For, Who We Sacrifice For* (Wei shei dazhang, wei shei xisheng), one of the troupe's most important *huaju* spoken dramas. Li Bozhao organized seventeen troupe members into a "propaganda team," which performed their new show up to three times a day.[28]

The drama told the story of a vegetable peddler, pressganged into the Guomindang army while his wife suffers abuse at home. After much misery, the peddler is "liberated" by the Communists and rejoins his wife in Ruijin, where husband and wife dedicate themselves to the Communist cause. According to Li Bozhao, hampered by poor lighting and unable to see the audience, actors feared their silent crowd was rejecting the show. As soon as the show ended, however, the soldiers started chanting for the overthrow of Jiang Jieshi (Chang Kai-shek) and the Guomindang, their mood "boiling over like a pot of water."[29] While Li Bozhao's lauding of the power of her show is perhaps overstated, in the future the Communist Party would rely on drama as one of its most

---

[25] Li Bozhao, "Suiyue mobuqu de huiyi," 61.

[26] Li Bozhao, "Wei diyi jie gongnongbing daibiao huiyi yanchu de jumu" [Playbill for the first worker–peasant–soldier representative meeting] HJSQ (1957), 93.

[27] Wang Yongde, "Suqu de yige zhongyao xiju yundong zuzhi – gongnong jushe" [The Worker-Peasant Drama Society – an important drama campaign organization in the Jiangxi Soviet] HJSQ (1983), 53.

[28] Li Bozhao, "Suiyue mobuqu de huiyi," 63.   [29] Ibid., 65.

important tools for "educating" enemy soldiers. Clearly, some in the audience found Red Drama moving.

Convinced by the usefulness of the August 1 Drama Troupe, cultural leaders moved to develop a broader and more systematic drama troupe system. Thus, in September 1932, less than a year after its founding, the August 1 Drama Troupe was reformed as the Worker-Peasant Dramatic Society (*Gongnong jushe*), under the control of the Red Army Political Department. This would prove to be the most important Red Drama performance organization, providing the official structure for overseeing the expansion of the drama movement in the base areas.[30] The troupe was a highly organized unit, with distinct sections for creation, direction, dance, song, and music. By April 1933, in addition to an eighty-member troupe the Worker-Peasant Dramatic Society would claim six county-level branches with over six hundred members, with five more branches established before the collapse of the Jiangxi Soviet.[31] This expansion would rely on activists, commonly called "cultural backbones," which in turn would lead to a new emphasis on cultural training within the Soviet.

Drama education in the Jiangxi Soviet

In order to train more "cultural backbones," the Worker-Peasant Dramatic Society founded its Blue Shirt Drama Troupe Training Class (Lanshan jutuan xunlianban) in April 1933. Led by Li Bozhao, the school hosted three types of instructors: artists from Shanghai and other "White Areas," including Hu Di, Qian Zhuangfei, and Sha Kefu; Red Army "cultural backbones," such as Zhao Pinsan; and artists, mostly musicians, captured from Guomindang units.[32] An ancestral hall, updated with an indoor stage for its students, served as the school's primary classroom. Most students were members of the Communist Youth League, although the school welcomed students as old as forty. When performing in the school's Blue Shirt Drama Troupe, students used symbols to signify progressive and reactionary characters, a technique Li Bozhao had picked up in the USSR.[33] All actors wore blue shirts and pinned triangular pieces of colored cloth to their lapels, with the color of the triangle signifying the nature of the character: red for revolutionary,

---

[30] Qu Qiubai, "Gongnong jushe jianzhang" [General regulations for the Worker-Peasant Dramatic Society] HJSQ (1934), 57.

[31] Wang Yongde, "Suqu de yige zhongyao xiju yundong zuzhi – gongnong jushe," 54.

[32] Li Bozhao, "Gaoerji Xiju Xueyuan" [Gorky Drama Academy] HJSQ (1979), 68.

[33] Zhao Pinsan, "Guanyu zhongyang geming genjudi huaju gongzuo de huiyi," 43.

white for counter-revolutionary, yellow for reformist (*gailiang pai*), and black for fascist.[34]

The training class developed further after Qu Qiubai, chosen by Mao to serve as Commissar of Education, arrived in Ruijin in early 1934. Qu immediately renamed the school the Gorky Drama Academy (Gao'erji xiju xueyuan), while the school's troupe became the Soviet Drama Troupe (Suweiai jutuan). Under Qu, the school held two distinct courses for drama students. The "local" course developed activists for branch drama troupes and trained the propagandists who would staff Red Army propaganda teams. The school's "normal" course, meanwhile, served the needs of newly arrived intellectual youths.[35] Li Bozhao would later emphasize Qu Qiubai's hands-on approach to running the school, with Qu personally convincing reluctant students to study with captured Guomindang artists.[36] Starting with an initial class of forty students, the school claimed to have eventually trained over one thousand students and organized some sixty drama troupes, most notably the model Xingguo County Blue Shirt Drama Troupe. Xingguo amateurs performed shows and dances learned at Gorky, including *huobaoju* living newspaper dramas and new content works that drew on the local Chu opera style.[37] As Judd has noted in her study of the Xingguo troupe, the Communist Party largely ignored folk artists, preferring to team urban intellectuals with peasant amateurs.[38] Not until the 1940s did the Party overcome its negative perception of folk artists; as explored in subsequent chapters, working with traditional performers proved a difficult but essential step in popularizing Communist directed dramas.

Drama on the eve of the Long March

The organization of multiple county branches of the Worker-Peasant Dramatic Society and sixty Blue Shirt Drama Troupes provided signs of clear progress, but overall cultural work was meager in light of the ten million people living in the base area.[39] Advances in the dramatic realm, moreover, were increasingly limited by the Guomindang's fifth and final encirclement campaign. After being forced to move in October 1933, the

---

[34] Chen Baichen and Dong Jian, eds., *Zhongguo xiandai xiju shigao: 1899–1949*, 451.

[35] Deng Bangyu, ed., *Jiefangjun xiju shi*, 48.

[36] Li Bozhao, "Huiyi Qu Qiubai tongzhi" [Remembering comrade Qu Qiubai] HJSQ (1950), 71.

[37] Liu Shousong, "Lao genjudi wenyi huodong" [Old base area literature and arts activities] HJSQ (1956), 127–128.

[38] Judd, "Revolutionary Drama and Song in the Jiangxi Soviet," 144.

[39] Liu Shousong, "Lao genjudi wenyi huodong," 122.

Gorky Academy finally shut down in August 1934 as Guomindang forces inched ever closer to Ruijin. During the final months of desperate fighting, the school's Soviet Drama Troupe attempted to perform for the Red Army on the frontlines, but after marching for three days the troupe was promptly sent back − soldiers were simply too busy to watch dramas.[40]

The Worker-Peasant Dramatic Society found more success with its Field Operation Drama Troupe, which it dispatched to the Guangchang front on the Jiangxi-Fujian border. There actors performed for Red Army and enemy troops alike, a feat only possible because of the blockhouse system that allowed the Guomindang to finally make progress in its attempt to destroy the Jiangxi Soviet. According to Red Drama veteran Zhao Pinsan, the blockhouse system stationed Guomindang soldiers directly on the frontlines, giving the troupe a captive audience. While attempts to use propaganda to defeat these advancing soldiers failed, Zhao claimed that enemy soldiers proved an appreciative audience, throwing performers pouches of tobacco in gratitude for their shows.[41] Even granted Zhao Pinsan's limited claims of success, the drama troupe's attempts to slow the Guomindang advance had grown truly desperate, revealing the limits of a cultural army in a losing military battle.

In October 1934, the main force of the Red Army departed the Jiangxi Soviet and began what would eventually be known as the Long March. Li Bozhao and Wei Gongzhi joined the march, but most of their Red Drama comrades remained in Jiangxi. Zhou Enlai had demanded total secrecy in his planning, and for rank and file actors the sudden departure of their superiors along with the bulk of the Red Army was totally unexpected. After learning that they had been left behind, the less than one hundred remaining members of the Worker-Peasant Drama Society divided into three troupes: the Single Spark, Red Flag, and Battle Call drama troupes. These troupes continued on despite increasingly grim odds, performing at markets and urging audiences to resist Guomindang forces. Eventually, the three troupes regrouped in early 1935 for a final and emotional performance for an audience that included their patron Qu Qiubai, Mao Zetan, and other leaders not included in the Long March.[42]

After this final show, troupe members dispersed into military units and attempted to evade Guomindang forces. The difficulties these artists

---

[40] Shi Lianxing, "Qiubai tongzhi, women yongyuan huainian nin" [Comrade Qiubai, we will forever cherish you] HJSQ (1980), 76; Shi Lianxing, "Nanwang de rizi" [Unforgettable days] HJSQ (1957), 131.

[41] Zhao Pinsan, "Guanyu zhongyang geming genjudi huaju gongzuo de huiyi," 46–47.

[42] Shi Lianxing, "Qiubai tongzhi, women yongyuan huainian nin," 77–78.

faced in the aftermath of the Soviet's collapse are vividly captured in the memoirs of the "red dancing star" Shi Lianxing. After teaming up with Zhao Pinsan and Cui Yinbo in the short-lived Single Spark Drama Troupe, she and her fellow troupe members found themselves adapting to military life as they marched with two thousand soldiers under Liu Bojian. All their equipment, save Cui Yinbo's precious violin, had to be discarded.[43] Marching alongside were two of the "child stars" (*tong xing*) Qu Qiubai had recruited for the Worker-Peasant Dramatic Society. One of these "child stars," the orphan Xiao Qiulan, had personally witnessed the deaths of her parents, leaving her with a sad disposition. Only seven in 1933 when she arrived at Gorky, Xiao studied dance and acting, slowly overcoming the loss of her parents and blossoming into an outgoing child actor, playing a key role in the drama *Li Baolian*. The two children struggled to keep up with their Red Army unit, choosing to march in their dancing costumes rather than abandon them on the roadside. But as Shi Lianxing later admitted, both children fell behind and were lost, assumed to have been killed by pursuing enemy forces.[44]

Drama troupes on the Long March

The collapse of the Jiangxi Soviet represented a severe blow to Mao's cultural army. Educational centers closed, propaganda teams and drama troupes scattered, and many artists lost their lives. But despite the tremendous pressures of encircling and pursuing enemy forces, Communist Party directed drama troupes would endure and even prosper as the Red Army slowly made its way to the Northwest. Even on this deadly trek, no self-respecting revolutionary leader would abandon the practice of patronizing a drama troupe, which only grew more important as the Long March progressed. While the exploits of Mao and his army as they made the circuitous trek to the Northwest are the best-known aspect of the Long March, there were three large armies traveling on individual but overlapping routes: the First, Second, and Fourth Front Red Armies. Each of these armies developed a signature drama troupe in spite of the hardship of the journey, a testament to unity in cultural practice, despite fierce factional divides. The Soldiers' Dramatic Society, traveling with the First Front Red Army, prospered thanks to the influence of military men shaped by the May 4th era. The Forward Drama Troupe, through its

---

[43] Shi Lianxing, "Nanwang de rizi," 132–134.   [44] Ibid., 135–138.

association with Zhang Guotao and the Fourth Front Army, suffered greatly as a result of factional divides within the Communist Party. Finally, the experiences of the Combat Dramatic Society, attached to He Long's Second Front Red Army, demonstrate the importance of patronage for drama troupes.

Traveling with Mao's Party Central: the Soldiers' Dramatic Society (Zhanshi jushe)

When Zhou Enlai planned the escape of top party leaders alongside the First Front Red Army, he did not include the Worker-Peasant Dramatic Society in his plans. But as the most important military force in the Red Army, the First Front Red Army had a high-quality propaganda team, which performed as the Soldiers' Dramatic Society. The initial creation of the team is largely attributed to Luo Ronghuan, head of the Red Fourth Army's Political Department and the originator of the "propaganda team" designation. Having organized dramas in the May 4th era when he was a youth in Qingdao, Luo initially staffed a small propaganda team with the talented soldiers performing in *wanhui* evening variety shows. The team's first performances, however, remained decidedly apolitical. Its lewd *huaguxi* flower-drum song show, staged in celebration of the Red Army's capture of Ji'an in October 1930, actually offended Luo Ronghuan.[45] Hoping to use drama as propaganda, Luo reformed the group as the Civilized Drama Amateur Performance Team. Under Luo's direction, the team made the difficult shift to the more politically correct form of *huaju* spoken drama, performing in support of the fight against the first encirclement campaign.

The difficulty in staging "civilized plays" stemmed in part from the fact that most of Luo's actors were only vaguely familiar with the concept of these modern style shows. Actors, furthermore, had to create their own works as well as their own props: team member Pan Zhenwu, for example, recalled fashioning a walking stick, glasses, and tall hat to create an imperialist character. Early shows all promoted the defense of the base area, including a rare Communist farce (*naoju*). In this spoken drama, enemy soldiers entered the base area but could not find food or water. In one of its most popular scenes, an enemy soldier finds a large vat of water only to discover his prize has been compromised by feces.[46] Mao

---

[45] Pan Zhenwu, "Zhan ge qun qiu" [Battle hymn of spring and autumn] HJSQ (ca. 1980s), 157–158.

[46] Ibid., 161–162.

Zedong and Zhu De were in the audience, and one can only imagine that Mao enjoyed the scatological humor.[47]

The troupe, renamed the Soldiers' Dramatic Society, was placed under the First Front Red Army's Political Department in January 1933. Officially the troupe remained a propaganda team, but used their "artistic name" (*yiming*) during performances. At this point, the troupe remained "amateur" in that all members had other duties, and while the troupe continued to perform spoken dramas, actors also used Peking opera in their shows. Pan Zhenwu, eager in his memoirs to emphasize the unique nature of Red Drama, thus notes that "modern Peking opera" was by no means a product of the Cultural Revolution. The troupe staged a handful Peking opera style shows, most notably *Cursing Jiang Jieshi* (Ma Jiang Jieshi) and *Jiang Jieshi Talks* (Jiang Jieshi zitan). The former show, based on a traditional cursing song, required minimal changes.[48] Built around the metaphor of enemy forces melting away like a mountain's snowcap, *The Snow of Mount Lu* (Lushan zhi xue) proved the most important of the troupe's earliest spoken dramas. In one particularly notable performance in March 1933, Red Army leaders Lin Biao, Nie Rongzhen, and Luo Ronghuan all acted in the show, an early instance of the blurring of the lines between the revolution and its dramatization. *August 1* (Ba yi), a thirteen scene drama written and directed by Nie Rongzhen, told the entire story of the Red Army from its inception to the fourth encirclement campaign.[49] According to Liang Biren, who played a bit part (*pao longtao*) in the show, Nie wrote a rough outline of the plot and actors improvised their lines. Many soldiers and officers were drafted to dramatize their revolution on stage, Luo Ruiqing among them.[50]

As Red Drama veterans from the Soldiers' Dramatic Society recalled at a 1980 conference, the troupe initially lacked costumes, makeup, curtains, and props. Eventually actors performed with set costumes that helped depict characters: imperialists sported top hats, cotton goatees, and big noses made out of dough; capitalists wore Western suits and big bellies; and landlords wore long gowns, mandarin jackets, and skull caps.

---

[47] For Mao's appreciation for scatological metaphors, see Michael Schoenhals, "Consuming Fragments of Mao Zedong: The Chairman's Final Two Decades at the Helm," in *A Critical Introduction to Mao*, ed. Timothy Cheek (Cambridge: Cambridge University Press, 2010).

[48] Pan Zhenwu, "Zhan ge qun qiu," 166–167.

[49] Zhu Ming *et al.*, "Hongjun shiqi de zhanshi jutuan jianjie" [Introduction to the Soldiers' Dramatic Society during the Red Army era] HJSQ (1958), 155.

[50] Liang Biren, "Hongjun shiqi de wenyi huodong" [Red Army era literature and arts activities] HJSQ (ca. 1980s), 174.

The troupe constructed stages with doors borrowed from villagers, while lighting, always a concern for rural actors, came from kerosene lamps or simple torches.[51] The troupe experimented with new forms of lighting by suspending bonfires with iron fishing nets. This proved effective at illuminating the stage, but by the end of the shows actors would have black nostrils and ash in the corners of their eyes.[52] The troupe, furthermore, lacked female members, forcing male actors like the young Shao Hua to play female roles in drag. Shao took this in stride, noting that "when you have no horse, ride the cow." Not until April 1939 did the troupe finally receive an influx of four female actors from a Shandong propaganda team.[53]

While in the Jiangxi Soviet, the troupe seldom worked as a full team. Members instead broke up into smaller units, which one troupe leader would later call "political work light cavalry teams" (zhengzhi gongzuo qingqidui).[54] These teams staged a wide range of dramatic performances, from simple costumed lectures (huazhuang yanjiang) to operas. The troupe also did standard propaganda work, distributing flyers and pasting slogans using homemade paint fashioned out of lime, black soot, or red earth. Sloganeering was particularly time consuming, with one painter noting in his diary that "all day my only contact is with lime and walls."[55] Troupe members, finally, performed before captive audiences: surrendered enemy soldiers. In Pan Zhenwu's account of one such show, held for between four and five hundred Guomindang captives, the audience was initially arrogant and refused to listen to the troupe. During a performance of For Whom Does Blood and Sweat Flow (Xuehan wei shei liu), which highlighted the abuse Guomindang soldiers received from their officers, audience members insisted that their commanders were not cruel and that discipline was needed, a view Pan felt betrayed their "slave mentality." But during the performance, soldiers slowly gravitated towards the stage, seemingly captivated by scenes depicting Guomindang officers pressing villagers into the army and even raping their wives. After the show, Pan claimed, some two hundred captured soldiers volunteered to join the Red Army.[56]

[51] Liu Yiran, "Yuan zhanshi jushe bufen hongjun lao zhanshi zuotan ceji" [Sidelights on the conference of old Red Army soldiers in the Soldiers' Dramatic Society Troupe] HJSQ (1980), 179–183.

[52] Pan Zhenwu, "Yi hong yi juntuan xuanchuan dui" [Remembering Red First Army Group Propaganda Team] HJSQ (ca. 1980s), 208.

[53] Pan Zhenwu, "Zhan ge qun qiu," 159.

[54] Liu Fenglin, "Yi zhi zhenggong qingqidui" [A political work light cavalry team] HJSQ (ca. 1980s), 257.

[55] Xie Fumin, "Cong Guangxi dao Jiangxi" [From Guangxi to Jiangxi] HJSQ (1931), 225.

[56] Pan Zhenwu, "Yi hong yi juntuan xuanchuan dui," 209–213.

After leaving the Jiangxi Soviet with the First Front Army on the Long March, the troupe quickly expanded its ranks and strengthened its organization by forming three sections: a speech unit to deliver lectures, an artistic unit staffed with members with good penmanship to write slogans, and a third unit to post slogans. This division of labor helped the troupe cover Zunyi, where Mao made his famous push to power, in slogans in only one night.[57] At the start of the Long March, the Soldiers' Dramatic Society functioned as a typical propaganda team, singing, shouting slogans, and performing simple *kuaiban* "wooden clapper" numbers to motivate soldiers and win over new recruits. The troupe specialized in agitation station (*gudongpeng*) work, setting up stations at river crossings, mountain passes, and other important points, including a performance during the famous crossing of the Luding Bridge. Troupe members rose early to paint slogans along the march route before setting up their agitation stations, where the troupe played music, sang motivational songs, and provided water for tired and thirsty soldiers. After soldiers passed through the agitation stations, the team would bring up the rear and ensure that no soldiers fell behind.[58] The troupe also worked with villagers, for example convincing locals that the Red Army was not a threat by performing the song "Three Disciplines and Eight Attentions" (San da jilu ba xiang zhuyi) to explain Red Army regulations. But they discovered many villages deserted, residents having fled into the mountains after hearing rumors of the Communists' plans to communize both property and wives; in such cases troupe members were asked to go into the mountains to find villagers and convince them to return home.[59]

In June 1935, Mao Zedong's First Front Red Army met up with Zhang Guotao's Fourth Front Red Army, which had started its own version of the Long March in Sichuan. Meeting in Lianghekou, Mao and Zhang disagreed over the march's direction; Mao wanted to head to Communist base areas in the Northwest, while Zhang insisted on returning to Sichuan. Seemingly oblivious to this factional divide, the Soldiers' Dramatic Society performed for the assembled marchers, while taking advantage of the respite to reorganize the troupe in an attempt to increase professionalism. As the armies split up, Li Bozhao, who had been traveling with the First Front Army, joined the Fourth Front Army to take control of its drama troupe. Mao and Zhang may have disagreed on the direction of their respective marches, but both were unwavering in the belief that

[57] Liu Fenglin, "Yi zhi zhenggong qingqidui," 260–261.
[58] Gao Li, "Hong yi juntuan xuanchuandui – zhanshi jushe" [The Red First Army Propaganda Team – The Soldiers' Dramatic Society] HJSQ (ca. 1980s), 196–197.
[59] Ibid., 198–199.

a revolutionary leader needed a revolutionary drama troupe. The First Front Army soon completed its Long March, arriving in the Northwest base areas in October 1935. The First Front Army's propaganda head, Deng Xiaoping, had made sure to provide for the troupe throughout the Long March.[60] Li Bozhao's trek, however, would reveal that not all drama troupes were so lucky.

Traveling with the "Fake" Party Central: the Forward Drama Troupe (Qianjin jutuan)

For Li Bozhao, taking over the Fourth Front Army's drama troupe meant performing for Zhang Guotao's forces. The Communist Party would later vilify Zhang as a "traitor," but in the early 1930s he was one of the most powerful figures in the party. Driven out of the E-Yu-Wan Base Area in late 1932, Zhang moved his Fourth Front Army into Sichuan, which had been torn apart by warlord misrule. Rural Sichuan proved highly susceptible to the Communist message, and the next two years would see "dazzling growth" for Zhang in Sichuan.[61] With the establishment of the Chuan-Shaan[62] Base Area, Zhang's General Political Department organized a handful of propagandists into what would eventually become the Chuan-Shaan Soviet Worker-Peasant Drama Troupe. But Sichuan locals called the troupe the "New Drama Troupe," highlighting the divergence of this unit from traditional xibanzi opera troupes. As the Chuan-Shaan Base Area expanded in the spring of 1933 so did the troupe, growing to over twenty members, with both male and female actors.[63]

While in Sichuan, the "New Drama Troupe" continued to grow. By May 1933, the troupe had about fifty members, mostly illiterate children, and a small music group playing drums, flutes, and brass instruments. Many performances supported Red Army recruitment campaigns, helping to increase the number of Red Army soldiers in the Chuan-Shaan Base Area to over eighty thousand. As the troupe expanded to nearly seventy members, the troupe organized sections for artistic creation, costumes, and scenery. With further development of the base area in 1934, the troupe divided into four smaller troupes, one of which was led by Liu Wenquan, who would go on to play an important role in drama education on the Long March. The height of the troupe's time in Sichuan

---

[60] Pan Zhenwu, "Zhanshi jushe de chuangjian he fazhan," 145–147.
[61] Benjamin Yang, From Revolution to Politics: Chinese Communists on the Long March (Boulder, CO: Westview, 1990), 130.
[62] Sichuan-Shaanxi.
[63] Lu Ying, "Hong si fangmian jun zongzheng jutuan" [The Red Fourth Front Army General Political Department Drama Troupe] HJSQ (1982), 395.

came in early 1935, when the Red Army captured a Guomindang *xibanzi* opera outfit. After agreeing to give up opium,[64] these traditional artists helped the troupe produce Sichuan operas, both historical and modern. Foreshadowing the later widespread use of local forms, these shows proved particularly popular with soldiers, most of whom were Sichuan natives.[65]

In March 1935, the troupe started its version of the Long March alongside Zhang Guotao and the Fourth Front Army, quickly meeting up with Mao Zedong and the First Front Army in June. Li Bozhao, sidelined from dramatic pursuits after joining a "Women's Work Group" under the First Front Army Health Department,[66] switched armies and took control of Zhang Guotao's prize drama troupe. In later years, many troupe members would call their old troupe the Worker-Peasant Dramatic Society in order to emphasize her leadership over that of Zhang Guotao.[67] But as its experiences in the Long March would prove, the unit was inexorably tied to Zhang. In August, as the two armies split apart, the troupe accompanied Zhang's left column for a brutal crossing of the "grasslands" (*caodi*), a swampy and deadly terrain. As one Long March veteran would later describe the marshy terrain:

That damn place was really strange! Just grass, no trees. It wasn't mountainous, just flat land. It rained every day and the sun came out every day. The ground was all wet. At first, the vanguard troops sank into the bog. If you tried to pull them out, you would sink, too. They couldn't climb out and they couldn't be rescued, either. You could only watch them die.[68]

After a disastrous trek through the grasslands, Zhang, frustrated with the difficultly of moving north, ordered the column to turn around and cross the grasslands a second time on the way back to Sichuan. In December 1935, Zhang established what would eventually be labeled a "fake Party Center" and changed the name of his troupe to the Central Forward Drama Troupe (Zhongyang qianjin jutuan) to further bolster his claim as the primary Communist leader. Only a few years after the Communist had first experimented with drama, troupes had already become an important marker of a leader's legitimacy.

In late 1935, the left column reached Chengdu, but failed to take the city. By February 1936, Zhang Guotao's Sichuan plan had proven

---

[64] As seen in the discussion of the Xiangyuan Rural Drama Troupe in Chapter 2, agreeing to give up opium was not the same as actually quitting the drug.

[65] Lu Ying, "Hong si fangmian jun zongzheng jutuan," 396–402.

[66] Young, *Choosing Revolution*, 191.

[67] Liu Wenquan, "Cong gongnong jushe dao zhandou jushe" [From the Worker-Peasant Dramatic Society to the Combat Dramatic Society] HJSQ, 420.

[68] Quoted in Young, *Choosing Revolution*, 211.

untenable, so his forces moved into Xikang, crossing the Dang'ling Mountains. During the dangerous crossing, Zhang Desheng, one of the leaders of the troupe, plummeted to his death while fellow troupe members looked on in horror. Arriving in Ganzi in February 1936, the Fourth Front Army halted its march until the June arrival of He Long's Second Front Army. The Central Forward Drama Troupe, which had been performing regularly in Ganzi, put on a show to celebrate the meeting of these forces, inspiring He Long to create his own drama troupe. In July, Zhang Guotao agreed to abolish his "fake Party Center" and march north to Shaanbei with He Long and the Second Front Army. The troupe's third crossing of the grasslands proved just as difficult as the first two: Li Bozhao had her horse killed to help feed her starving troupe.[69]

The Long March finally came to an end in October 1936 when the First, Second, and Fourth Front Armies converged in Gansu's Huining County. Li Bozhao, understandably ill after her third crossing of the grasslands, was sent to the Shaanbei Base Area for treatment. Her illness proved fortuitous. In 1937, most of her former troupe followed the West Road Army, composed of soldiers from the Fourth Front Army, into Gansu's Hexi corridor. This was the territory of the powerful warlord Ma Bufang, and the troupe quickly found itself isolated and surrounded by enemy cavalry. As described by Wang Dingguo in his memoirs concerning fellow performer Liao Chijian, the troupe ended up trapped in an abandoned tower, desperately fighting off attackers. An attempt by the Red Army to use captured horses against the warlord's forces immediately failed when Ma Bufang's soldiers simply called the horses back to them, throwing off their Red Army riders. The drama troupe was eventually smoked out of its tower, but not before Liao Chijian was killed.[70]

Seeing a valuable prize, Ma Bufang ordered the troupe of twenty women and ten men to be treated politely, with the women sent to his headquarters in Xining. In this they fared better than the women soldiers and nurses attached to the West Road Army, who were distributed to officers and men as concubines, with the youngest and most attractive captives given to high-ranking officers.[71] In Xining, the women actors agreed to perform for Ma Bufang and his troops, negotiating for their male musicians to join them in the warlord's capital. Reformed as his 100th Division Dance Team, they remained in Ma Bufang's custody

[69] Lu Ying, "Hong si fangmian jun zongzheng jutuan," 403–407.
[70] Wang Dingguo, "Ta – zhidaoyuan jian yanyuan" [Her – Political instructor and actor] HJSQ (ca. 1980s), 427–428.
[71] Yang, From Revolution to Politics, 234.

until the Communist Party was able to negotiate their release during the Second United Front.[72] While the details of their captivity remain unclear, their relatively benign treatment under Ma Bufang suggests that even warlords afforded special honors to cultural performers.

The bandit's players: the Combat Dramatic Society (Zhandou jushe)

The final Red Drama troupe of note on the Long March was the Combat Dramatic Society, which evolved from the Second Front Red Army Propaganda Team. But the unit's origins can be traced back to 1926, when Zhou Enlai sent the Left Wing Army Propaganda Team, led by early Communist Party member Zhou Yiqun, to carry out ideological work among the Revolutionary Army forces under the charismatic bandit turned revolutionary, He Long. He Long, taking a strong liking to Zhou Yiqun and pleased with the work of the propaganda team, made Zhou the director of his Political Department. As Richard Kraus has noted, many Communist leaders were "artistically inclined" and eager to serve as patrons of the arts, yet surprisingly few had a deep love for traditional opera.[73] He Long was one of these rare figures, making him a natural patron for a drama troupe. After He Long joined in the Nanchang Uprising, he formed the Western Hunan Worker-Peasant Red Army, a force of around three thousand soldiers that later formed the basis of his Red Second Army Group. Zhou Yiqun continued to lead propaganda work for He Long, with his greatest achievements in composing revolutionary songs based on foreign melodies from places as far away as Scotland and the United States. But "leftist deviations" led to the loss of much of He Long's base area, and with Zhou Yiqun himself killed in 1931, meaningful propaganda work ground to a halt.[74]

While propaganda activities increased after Xiao Ke and Ren Bishi's Sixth Army Group joined with He Long's Second Army Group to establish the Hunan-Hubei-Sichuan-Guizhou Soviet Base Area in October 1934,[75] propagandists remained decidedly limited in their activities, which mainly consisted of pasting slogans. The team also organized agitation

---

[72] Lu Ying, "Hong si fangmian jun zongzheng jutuan," 409–413.

[73] Richard Curt Kraus, *Brushes with Power: Modern Politics and the Chinese Art of Calligraphy* (Berkeley, CA: University of California Press, 1991), 65.

[74] Chen Jing, "Zhandou jushe yuanyuan liuchang" [The long standing and well established Combat Dramatic Society] HJSQ (ca. 1980s), 289–295.

[75] The flight of the Sixth Army Group from the Hunan-Jiangxi Soviet Base Area to join with He Long may be considered the earliest component of the Long March. Over three months of fighting, the ninety-five thousand troops who left the base area were reduced to around four thousand. See Young, *Choosing Revolution*, 73.

stations, foreshadowing later Long March cultural performances. He Long was a tireless recruiter, and soldiers that displayed a talent for performance might find themselves drafted into his propaganda team. Chen Jing was drafted after singing a ditty from his hometown and playing a melody by fashioning a makeshift musical instrument out of a leaf during a victory celebration.[76] But while He Long was consistent in his support of propaganda, cultural work was severely constrained by Guomindang encirclement campaigns and incursions: the three county seats at the heart of the base area were taken and retaken six times in a single year.[77]

The Second and Sixth Army Groups, which would eventually be merged into the Second Front Army, did not begin their own Long March until November 1935, one month after Mao and the First Front Army completed its far more famous journey. Pushed the furthest west and forced to traverse through Yunnan and the Tibetan highlands of Western Sichuan, He Long's forces initially fielded a small propaganda team with only around fifteen members, although female marchers were often mobilized for posting notices and other light propaganda work.[78] In addition to typical propaganda work, team members also served as diplomatic envoys. For example, after entering the Tibetan region near Zhongdian where hostile forces attacked the Red Army, the Political Department gave the team a letter to deliver to a local Lama Temple. Their words and a couple of shows helped smooth their passage through the region.[79] But for the most part, this was a typical propaganda outfit, with member duties defined by the team's three-part structure: one unit went ahead to prepare propaganda for marching soldiers, one unit set up agitation stations, and one unit brought up the rear to collect any stragglers. During longer respites, the propaganda team performed short dramas for resting soldiers, but also experimented with "flying performances." Quick ten-minute shows, these "flying performances" were staged when the army took short rests, although enemy attacks often interrupted shows.[80]

In June 1936, the Second and Sixth Army Groups, having traveled separately from Zhongdian, met up with Zhang Guotao and his Fourth Front Army in Ganzi; in July, the Second and the Sixth Army Groups merged into the Second Front Army under He Long's control.

---

[76] Chen Jing, "Gengjia zhongzhi cheng cheng" [The people's will unites like a fortress] HJSQ (ca. 1980s), 273–274.
[77] Young, *Choosing Revolution*, 30.   [78] Ibid., 45.
[79] Chen Jing, "Gengjia zhongzhi cheng cheng," 278.
[80] Chen Jing, "Zhandou jushe yuanyuan liuchang," 295–299.

In celebration of the meeting of these forces, Li Bozhao
Forward Drama Troupe performed for the new arrivals.
and professionalism of Li Bozhao's troupe, He Long
decided to turn their propaganda team, which barely ha
instruments, into a proper drama troupe. But while establ
was critical to demonstrate their worth as revolutionary lea
was not an easy one. At the start of the Long March, the tea
than twenty members and was now down to seven or eight. N ansfers
raised that number to fifty-seven, split into three units: drama, music,
and dance.

Li Bozhao helped train the expanded troupe while the two armies
prepared to cross the grasslands. He Long also convinced Li Bozhao to
send Liu Wenquan, a mainstay of the Forward Drama Troupe, to join his
troupe as a "temporary instructor" (*linshi jiaoyuan*). Under the direction
of Li and Liu, the troupe studied songs, dances, and dramas, with the
goal of motivating soldiers as they navigated through the difficult grasslands. The two drama troupes crossed the grasslands with their respective armies, but their experiences followed a similar trajectory. As He
Long's young team entered the grasslands, members first focused on
typical propaganda work: writing slogans, singing revolutionary songs,
staging short shows, and setting up agitation stations. But as Liu
Wenquan recalled in his memoirs, soon the team's only concern was
survival. Enduring great suffering and hunger, some younger members
attempted to alleviate their pains by eating un-ripened grain and died.[81]
Zhang Guotao's larger force had entered the grasslands first in three
columns, with the Second Front Army tracing their steps in a single
column; as the marchers discovered, their comrades had picked the
grasslands clean of all food and supplies, leaving them to starve.[82]
Of the fifty-seven propaganda team members to enter the grasslands,
only eleven would exit.[83]

The decimation of his propaganda team was thus fresh in He Long's
mind when his column arrived in the Northwest. After watching Wei
Gongzhi's People's Dramatic Society put on a show welcoming his
soldiers, He Long, impressed by the quality of the performance and
convinced of drama's power, moved to rebuild his troupe.[84] In one of
the most unique moments in casting history, He Long positioned himself
on a good vantage point overlooking his soldiers as they marched out,

---

[81] Liu Wenquan, "Cong gongnong jushe dao zhandou jushe," 421–423.
[82] Yang, *From Revolution to Politics*, 213.
[83] Chen Jing, "Gengjia zhongzhi cheng," 279–281.
[84] Chen Jing, "Zhandou jushe yuanyuan liuchang," 289.

personally selecting the best-looking young men and drafting them into his new troupe, now called the Combat Dramatic Society.[85] Zhou Enlai then took the troupe to Bao'an for a round of training with Wei Gongzhi and her People's Dramatic Society. While in Bao'an, the Combat Dramatic Society performed for top Communist Party leaders and dabbled in creation, writing *Capturing Jiang Jieshi Alive* (Huozhuo Jiang Jieshi), a "living newspaper drama" depicting the Xi'an Incident. Zhou Enlai then dispatched the two troupes to the new Communist capital of Yan'an to carry out mass work.[86] This work was in fact needed, as Yan'an residents fled when they first saw the troupe.[87] But by the time troupe left Yan'an, actors could perform a wide range of, dances, songs and dramas. Boasting their own dance instructor and a respectable curtain, they had finally become the type of drama troupe that He Long had so longed for.[88]

In relative safety in the Northwest, the Combat Dramatic Society further developed its organization, establishing sections for drama and dance, as well as a general affairs section that handled cooking, transport, and communications. Skilled musicians were still lacking, with music largely provided by harmonicas, *erhu*, and simple percussion instruments. But the spoken dramas the troupe specialized in did not require elaborate musical accompaniment. The troupe also had a propaganda section that handled the basic tasks of painting slogans and conducting street corner propaganda. Typically, teenagers and young adults staffed the propaganda and drama sections, while the dance group was mostly staffed by unschooled children. Overall, the troupe had tight party control, with a party branch committee for the entire troupe and small party groups (*dang xiaozu*) at the sectional levels.[89] The main problem the troupe faced was the continued lack of female members; during this time, the troupe only had one female member, Fan Ermei, but she refused to go on stage. As a result, it fell to the men to play female roles, with Yu Xun often cast in elderly female roles. A young man himself, Yu grew angry when soldiers started calling him "Old Aunty" (Lao Taitai or Lao Popo). As he later recalled, he "didn't like the taste" of the new moniker, although he did learn to accept it.[90]

[85] Chen Jing, "Gengjia zhongzhi cheng cheng," 282.
[86] Liu Wu, "Zhandou jushe de jianjie" [Introduction to the Combat Dramatic Society] HJSQ (ca. 1980s), 286.
[87] Gong Guifan, "Huiyi hong er fangmian jun de gewu yanyuan" [Remembering song and dance actors of the Red Second Front Army] HJSQ (ca. 1980s), 317.
[88] Chen Jing, "Gengjia zhongzhi cheng cheng," 283.
[89] Yu Xun, "He Long yu zhandou jushe" [He Long and the Combat Dramatic Society] HJSQ (ca. 1980s), 325–326.
[90] Ibid., 329.

Conclusion: the sprouts of revolutionary drama

Three consistent trends characterized early cultural performances under Communist direction. First, drawing on both Chinese tradition and May 4th reformist theories, Communist leaders were unwavering in their conviction that drama had the power to influence audiences. This conviction, forcefully espoused by Mao Zedong at early party conferences in Sanwan and Gutian, was widespread among leading Communists. Soviet-trained artist Li Bozhao and bandit turned revolutionary He Long were thus united in their firm and fervent belief that dramatic performances were one of the keys to eventual Communist victory. The factional divide between Mao Zedong and Zhang Guotao nearly destroyed their Communist Party, yet both men adhered to a vision of Communist leadership that demanded the patronage of revolutionary drama troupes.

Yet this theoretical belief in the power of drama existed in sharp juxtaposition with a second salient characteristic of Red Drama: the continuing undervaluing of cultural work in practice. At a time when the precarious military situation of the Red Army meant that the Communist movement was seemingly on the verge of total defeat, it is perhaps not surprising that the party preferred to channel its resources into the military and political realms. The tensions between the stressed importance of cultural work and the sorry state of cultural workers peaked during the late 1920s and early 1930s, when critics despised propagandists as incompetent deserters. With the arrival of Soviet trained intellectuals, the quality of propaganda work increased significantly. Yet these talented individuals were often persecuted for their intellectual status, an unfortunate trend typically blamed on the leadership of Wang Ming and Zhang Guotao. As Zhu De's wife Kang Keqing later noted, "only if you have a fountain pen in your front pocket do you face the danger of being persecuted as an intellectual; only if you wear eyeglasses do you encounter difficulty."[91] Even when not held in suspicion for their learning, elite artists always remained in the minority, surrounded as they were by village children too young for the frontlines. Until He Long took casting into his own hands, few able-bodied men found their way into the world of Red Drama.

The disjunctions between the perceived power of Red Drama and the limited support given to its practitioners only underlines the third characteristic of early Communist drama: the sheer difficulty in staging dramatic performances in support of the party. The limiting factor most

---

[91] Quoted in Hong Yung Lee, *From Revolutionary Cadres to Party Technocrats in Socialist China* (Berkeley, CA: University of California Press, 1990), 22.

Figure 2 Propaganda team members shouting slogans at Guomindang soldiers

afflicting Red Drama practitioners was the simple fact that there were far too few of them. Operating in base areas home to millions, the Communists could not create a meaningful network of cultural institutions that could reach Jiangxi Soviet villages. The fact that the Communists were active in mountainous regions with troublesome transportation networks only further constrained the reach of their drama troupes. Taking the most optimistic claims of troupe development, advanced by Wei Gongzhi to Edgar Snow after the Long March, Jiangxi Soviet cultural leaders were only able to train around sixty drama troupes.[92] Even making the very questionable assumption that these troupes existed, performed regularly, toured widely, and staged propaganda-heavy shows, this was a miniscule cultural army.

The men, women, and children of Red Drama made concrete contributions to the military efforts that kept the Communist cause alive. Theatrical shows were rare, but served as a welcome respite from the drudgery and danger of military service, while offering reminders of why the Red Army fought its seemingly unwinnable war. Performances during marches, especially at agitation stations, provided encouragement and refreshment for exhausted soldiers. But despite improvements in training and expanded membership, propaganda teams found themselves engaged in increasingly desperate measures as the Jiangxi Soviet collapsed and the Red Army fled to the Northwest. Besides the agitation station, the most paradigmatic form of propaganda of this era was the simple shouting of slogans at enemy soldiers camped across enemy lines. The attempts at propaganda seen on the frontlines of Zhang Guotao's doomed Chuan-Shaan Base Area were even more pathetic. Members of what locals called the "New Drama Troupe" constructed raft slogans, fashioning bamboo stalks into characters and tying them together to float downstream towards the enemy forces that had encircled their base area. If these bamboo rafts ever reached the enemy, their message to "turn all of Sichuan red" (*chi hua quan* Sichuan) went unheeded.[93]

---

[92] Edgar Snow, *Red Star over China* (New York: Grove Press, 1968),122.

[93] Xiong Yun, "Hong si fangmian jun wenyi xuanchuan gongzuo suoyi" [Trivial recollections of Red Fourth Front Army literature and arts propaganda work] HJSQ (ca. 1980s), 381.

2   Acting against Japan
Drama troupes in North China

By the late 1930s, the Combat Dramatic Society, under the patronage of the reformed bandit He Long, had emerged as one of the finest drama troupes in Mao Zedong's young cultural army. During the eight-year Sino-Japanese War, the troupe, now attached to the newly created 120th Division of the Eighth Route Army,[1] toured throughout North China, supporting the fight against Japan and helping develop the Jizhong,[2] Jin-Cha-Ji,[3] and Jin-Sui[4] border regions. Throughout the conflict, He Long took an active interest in promoting cultural production, personally intervening to ensure the safety and wellbeing of the troupe, especially his beloved Peking opera actors.[5] The troupe, meanwhile, grew acclimatized to the realities of war impinging on their performances – its actors were able to dismantle their stage and change out of their costumes in less than five minutes.[6]

In September 1939, for example, an unexpected Japanese offensive interrupted the troupe's planned evening show. The attack, which signaled the start of a six-day skirmish now known as the Battle of Chen Village, forced the troupe to stash its theatrical equipment and flee for their lives. According to troupe member, Chen Kai, after a harrowing two-day forced march the troupe finally reached the safety of the rear lines where actors performed by night, hoping to raise morale by mixing drama with reports from the battlefront. Without the benefit of proper lighting or even a microphone, the actors relied on a few borrowed props and a bullhorn to entertain their audience. Always a firm believer in the

---

[1] The Second United Front brought about structural changes in military command structures. Under its agreement with the Guomindang, the Eighth Route Army had three divisions: the 115th under Lin Biao, the 129th under Liu Bocheng, and the 120th under He Long. The Combat Dramatic Society, fitting given its relationship with He Long, was directly attached to Division Headquarters (*shibu*). The 120th was divided into four brigades, each with its own drama troupe.

[2] Central Hebei.   [3] Shanxi-Chahar-Hebei.   [4] Shanxi-Suiyuan.

[5] Dong Xiaowu, "Zhanxian jushe and zhandou jushe zai Jin xibei" [The Battle Line Dramatic Society and the Combat Dramatic Society in Northwest Shanxi] BLZK (ca. 1980s), 568.

[6] Ibid., 570.

power of drama, He Long coordinated shows with battle rotations so that resting soldiers had an opportunity to view the troupe's performances. As Chen Kai later insisted, she and her fellow actors "did not perform for the sake of performing, we performed for the war."[7]

Political leaders would have agreed with Chen's assessment. Deng Xiaoping, in a report to propaganda teams attached to his 129th Division, insisted that all cultural work remain subordinate to political responsibilities, which meant above all promoting the war effort and defense of the base areas.[8] Elsewhere Deng stressed the danger of traditional *xibanzi* opera troupes, warning that the Japanese invaders were using popular dramas to draw crowds, giving the enemy the opportunity to promote a "traitor culture" in China.[9] As dramatist Fu Duo made clear in his declaration that "art is a weapon and the stage a battlefield,"[10] the war against Japan was a cultural as well as military conflict. Fu Duo was speaking metaphorically, but Zhang Zhenshan, an actor specializing in "Japanese devil" characters, knew the dangers of acting first hand. During his performances, particularly when his "Japanese" character sexually assaulted Chinese women, audiences would often hurl bricks and rocks on stage.[11] But as drama troupes on the frontlines quickly realized, any stage could turn into a literal battlefield. Not merely playing revolution, the reality was that many members of Mao's cultural army would not survive the war.

Despite the dangers of performance, studies of Chinese culture have repeatedly stressed the rapid and transformative development of drama during the Sino-Japanese War.[12] But when scholars call the early 1940s a "golden age" (*huangjin shidai*) for drama, they are typically investigating the artistic community based in Yan'an, the Communists' wartime capital.[13] As Paul Clark and David Holm have demonstrated, the influx

---

[7] Chen Kai, "120 shi zhandou jushe zai Ji zhong" [The 120th Division's Combat Dramatic Society in Central Hebei] BLZK (ca. 1980s), 559.

[8] Deng Xiaoping, "129 shi wenhua gongzuo de fangzhen renwu ji qi shili fangxiang" [Policies and direction for cultural work in the 129th Division], in *Deng Xiaoping wenxuan di yi juan* [Selected works of Deng Xiaoping: Volume I] (Beijing: Renmin chubanshe, 2005), 22–25.

[9] Deng Bangyu, ed., *Jiefangjun xiju shi*, 77–79.

[10] Fu Duo, "Yi Jizhong wenyi huodong" [Remembering Central Hebei literature and arts activities) BLZK (ca. 1980s), 554.

[11] Ibid., 553.

[12] On a broader scale, scholars of modern China have increasingly highlighted the importance of war in spreading mass culture. See Matthew David Johnson, "International and Wartime Origins of the Propaganda State: The Motion Picture in China, 1897–1955" (doctoral dissertation, University of California, San Diego, 2008).

[13] For example, see Cheng Baichen and Dong Jian, eds., *Zhongguo xiandai xiju shigao: 1899–1949*, 285.

of elite artists into Yan'an fueled a craze for Western style spoken drama.[14] After initially welcoming these "big shows" (*daxi*) to his stages, Mao reversed course in his 1942 "Talks at the Yan'an Forum." In these highly influential lectures, Mao began a forceful push for cultural workers to create art for the peasant masses, not the petit bourgeois of Greater Rear Area.[15]

Through the difficult process of rectification (*zhengfeng*), Yan'an artists were slowly but surely bent to Mao's will, creating works that drew on Chinese traditions to promote the Communist cause. But with an extreme concentration of intellectuals living in the capital, Yan'an was the most unique of all Communist held territories, especially in the artistic realm. While theoretical debates over "national forms" and the resulting shifts in artistic styles were of great importance for party intellectuals living in Yan'an, their significance outside the capital during the Sino-Japanese War should not be overestimated. Local cadres simply did not find cultural work particularly important. As Hong Yung Lee has argued, lower-level cadres in the Shaan-Gan-Ning Border Region were almost always of peasant origin with little cultural education.[16] And as Ellen Judd astutely noted, while the party attempted to bring high-ranking cadres to the countryside through its "mass line" policy, getting elite artists into the countryside was a painfully slow process. Professional artists only went down to the village level "on a truly large scale toward the end of the 1940s when they spread throughout the country, along with the advancing armies, in propaganda teams or in land reform teams."[17] With most scholarship focused on debates over artistic theory in the Yan'an, the deployment of the Communists' cultural army in the vast North China countryside during the fight against Japan has escaped academic investigation.[18] The most enduring depiction of a drama troupe during the Sino-Japanese War remains Edgar Snow's contemporary

---

[14] Clark, *Chinese Cinema*, 9; Holm, *Art and Ideology in Revolutionary China*, 47–48.

[15] For a translation and full analysis of these talks, see Bonnie McDougall, *Mao Zedong's "Talks at the Yan'an Conference on Literature and Art": A Translation of the 1943 Text with Commentary* (Ann Arbor, MI: Center for Chinese Studies, University of Michigan, 1980).

[16] Hong Yung Lee, *From Revolutionary Cadres to Party Technocrats in Socialist China*, 32–33.

[17] Ellen R. Judd, "Prelude to the 'Yan'an Talks': Problems in Transforming a Literary Intelligentsia," *Modern China*, Vol. 11, No. 3 (July, 1985), 401.

[18] One rare examination of drama troupes outside of Yan'an is David Holm's 1980 investigation of the push to build village drama troupes in Northwest Shanxi. Tellingly, Holm's attempt to look past the formulation of policy and see its implementation at the local level is largely based on a handful of documents promoting Hua Guofeng's close relationship with the masses in Jiaodong County. David Holm, "Hua Guofeng and the Village Drama Movement in the North-West Shanxi Base Area, 1943–45," *The China Quarterly* No. 84 (December, 1980), 669–693.

portrayal of the People's Anti-Japanese Dramatic Society, led by Wei Gongzhi.[19] Yet this drama troupe, directly under the patronage of Zhou Enlai, largely existed to entertain top leaders in Yan'an. Understanding the role of culture in the Sino-Japanese War requires a broader field of inquiry, one that investigates the actual workings of Mao's cultural army in the field and at the local level.

This chapter moves outside of the rarified air of the Communists' wartime capital in order to understand the inner workings of propaganda teams and drama troupes in the war-torn countryside, focusing on the base areas in and around Shanxi. Because Mao's cultural army grew increasingly complex during these years, this chapter analyzes the activities of three troupes, each representing a distinct organizational model. The Taihang Mountains Drama Troupe exemplifies the "big drama troupe" (*da jutuan*). Typically attached to military organizations and base area governments, "big drama troupes" were the largest and most prolific revolutionary drama troupe organizations. The Xiangyuan Rural Drama Troupe represents professional drama troupes (*zhiye jutuan*), private outfits that could choose to perform politically charged shows in exchange for government support. Finally, the High Street Drama Troupe allows the investigation into amateur rural drama troupes (*yeyu nongcun jutuan*), simple organizations of talented villagers staging free performances for their neighbors.

Taken together, drama troupe activities during the Sino-Japanese War reveal a number of important themes concerning cultural mobilization during wartime. First, while the Communist Party often boasted of thousands of rural drama troupes,[20] any pretense of creating a dense infrastructure of Communist directed performance organizations is overstated. Second, despite the best efforts of the party, the line between professional and amateur remained a fuzzy and permeable barrier. Traditionally, many "amateur" performers collected money or goods in return for their shows, with the most talented village troupes pursuing professional status. The party was desperate to increase farm yields while

---

[19] After describing a raw and emotion-provoking performance from Wei's troupe, Snow claimed that there "was no more powerful weapon of propaganda in the Communist movement than the Red's dramatic troupes, and none more subtlety manipulated." Snow, *Red Star over China*, 123–124.

[20] In his study of the Village Drama Troupe Movement, for example, Holm notes that in the Taihang base area in 1940 the Communist Party controlled around 100 drama troupes and "exercised some leadership over a further 300"; within two years the Central Hebei area would have 1,700 village-level drama troupes, while Beiyue area (West Hebei and the Northeast corner of Shanxi) had another 2,124 troupes. Holm, "Hua Guofeng and the Village Drama Movement in the North-West Shanxi Base Area, 1943–45," 671.

still reaping the cultural fruits of amateur performance, but failed to keep amateurs from moving towards professional status. Third, while the growth of Mao's cultural army was largely predicated on adapting local cultural forms, rural audiences continued to favor traditional operas. As a result, local culture often hampered the Communists, even after Mao led the push to use local forms to serve the revolution. Finally, throughout this era dramatic performance was largely divorced from the revolutionary process under the assumption that cultural campaigns should follow "liberation." During the Sino-Japanese War, the party used drama troupes to mobilize soldiers and enlighten "liberated" peasants. Critically, not until the full development of land reform was drama truly brought into the actual process of rural revolution.

A "Big Drama Troupe": the Taihang Mountains Drama Troupe (Taihangshan jutuan)

In November 1937, Zhu Rui, a "Soviet-trained organization expert attached to the 129th Division,"[21] was busy laying the foundations for what would eventually become the Jin-Ji-Lu-Yu Border Region. An important but understudied Communist base area,[22] the border region grew out of its relatively secure core in Shanxi's Taihang Mountains region. Never one to neglect party organization, Zhu established his North China Military and Administrative Cadre Institute, commonly known as Hua Gan, in the recently "liberated" city of Jincheng. The school proved popular with educated youths unable or unwilling to make the trek to Yan'an. With about one thousand students at Hua Gan, Zhu Rui formed a number of cultural units, including the Spoken Drama Group under party member Zhao Luofang. Under Zhao's direction, the team staged a number of small street performances in and around Jincheng, including *Lay Down Your Whip* (Fang xia ni de bianzi), a well-known anti-Japanese drama that was popular in both Communist and Guomindang held areas.[23] In March 1938, these performers merged with a Communist Party propaganda team to form the United Anti-Japanese Mobile

---

[21] David S.G. Goodman, "JinJiLuYu in the Sino-Japanese War: The Border Region and the Border Region Government," *The China Quarterly* No. 140 (December, 1994), 1011.

[22] As Goodman notes, the Taihang region is part of the Jin-Ji-Lu-Yu Border Region, which is associated with Mao's later political rivals (Deng Xiaoping, Peng Dehuai, Yang Shangkun, Bo Yibo, and Li Xuefeng) and is thus not as famous. See David S.G. Goodman, *Social and Political Change in Revolutionary China: The Taihang Base Area in the War of Resistance to Japan* (New York: Rowman & Littlefield Publishers, 2000), 14.

[23] For a discussion of the significance of this spoken word drama, see Hung, *War and Popular Culture: Resistance in Modern China, 1937–1945*, Chapter 2.

Drama Troupe. Around the same time, a handful of Hua Gan cadres established a children's propaganda team in nearby Lingchuan County, quickly bringing their young troupe to Jincheng, performing dance dramas (*wuju*) in towns and villages along the five-day journey.[24]

On May 7, Zhu Rui, after seeing these two troupes perform together, formally joined the two units into the Taihang Mountains Drama Troupe. This military troupe, its members all enlisted in the Eighth Route Army, would prove the region's most important cultural unit. Led by Zhao Luofang, the new troupe initially boasted some thirty members, including twelve middle school students. Ruan Zhangjing, a promising playwright and director, served as the troupe's artistic director (*yishu zhidaoyuan*), providing the voice behind most of its original creations. Ruan, who would later pen the seminal land reform opera *Red Leaf River*, was remembered by his fellow troupe members as a serious and demanding director, criticizing actors until they broke down in tears.[25] The troupe was a volatile mixture of elite intellectuals and impoverished village children performing during dangerous wartime conditions. These child actors would have to grow up quickly.

The troupe bonded quickly in face of shared hardships and members often addressed each other using kinship terms. But this was a decidedly young family. While not a true member of the troupe, patron Zhu Rui was the designated "head of the family" (*jiazhang*) and often joked with his child actors, even telling them that he was Zhu De's brother.[26] But "Uncle Zhu" could be a stern uncle, delivering harsh lectures to ensure his young actors did not dare to leave the troupe and return home.[27] "Elder Brother" Zhao Luofang and "Elder Sisters" Zhang Wenru and Zhang Jieru, all in their twenties, were the most senior members of the troupe; the youngest player, Zhang Shangren, was only eleven-years old and often had to be carried during difficult marches.[28] "Elder Sister" Zhang Jieru, a party member, served as the troupe's political director. One of the clearest speakers in the troupe, she was given the assignment of reminding actors of their lines on stage; according to her comrades she

---

[24] Zhang Shangren, "Huiyi Zhu Rui tongzhi" [Remembering comrade Zhu Rui] THFY (1982), 196–197.

[25] Tian Jing, "Miao" [Sprout] THFY (ca. 1980s), 221.

[26] Zhao Ziyue, "Wo he Taihangshan jutuan" [I and the Taihang Mountains Drama Troupe] THFY (1995), 174.

[27] Zhang Shangren, "Huiyi Zhu Rui tongzhi," 198.

[28] Zhang Wenru and Zhang Jieru were fictive sisters. Originally from Hebei's Baoding, "Zhang Wenru" had been Zhang Jieru's servant girl and close friend. When Zhang Wenru decided to flee from an arranged marriage, Zhang Jieru joined her, changing her name to become "sisters." Zhao Luofang, "Zhu Rui jiangjun yu Taihangshan jutuan" [General Zhu Rui and the Taihang Mountains Drama Troupe] THFY (ca. 1980s), 171.

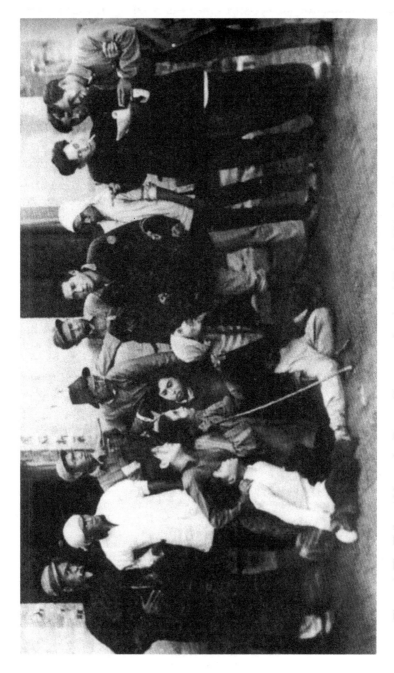

Figure 3 The Taihang Mountains Drama Troupe performing *A Hatred of Blood and Tears*

was quite accomplished in this role, able to communicate lines without disrupting shows. Very seldom appearing on stage, she only played bit parts in a handful of shows.[29] The care she provided for her "little sisters" comes through in an account of the troupe by Tian Jing, then a young girl. According to Tian, during the summer of 1939 the troupe learned how to swim, wisely anticipating that this skill might prove useful during wartime. Zhang Jieru made sure that Tian had the appropriate clothing to practice swimming, but did not learn herself,[30] decisions that would have life and death implications for both women.

Building ties of kinship helped bond the diverse and multi-generational troupe, but other problems remained. While the formation of the troupe allowed Zhang Shangren and other child members to finally purchase much longed for shoes, the larger financial story, as was the case with all Communist troupes, was one of scarce resources.[31] According to troupe leader Zhao Luofang, during its first months of existence his troupe only had two gas lights, a basic percussion set, and a few wooden guns for props.[32] While the situation of the troupe would improve, financial support was always uneven and ad-hoc. Shortly after the troupe was founded, for example, patron Zhu Rui gave the troupe the "liberated" property and cash of a Jincheng "traitor," enabling the troupe to obtain musical instruments and enough cloth to create its prized red curtain.[33] The patronage of Zhu Rui proved decisive for the troupe, and his capital investments were not in vain. As the perceived importance of cultural work grew over the course of the Sino-Japanese War, Zhu's patronage helped legitimize him as a proper revolutionary leader.

During the summer of 1938, just a few months after its formation, the troupe traveled to the Taihang base area's temporary headquarters in Qin County. Settling into a hillside temple that served as a rehearsal hall, the troupe performed for Zhu De, Peng Dehuai, and other leaders. At this early stage, the troupe was divided into two basic units, a drama unit and dance unit – the latter predictably staffed with child members. In August, the troupe expanded to sixty members, establishing its own Lenin Club and Luyi Training Class, although students primarily focused on politics as opposed to culture; in accordance with the prece-dent set by Mao Zedong during the era of Red Drama, Zhu Rui insisted on the primacy of party control over his personal cultural army. That

---

[29] Song Guang and Wang Yantan, "Yi zhanyou Zhang Jieru" [Remembering Zhang Jieru, our friend in war] THFY (1986), 179–180.
[30] Tian Jing, "Miao," 219.   [31] Zhang Shangren, "Huiyi Zhu Rui tongzhi," 197.
[32] Zhao Luofang, "Zhu Rui jiangjun yu Taihangshan jutuan," 163
[33] "Taihang fengyu" [Taihang wind and rain] THFY (ca. 1990s), 9.

autumn Ruan Zhangjing created *Defending the Anti-Japanese Base Area* (Baowei kangri genjudi), a three-act drama concerning the need to organize all efforts against the ongoing Japanese offensive. This drama, the troupe's first important show, showcased Ruan's talent, which would eventually lead to his transfer to ever-higher positions of cultural power. While Ruan emerged as the most eminent of the troupe's elite intellectuals, he still had to work with the many poor village children under his direction. The connections between these children and the "child stars" of Red Drama were more than theoretical: the party dispatched Luo Wenying, a member of the Single Spark Drama Troupe, another "big drama troupe," to the Taihang Mountains Drama Troupe to teach dance. A veteran of the Long March, Luo taught the Taihang children a handful of dances from the Jiangxi Soviet era.[34]

After training in Qin County, the troupe departed in October 1938 for a three-month tour featuring over thirty performances. Later accounts, clearly exaggerated, estimate that these shows reached a total audience of between 200,000 and 300,000. But those who did attend the performances from the troupe's first tour saw an excellent show. The troupe performed a number of songs, dances, and dramas, culminating in their *Defending the Anti-Japanese Base Area*. With this timely topic, Ruan Zhangjing's first important creation inspired great emotion among the crowd, with audience members said to shout out in anger during performances. But these shows were just part of the tour's attractions. The troupe brought along two Japanese captives and an interpreter; this Japanese entourage, most certainly composed of former soldiers, delivered anti-war speeches as part of the troupe's performances. And audiences also saw women on Taihang stages for the first time. Interestingly, villagers quickly accepted female acting, even joking with female performers about their marriage status.[35]

After returning to Qin County at the end of 1938, the troupe traveled to Changzhi in early 1939, performing in support of the Second United Front. But the real purpose of this trip to Taihang's largest city was another round of intensive training. Changzhi was now home to the Southwest Shanxi People's Revolutionary Art Academy, established in February 1939 by Li Bozhao and other cultural leaders from the Yan'an Luyi. This academy, also known as Front Line Luyi (Qianfang Luyi) or Little Luyi (Xiao Luyi), held its classes in Changzhi Normal Academy. Under Li Bozhao's personal direction, the troupe studied her *Song of the Countryside* (Nongcun qu), which had won much acclaim due to Li's

---

[34] Zhang Shangren, "Huiyi Zhu Rui tongzhi," 198.
[35] "Taihang fengyu," 27–28.

pioneering use of folk songs. Li Bozhao would become the troupe's second great patron, writing, directing, and even acting in shows.[36] But senior members of the troupe also took leadership roles in the academy, especially the troupe's own emerging star, Ruan Zhangjing. Working with five other drama troupes drawn to the academy, troupe leaders helped form an eleven-person preparatory committee, which laid the foundations for the subsequent formation of the Southwest Shanxi Branch of the Chinese Dramatic Circles Anti-Japanese Association. Planning a cultural offensive, the Association's sixty representatives discussed myriad plans for all aspects of drama in the Taihang region.[37]

Yet these plans were sidelined due to the war, with both the academy and the troupe forced to head north to Liao County in May 1939 after Japanese attacks associated with the second Ninth Route Siege.[38] Ensconced in the most secure county in the heart of the Taihang base area, the troupe continued to develop despite the uncertainty of the base area's very survival. Sometimes development came with laughs, as it did when the troupe experimented with stage makeup. As will bediscussed in Chapter 5, drama troupes often had to improvise when dealing with makeup, and the Taihang players were no exception. According to Tian Jing, while in Liao County the troupe staged Ruan Zhangjing's latest drama, a show concerning Hitler and Chamberlin in Munich. This was one of the first times the troupe had attempted to create foreign noses, and the experience went poorly. The gluten (*mianjin*) actors used for their fake noses began to rise during the performance, so that the noses of the foreign characters grew ever longer and ended up looking like "elephant trunks." As might be expected, the audience found this show particularly amusing.[39] Yet these "elephant noses" serve as a reminder of the tension between entertainment and propaganda that so plagued Mao's cultural army: the troupe's audience may have been entertained, but the show's educational message could easily be sidelined by humorous but unscripted moments.

In November, after a short tour in the countryside that left many actors in bad health, the troupe settled into Liao County's Siping Village. Here a local Dragon King Temple provided an ideal space for both living and rehearsing, and would remain the troupe's headquarters until the spring

---

[36] Zhu Hua, "Zhandou zai Taihangshan shang Taihangshan jutuan" [Battling in the Taihang Mountains: The Taihang Mountains Drama Troupe] THFY(1985), 192.

[37] "Taihang fengyu," 35.

[38] This county was renamed Zuoquan in September 1942, in honor of Zuo Quan, a Communist leader that was killed during a Japanese offensive deep into the Taihang base area.

[39] Tian Jing, "Miao," 216.

of 1940. A large village with some three hundred families and over one thousand residents, Siping offered the troupe a rare respite. But instead of simply focusing on artistic training, the Taihang players carried out "mass work" (*qunzhong gongzuo*) in the countryside, foreshadowing the importance of drama troupes during later rural revolutionary campaigns. Thanks in part to its secure location, Liao County had been chosen as the Jin-Ji-Yu Border Region's model county in November 1939, making its transformation all the more important. The troupe split up into small teams with three to five members each to work in Siping and six nearby villages.[40]

Troupe members primarily focused on carrying out Double Reduction, a campaign to lower interest rates and rents in the countryside, severely limiting their ability to perform. Troupe members also worked on more domestic issues. One local "activist," for example, had wanted his wife to cut her hair in the modern style, and when she resisted he simply cut it for her as she slept; the wife ran crying to the troupe, forcing them to mediate.[41] But despite the demands of political work, troupe members insisted that they carry on as cultural warriors. Troupe leader Zhao Luofang thus claimed that the troupe established one amateur troupe in each of the seven villages where they had carried out Double Reduction.[42] And troupe members, following the suggestion of Luyi's An Bo, also collected local folk songs.[43] While the degree to which any of this cultural work was meaningful is uncertain, the troupe had clearly branched into new territory by carrying out mass work in the Liao County countryside.

In February 1940, the troupe shifted its attention back to the military, which was then fighting off Guomindang harassment. But the troupe also began to create branch troupes, renaming itself the "Central Troupe" (*zongtuan*), with plans to establish branches in all seven Taihang area prefectures. The troupe sent one of its own, Dong Shiyan, to establish its first branch in March 1940. Based on the existing Beiping-Hankou Line Drama Troupe, this branch had very close ties with the "Central Troupe," with most members trained at one of the Taihang troupe's many training courses.[44] But only five prefecture branch troupes were

[40] Chen Houyu and Xing Shaosi, eds., *Balujun zongbu zai Zuoquan* [The Eighth Route Army in Zuoquan] (Beijing: Zhongyang wenxian chubanshe, 2008), 350–352.

[41] "Taihang fengyu," 47.

[42] Zhao Luofang, "Zhu Rui jiangjun yu Taihangshan jutuan," 165.

[43] "Taihang fengyu," 39.

[44] Hua Qing, "Taihangshan jutuan yu Taihangshan jutuan yi fentuan" [The Taihang Mountains Drama Troupe and the first branch of the Taihang Mountains Drama Troupe] THFY (1999), 272.

ever created, a sign of infrastructural weakness in the Taihang region. The third branch, founded in April 1940, was actually disbanded in 1942 under the call to "simplify the military and the government."[45] Despite its ceaseless touring for soldiers and forays into mass work in the countryside, the Taihang Mountains Drama Troupe still had to fight for recognition.

The year 1940 was a particularly important time of transition for the Taihang Mountains Drama Troupe. That April the troupe moved to Licheng County and reorganized, admitting some new members while sending some child actors to a local school. Further and far more foundational changes occurred over the summer, when Li Bozhao transferred the military troupe to government control under the Communist Party's Central North China Bureau, where she oversaw cultural affairs. Li, now displacing Zhu Rui as the troupe's most important patron, instructed her charges to "struggle to create the North China model drama troupe." Under Li, the troupe launched a new round of training. According to Guo Wei, who joined the troupe in June 1940 to serve as political director, the troupe had a rigorous schedule, with daily jogging, voice exercises, and rehearsals. Political studies were particularly important during times of bad weather and agricultural busy seasons.[46]

The troupe's rigorous training, captured in Guo Wei's memoirs, was put to the test later that year when Japanese forces redoubled their attacks on the base area. After the Hundred Regiments Campaign of August 1940, the troupe found itself on the frontlines performing for the 129th Division, twice taking part in battle in October 1940. Ruan Zhangjing, seemingly intent on proving himself more than an armchair intellectual, led a dozen actors to the front to throw grenades and provide encouragement to frontline soldiers. Yet if he aimed to prove his martial valor, he was disappointed, as he and his fellow players arrived to find that the 129th Division had already retreated. Ruan and the troupe fled to a mountain cave until they were able to rejoin the main force; later, Liu Bocheng and Deng Xiaoping ensured troupe members had horses during a dangerous winter river crossing.[47] During this moment of military danger, ties with party leadership proved to be of decisive help, but what would happen if the troupe found itself without its protectors?

---

[45] Su Feng and Su Ji, "Taihangshan jutuan san fentuan de jianlue huigu" [Some memories from the third branch of the Taihang Mountains Drama Troupe] THFY (2000), 277–279.

[46] Guo Wei, "Yi duan meihao de huiyi: ji Taihangshan jutuan zhandou shenghuo pian" [A beautiful memory: recalling a slice of battling life in the Taihang Mountains Drama Troupe] THFY (1985), 186–187.

[47] Zhu Hua, "Zhandou zai Taihangshan shang taihangshan jutuan," 193–195.

The answer to this question would have to wait. After surviving the aftermath of the Hundred Regiments Campaign, it was time to return to Liao County, where troupe members engaged in another winter of mass work, their political skills increasingly valued. In early 1941, the troupe rehearsed and staged new spoken dramas by new patron Li Bozhao and star playwright Ruan Zhangjing. Special performances were held in honor of Women's Day and to celebrate the establishment of the new Jin-Ji-Lu-Yu Border Region in April. In May, the troupe, celebrating its three-year anniversary, opened a shop that sold mules in She County, demonstrating that funding remained a serious concern. But the search for funds led directly to the Taihang Mountains Drama Troupe's greatest success: the creation of its Shanxi Opera Team under Zhao Ziyue. Where the main troupe typically focused on mobilizing its audiences for the war, this group performed traditional operas for profit. The team's non-political shows, foreshadowing future collaboration between the Communist and local opera actors, proved the most popular performances ever staged by the Taihang players.

Established in the spring of 1941, the Shanxi Opera Team directly appealed to the popular tastes of Taihang soldiers and citizens. According to Zhao Ziyue's memoirs, locating musicians proved the most difficult aspect of organizing the team. Amazingly, not only did he find the needed musicians, but Zhao also was able to recruit two women for his new unit, including a professional female actor trained in local opera. The other woman, Li Peilin, fearing that others would look down on her for being an opera performer, was less than thrilled by her new assignment; the Communists' bias against opera performers was alive and well. According to Li, Zhao Ziyue shot down her suggestions that the troupe perform modern shows, arguing that it was imperative to follow the dictates of popular taste.[48] His argument, made a year before Mao Zedong's "Talks at the Yan'an Forum" made a similar point, quickly proved correct. These shows were among the troupe's most popular, and while the Shanxi Opera Team occasionally performed for free, its primary function was to raise money, not just for the troupe but for the Taihang government as well. Led by the short and rotund Zhao Ziyue, a natural comic actor, the team's shows were enjoyable affairs that attracted sizeable audiences with Du Runsheng and other high-ranking party leaders among the many to turn out for Shanxi opera classics. By enjoying these traditional shows alongside huge rural audiences, Du and his comrades were admitting that there were times when political

---

[48] Li Peilin, "Yi Taihanshan Jutuan de Jinju zu" [Remembering the Taihang Mountains Drama Troupe Shanxi Opera Group] THFY (ca. 1980s), 210–213.

messages had to be shelved in order to entertain audiences and raise funds.

Yet the success of the troupe's Shanxi Opera Team was more than offset by losses in the field. In 1942, the base region suffered through a series of Japanese military offensives, resulting in the most difficult year of the troupe's existence. While staying in She County's Xuanzhong Village, home to the mule shop, the troupe received orders to perform for soldiers who were staving off Japanese attacks. But after days of marching, Japanese harassment forced the troupe to abandon its equipment and flee to Pingshun County, where a two-hundred-strong officer training unit offered a modicum of safety. According to troupe member Xia Hongfei, the troupe faced a difficult decision: Ruan Zhangjing, now serving as the head of the troupe, saw the danger of the moment and advised dispersing the troupe into the countryside, while nearly everyone else favored remaining with their newly found military escort.[49] Going with the majority opinion, the troupe overruled Ruan and followed the soldiers through a region rife with Japanese and Guomindang soldiers, eventually arriving at Jingdi Village on June 26.

Entering the Jingdi Village from the north, the troupe, exhausted from its journey, naturally gravitated towards the village stage to rest. But just as the weary marchers started to relax, the sound of shouting and gunfire filled the air: their military escort had accidently run into enemy forces at the south entrance of the village. Finding both main village entrances now blocked, troupe members scattered in a panic. As vividly captured in dramatist memoirs, the flight from Jingdi Village was chaotic and deadly. Zhao Ziyue had it relatively easy, racing down terraced fields to safety.[50] Tian Jing, a young female actor, also ran down terraced fields, only to run into a dead end as she found herself on a cliff high above deep water. Fearing being captured alive, as another female troupe member would be, Tian managed to climb halfway down the cliff before jumping into the water, her earlier swimming lessons now saving her life.[51] Other troupe members who found themselves stuck on the same cliff were not so lucky. "Elder sister" Zhang Jieru, shot in the abdomen and having never learned to swim, drowned, as did three other troupe members. Ruan Zhangjing was among six troupe members injured in the altercation, but he survived a shot to his buttocks and helped guide the remaining troupe members to safety.[52]

---

[49] Xia Hongfei, "Jingdi ju xue ji" [Record of blood in Jingdi] THFY (ca. 1980s), 254.
[50] Zhao Ziyue, "Wo he Taihangshan jutuan," 178.
[51] Tian Jing, "Miao," 226–228.   [52] Xia Hongfei, "Jingdi ju xue ji," 256.

The troupe returned to Xuanzhong Village to commemorate its fallen and to regroup, its strength further depleted by the subsequent loss of the Shanxi Opera Team. While by most metrics the troupe's most successful unit, the team was forced to disband in early 1943 after losing its two female actors to a Peking opera troupe organized by the Eighth Route Army Headquarters.[53] The troupe continued to perform for money, but raising funds became much more difficult without the ability to stage traditional Shanxi operas. In April, the troupe again returned to Xuanzhong Village, finally reading Mao's "Talks at the Yan'an Forum" and undergoing "rectification" for the first time in June. While the troupe had indeed performed some "big shows," its emphasis on local styles, especially the highly successful staging of Shanxi operas, allowed them to insist that rectification only reinforced previous work.[54] For the Taihang Mountain Drama Troupe, the "Talks at the Yan'an Forum" meant little in terms of altering its approach to drama; much more meaningful was the departure of its star playwright. In September, Li Bozhao helped transfer Ruan Zhangjing to her Jin-Ji-Lu-Yu Cultural Federation, an organization of party artists that oversaw cultural work in the base area during the Sino-Japanese War.

With Ruan Zhangjing's transfer, Zhao Ziyue from the defunct Shanxi Opera Team became the troupe's new leader, a fitting choice in the aftermath of the "Talks at the Yan'an Forum." But after a move to the base area's new Eighth Prefecture, the dictates of mass work kept the troupe off stage. Formally transferred back to military control, the troupe became the Eighth Prefecture Propaganda Team but kept its old Taihang Mountains artistic name. According to Tian Jing, carrying out mass work in the new prefecture proved one of the most difficult assignments of the war. The region, still reeling from Japan's "Three Alls" campaign, was a wasteland scattered with corpses. With wolves feeding on the dead, the troupe mandated that trips to the bathroom after dark had to be done in groups. Dispatched to a remote village to promote production, Tian Jing's work team found the village, once home to over twenty families, had only four residents left.[55] Given the tattered state of the local society, the troupe largely focused on increasing production not through performance but by actually engaging in hard labor opening up the wasteland. This difficult and unfamiliar work led to injuries, with one troupe member hospitalized after breaking a foot. The troupe's time in the new Eighth Prefecture serves as a stark reminder that the demands of the war against Japan often kept the Communists' cultural army far away from artistic endeavors.

[53] Zhao Ziyue, "Wo he Taihangshan jutuan," 176–177.
[54] "Taihang fengyu," 101–103.   [55] Tian Jing, "Miao," 230–232.

Figure 4 The Taihang Mountains Drama Troupe in the Eighth Prefecture, 1944

In early 1945, the troupe celebrated the official formation of the Eighth Prefecture, and before long the struggle against Japan was finally coming to a close. As the balance of power in North China shifted and the Communists went on the offensive, the Taihang players accompanied their military comrades towards Henan, but by the end of the year the troupe was dispersed, formally bringing the history of the Taihang Mountains Drama Troupe to a close. Despite the challenges of wartime, the achievements in cultural creation and performance were considerable. Aside from numerous songs, musical numbers, and dances, the troupe's dramatic output was impressive. Largely under the direction of Ruan Zhangjing, the troupe staged fifty-eight different dramatic works, thirty of which were original creations. But as seen in the carnage of Jingdi Village, the cost was great. One troupe member would later claim that Japanese germ warfare infected the entire troupe with malaria.[56] Eight troupe members were martyred over the long-course of the war, some buried alive.[57] Yet the experiences of this little known troupe reveal that the mixture of elite intellectuals and poor village children that typified so many Communist troupes proved adept at both cultural performance and mass work in the countryside, a double burden that future cultural workers would have to embrace. And despite powerful patrons in Zhu Rui and Li Bozhao, funding proved a serious concern for performers of revolutionary dramas. Tellingly, the enduring popularity of traditional opera offered the troupe its best hope for raising money through its Shanxi Opera Team. Mao's cultural army would learn to embrace local opera, but the relationship between traditional culture and revolutionary politics was eternally fraught with complications.

A professional troupe: the Xiangyuan Rural Drama Troupe

While "big drama troupes" were the most prolific performers of Communist dramas during the Sino-Japanese War, their scarcity kept their performances from reaching far beyond Eighth Route Army soldiers. Even in the Taihang region, the relatively secure and well-governed core of the Jin-Ji-Lu-Yu Border Region, few villagers had the chance to see "big drama troupe" shows. And although Taihang cultural leaders had grand plans for a network of amateur village drama troupes in the Taihang region, the border region ultimately lacked the organizational power to construct this cultural infrastructure. As David Goodman has

---

[56] Ibid., 230.
[57] Zhu Hua, "Zhandou zai Taihangshan shang Taihangshan jutuan," 194.

noted, the border region "had little cohesion and consequently little clear identity before 1945. It was not until the Civil War period that the border region government could reasonably claim to act as a government for much, if not all, of the border region."[58]

In the Jiangxi Soviet, Mao had envisioned a cultural army that relied on party-run troupes and amateur performers in order to sidestep professional drama troupes, imagined to be hotbeds of immorality and feudalism. In the Taihang region, government weakness made this unrealistic. Zhang Panshi, a leading propaganda and education cadre, conceded that that the Communist Party would have to rely on professional troupes to staff the Taihang cultural army during the fight against Japan. Speaking in the aftermath of rectification, when using local culture to mobilize the masses was a leading priority of the party, Zhang noted that the Taihang region was home to three types of drama troupes: "big drama troupes," professional troupes, and amateur village troupes. According to Zhang, the popularity of professional troupes made them the natural foundation for the rural drama troupe movement, while amateur troupes were to focus on production and not leave their home villages.[59] But relying on professionals often left Communist leaders dismayed. Local popular culture ensured that professional troupes continued to function in ways reminiscent of old-style *xibanzi* outfits, even when they staged revolutionary dramas. The experiences of the Xiangyuan Rural Drama Troupe, for example, suggest that professional entertainers were not the most reliable of soldiers in Mao's cultural army.

Like most professional troupes that came under Communist Party control, the Xiangyuan players started as a *xibanzi* outfit, performing local operas for profit in the Changzhi region. But traveling troupes need a peaceful countryside, and Japanese invasion disrupted tours and kept the troupe idle until the establishment of the Taihang base area in 1938. Hearing that the Fourth District wanted to form a drama troupe, the troupe changed its name to Xiangyuan Fourth District Rural Drama Troupe and found a patron in the new government. While boasting a new name and affiliation with the base government, the troupe continued to only perform traditional shows. Despite powerful examples from the Taihang Mountains Drama Troupe and other "modern" outfits in the region, the Xiangyuan troupe failed to add a single modern show to its repertoire. Equally troubling, troupe members continued to behave

---

[58] Goodman, "JinJiLuYu in the Sino-Japanese War: The Border Region and the Border Region Government," 1010.
[59] Zhang Panshi, "Panshi tongzhi zongjie baogao" [Comrade Panshi's summary report] SGWZ (ca. 1940s), 209–210.

like "hooligans," a problem the Communists often ascribed to *xibanzi* players. According to a 1938 report on the troupe, its actors and musicians continued to gamble, consort with prostitutes, and smoked opium. In a sign of how little control the base region had over the drama troupes that bore their names, this state of affairs lasted a full two years until the Communists finally intervened.[60]

Of the changes the Communists forced on the troupe in 1940, most challenging was getting troupe members to give up opium, a problem plaguing North China but particularly common among actors and musicians. The Communists typically approached the problem of addiction with a methodological mixture of persuasion and coercion.[61] Using methods of group criticism helped start the process, but actors and musicians simply took to smoking in private. With further efforts to stamp out smoking, troupe members found new ways to consume the drug, a testament to the depths of their addictions as well as their refusal to submit to Communist supervision. Opium addicts first began secretly drinking "mud water" (*tushui*), a liquid mash of opium. When "mud water" was suppressed, players moved on to discretely consuming opium poppy shells (*yinsu ke*). Eventually, cadres realized that state power alone could not force obstinate actors and musicians to give up their opium. They could, however, pay the salaries of opium addicts directly to their wives. This proved effective.[62]

Changing the troupe's old recruitment and education system also vexed the Communists. In a traditional *xibanzi* troupe, students were indentured to teachers, who were free to treat their charges cruelly while training them in the dramatic arts. This harsh arrangement served to propagate abuse and was frequently labeled "feudal." Despite the negative connotations associated with this system, it was not until 1943, five years after the troupe first attached itself to the Taihang border government, that any changes were made. Even then, troupe elders fiercely resisted these changes, resulting in a divisive generational clash within the troupe.[63] Thus, while the Communist Party was able to reform the Xiangyuan troupe, the fit of the party with professional actors was from the start a difficult one.

---

[60] Ye Feng and Yu Ming, "Xiangyuan nongcun jutuan de gaizao" [The reform of the Xiangyuan Village Drama Troupe] SGWZ (ca. 1940s), 220.

[61] Suzanne Pepper, *Civil War in China: The Political Struggle 1945–1949*, 2nd edn. (Lanham, MD: Rowman & Littlefield Publishers, Inc., 1999), 346.

[62] Ye Feng and Yu Ming, "Xiangyuan nongcun jutuan de gaizao," 221.

[63] Ze Ran, "Nongcun jutuan de qizhi – ji Taihang jutuan de chengzhang" [The banner of rural drama troupes – remembering the Taihang Drama Troupe's growth] SGWZ (1947), 475.

Once firmly under the thumb of the district government, the Xiangyuan troupe was quickly elevated to model status. Blessed with talented actors, the troupe toured widely and earned a respectable salary through performances. While this was a professional troupe that charged for shows, occasional free performances were said to be highly valued by impoverished villages. The troupe also invested in small industry and commerce in order to gain additional income streams.[64] While the troupe continued to stage traditional shows, its repertoire now included *The White-Haired Girl* and other revolutionary dramas. The troupe, finally, was also said to have helped form around a dozen village drama troupes in Xiangyuan.[65] When the troupe received a new banner from party leader Bo Yibo, its transformation from unruly *xibanzi* outfit to model troupe was complete.

The Xiangyuan Rural Drama Troupe would have a long and fruitful collaboration with the Communist Party. But coopting the troupe was a rare victory. The Communists' attempt to bring order to local culture in the Taihang region through a rural cultural campaign in the early 1940s, in contrast, flopped miserably. The campaign's failure was first caused by the inadequate reach of the cultural infrastructure needed for rural cultural campaigns. The Taihang Cultural Federation did not launch its journal, *North China Culture* (*Huabei wenhua*), until 1942, a full four years after the establishment of the base area. As detailed in Hua Shan's September 1943 report "Thoughts on Literature and Arts Going to the Countryside," cultural knowledge had not penetrated rural areas. After traveling extensively in the countryside and speaking with cadres and villagers, Hua Shan discovered that despite almost five years of cultural activities in the region, only county-level cadres specializing in education and propaganda had even heard about the region's most famous artists and works. Even more troubling, many village schoolteachers were unaware of the existence of the Cultural Federation, which in theory was organizing the rural cultural campaign.[66] Cultural leaders seemed well aware of this problem, admitting that they had no means of reaching out to the village intellectuals, who were to play the lead role in developing local cultural institutions.[67]

---

[64] Ye Feng and Yu Ming, "Xiangyuan nongcun jutuan de gaizao," 223–226.

[65] The quality of these units is unclear. Ze Ran, "Nongcun jutuan de qizhi – ji Taihang jutuan de chengzhang," 478.

[66] Hua Shan, "Wenyi xiaxiang zatan" [Thoughts on literature and arts going to the countryside] SGWZ (1943), 133.

[67] Xu Maoyong, "Wenlian yijiusier nian de gongzuo zongjie ji yijiusisan nian de gongzuo jihua" [Summary of Wenlian work in 1942 and work plan for 1943] SGWZ (1943), 158.

Second, over the course of the Sino-Japanese War, cultural leaders in the base area raised serious concerns regarding the role and abilities of their cultural workers. Looking at the limited successes of 1942 to 1943, Zhang Xiuzhong suggested that "campaign" (*yundong*) was too strong a word to describe area cultural work. In Zhang's view, advances had been made, but overall there was very little real progress to speak of.[68] Hua Shan placed particular doubt on female cultural workers, noting that while some women truly became one with the masses, many preferred to "wash their faces" and "brush their teeth" while spending most of their time alone writing.[69] This problem was never solved during the war against Japan: in mid-1947, cultural leaders were still accusing cultural workers of acting like "guests" in the base area, divorced from the masses.[70] With a limited cultural infrastructure and cultural workers of questionable quality, it is little surprise that cultural work failed to keep pace with political work.[71]

Third, the "campaign" also revealed the uneasy relationship between the Communist Party, traditional *xibanzi* troupes, and amateur performers. In 1941, in his "Opinions" on the region's drama movement, party leader Xu Guang emphasized the need to work with and win over *xibanzi* troupes.[72] If, as some cultural cadres claimed, the masses truly wanted shows that focused on real-life events,[73] the Communist Party's plan for using professionals as propagandists would have made perfect sense: the market would encourage professionals to stage modern works. But troupes like the Xiangyuan Rural Drama Troupe, willing to work with the Communists, proved the exception. In mid-1947, cultural leaders were still bemoaning the popularity of old-style "big shows" of questionable content.[74] The continued love for traditional shows created financial opportunities that talented drama troupes found hard to ignore. This led to a troubling trend as professional drama troupes continued to perform as *xibanzi* units, while amateur troupes aspired to *xibanzi* status. As Zhu

---

[68] Zhang Xiuzhong, "Yi nian lai benqu wenyi yundong de huigu yu qianzhan" [Reflections and projections after one year of area cultural work] SGWZ (1943), 187–191.

[69] Hua Shan, "Wenyi xiaxiang zatan," 135.

[70] Xiao Qiu, "Dangqian xiju jie de jige wenti" [Some problems with the current drama circles] SGWZ (1947), 205.

[71] Goodman argues that by the end of the Sino-Japanese War, considerable progress had been made in the transformation of social and political institutions. See Goodman, *Social and Political Change in Revolutionary China*, 225.

[72] Xu Guang, "Xin de shiqi yu xin de fangxiang – dui benqu juyun de ji dian yijian" [New times and new directions – some opinions on our area drama movement] SGWZ (1941), 132.

[73] Hua Shan, "Wenyi xiaxiang zatan," 134.

[74] Xiao Qiu, "Dangqian xiju jie de jige wenti," 204.

Muzhi warned cultural workers in a speech on rural drama troupes in mid-1946, this was not an isolated problem: "all rural drama troupes have a tendency to develop towards professional drama troupes." To make things worse, "in the best rural drama troupes, this tendency is particularly clear."[75]

Cultural leaders, finally, envisioned a rural cultural campaign that held drama as distinct from the process of rural revolution. Throughout the Sino-Japanese War, party leaders continually emphasized the importance of drama troupes, but tended to promote a Marxist view of cultural change. While drama was believed to have great power, ideological and cultural transformation was ultimately a byproduct of economic forces. Zhu Muzhi was particularly clear in discussing the relationship between economic *fanshen* and the drama troupe movement. According to Zhu, the some seven hundred village drama troupes dispersed among the twenty-two counties in the Taiyue region constituted a "formidable dramatic army" (*qiangda de xiju dajun*). But Zhu also argued that "rural drama troupes are not organized through the process of the *fanshen* struggle, but are organized after the victory of the *fanshen* struggle."[76] Without a "quality *fanshen*," it was impossible to establish a modern *jutuan* drama troupe. Without a "quality *fanshen*," Zhu argued, all that existed were traditional *xibanzi* opera troupes that tricked the people. Once *fanshen* occurred, people would turn away from the old stories and prefer the new-style shows staged by *jutuan* drama troupes. Popular preference for *xibanzi* opera troupes and their traditional shows, however, did not simply vanish with *fanshen*. If anything, peace and prosperity brought about increased demand for traditional operas.

An amateur example: the High Street Village Drama Troupe (Gaojiecun jutuan)

Along with the Shaan-Gan-Ning Border Region, the Jin-Cha-Ji Border Region was a rare "officially" recognized Communist government, and far more secure than the oft-invaded Jin-Ji-Lu-Yu Border Region. As described by Kathleen Hartford, Jin-Cha-Ji served as a "policy model for other resistance bases," while also showing the power of Japanese repression "even when the revolutionaries did just about everything right."[77]

---

[75] Zhu Muzhi, "Qunzhong fanshen, zichang zile" [When the masses fanshen, they sing of their happiness] SGWZ (1946), 441.

[76] Ibid., 431.

[77] Kathleen J. Hartford, "Repression and Communist Success: The Case of Jin-Cha-Ji, 1938–1943," in *Single Sparks: Chinas Rural Revolutions*, eds. Kathleen J. Hartford and Steven M. Goldstein (New York: M.E. Sharpe, 1987), 94.

In Hartford's analysis, the Jin-Cha-Ji Border Region provides a best-case scenario for the implementation of Communist Party programs. To be sure, morale in the region was severely dampened by Japanese attacks after the Hundred Regiments offensive during the late summer of 1940. As Hartford describes the four major extermination campaigns carried out by the Japanese:

> Savage, protracted, repeated sweeps of base areas and guerrilla bases were conducted. In the heartland of the border region, these sweeps were designed to drag off, burn, shoot, bury alive, eviscerate, or otherwise eliminate any inhabitants of potential use to the border region. Any grain that could not be carried off was burned. Standing crops were burned or trampled. Villages were razed, livestock slaughtered or stolen, trees chopped down, irrigation works destroyed.[78]

Yet while these incursions brought the Jin-Cha-Ji to the "brink of disaster," by 1943 the strategy had failed and Japanese troops were caught in a stalemate.[79] Jin-Cha-Ji saw relative security, adequate staffing, and widespread mass activism. With these factors allowing ever-greater opportunities to carry out rural cultural work, the Jin-Cha-Ji Border Region moved to develop a network of amateur drama troupes to supplement the work of the region's professional drama troupes, the same goal that proved impossible in the Taihang Mountains.

The first salvo in the attempt to mobilize a village cultural army was the Jin-Cha-Ji Rural Cultural Movement, launched in 1940 through the government's Culture and Education Association (Wenjiao hui). With a focus on popularizing Communist-friendly performances throughout the countryside, cadres and professional drama troupes were assigned the task of bringing the long-desired amateur cultural army to life. Working under the slogan "struggle to create model village drama troupes," the campaign boasted of the formation of thousands of village troupes. But a 1942 report by the Jin-Cha-Ji Drama Association Branch strongly questioned the quality of these units, finding their organization, artistic level, and work output all of dubious value. Referencing the oft-repeated claim of the three thousand village amateur troupes established in the Beiyue and Jinzhong regions, the report bluntly admitted that "fewer than one hundred" village drama troupes lived up to expected standards.[80] Given that this was the most severe era of Japanese

---

[78] Ibid., 107.   [79] Ibid., 95.

[80] Jin-Cha-Ji bianqu juxie fenhui, "1942 niandu wei chuangzuo mofan cun jutuan er douzheng" [In 1942 struggle to create model village drama troupes] JCJX (1942), 325.

repression, the failure of even the "secure" Jin-Cha-Ji Border Region to develop amateur cultural activities is hardly surprising.

Two years later, the Jin-Cha-Ji regional government was ready to again push the development of a rural amateur drama troupe network. This renewed campaign primarily benefited from an increasingly secure base area, but was also well served by the development of a handful of model troupes, especially the High Street Village Drama Troupe. Formed in Fuping County in 1944, the High Street troupe rose to fame on the basis of its original creation, *Happiness of the Poor* (Qiongren le). A mixture of *huaju* spoken drama and local opera, the show depicted life in a Shanxi village over the course of nearly a decade. Over its fourteen scenes, villagers suffer under a Lama landlord, find liberation under the Eighth Route Army, carry out rent reduction, and elect a democratic village government. The second half of the drama focuses on various efforts to raise production in order to support the war against Japan, including spring planting drives and a campaign to kill locusts.[81] The show opens on a depressing note, with a peasant forced to sell his daughter as a servant girl (*yatou*) to the village landlord, foreshadowing the skillful use of gender tropes that would become a hallmark of land reform opera. Yet the majority of the show was upbeat: only one of the opera's fifteen songs was a lament.

Announcing the selection of *Happiness of the Poor* as a model work in late 1944, the Jin-Cha-Ji cultural authorities noted that the opera accurately reflected the process of *fanshen*, and emphasized how the High Street dramatists had correctly complied with Mao's dictates concerning artistic production. This decision to promote the opera heralded fame and even a modicum of fortune for troupe members. Their script would be published and distributed throughout the border region, while the local border government gave the troupe a curtain to use in future shows.[82] And when the border region launched a second village drama troupe campaign, all Jin-Cha-Ji villages were instructed to "follow the *Happiness of the Poor* direction." As explained in an editorial in the *Jin-Cha-Ji Daily*, the High Street Drama Troupe solved the challenges of rural artistic creation by using local artistic forms and drafting villagers to play peasants on stage. The troupe was also praised for the integration of creation and performance: the amateur dramatists started with a simple

---

[81] Gaojiecun jutuan, *Qiongren le* [Happiness of the poor] JCJX (1944).

[82] "Zhonggong zhongyang Jin-Cha-Ji fenju guanyu Fuping xian Gaojiecun jutuan chuangzuo de "*Qiongren le*" de jueding" [Central Committee of the Communist Party of China, Jin-Cha-Ji Branch Office's decision regarding the Fuping County High Street Village Drama Troupe's creation *Happiness of the Poor*] JCJX (1944), 314.

Figure 5 The High Street Village Drama Troupe performing *Happiness of the Poor*

outline, which was continuously reworked during early performances through audience feedback.[83]

In the wake of the 1944 rural culture campaign, calling for villages to follow the High Street example, once again the Jin-Cha-Ji Border Region would boast of the creation of a rural drama troupe network that contained thousands of village performing units. According to a late 1945 report in *Education Battleground*, the campaign had proved a huge success: in one district, half of all villages now enjoyed their own drama troupe. While noting that more leadership was needed, especially from intellectuals and local cadres, these village troupes were praised for following the "*Happiness of the Poor* direction" by describing the *fanshen*

[83] "Yanzhe *Qiongren le* de fangxiang, fazhan qunzhong wenyi yundong" [Develop a literature and arts campaign in the direction of *Happiness of the Poor*] JCJX (1944), 315–317.

of the laboring masses while using a variety of local cultural forms.[84] With the "*Happiness of the Poor*" direction, it would seem that the Communists had finally found the key to organizing amateur performance.

But when Jin-Cha-Ji cultural leaders launched a third rural arts movement in 1946, the deficiencies of the 1944 campaign were slowly but surely dragged into full view. As explained in late 1946 by Man Qing in *New Masses*, quality village drama troupes were in fact still extremely rare and not widely disseminated. Their performances, moreover, were largely confined to the holiday season. Man Qing, of course, assured readers that with the 1946 campaign, these problems had been solved, boasting that the 1,381 drama troupes then operating in the Hebei-Shanxi region were preforming throughout the year, with spring performances at festivals and autumn and winter shows in periodic markets.[85] According to Man Qing, the border region government had finally installed an infrastructure of amateur drama troupes, a network that could be relied on to perform in support of political movements, which in 1946 meant the burgeoning "settling accounts struggle" (*qingsuan douzheng*), a forerunner to all-out agrarian revolution. With one Central Hebei local cadre declaring a single show to be worth ten days of traditional propaganda, the Communist Party surely had achieved its dream of creating a true cultural army in village China.[86]

Yet as studies of Communist mass campaigns from land reform to Great Leap Forward have made clear, the party's declarations of victory often prove premature or simply fabricated. Similarly, the apparent successes of amateur village troupes in Jin-Cha-Ji had once again been wildly overstated. Nowhere are the limitations and ultimate failure of rural cultural infrastructure building clearer than the case of the Dongyang Village Drama Troupe, located in Hebei's Xintang County. Created in 1943 during a push for rural cultural campaigns in the aftermath of Mao's "Talks at the Yan'an Forum," the early years of the troupe's history demonstrate that coordinated action by village activists was critical to the success of rural drama troupes. According to Sun Ying's post-Cultural Revolution account, the troupe's creation was a result of the initiative taken by the village party branch. Because Dongyang Village had no dramatic traditions, the party branch dispatched students to a nearby village to study the local "rattle stick dance." This dance team

[84] Feng Suhai and Hou Jinjing, "Dui muqian xiangcun wenyi yundong de ji dian yijian" [Some opinions on the current rural literature and arts movement] JCJX (1945), 330–335.
[85] Man Qing, "Ji-Jin qu yi nian lai de xiangyi yundong" [One year of the Hebei-Shanxi rural arts movement] JCJX (1946), 347–350.
[86] Wang Lin, "Wei Jizhong cun jutuan jiang yi yan" [Thoughts on Central Hebei village drama troupes] JCJX (1946), 337.

quickly expanded into a drama troupe, performing local operas alongside original creations. Between 1943 and 1947, the troupe created over 120 shows, consistently used local forms, and even brought villagers on stage to play themselves. Yet despite perfectly adhering to the "*Happiness of the Poor* direction," the troupe's performances ground to a complete and final halt in 1947.[87]

Sun Ying provided three reasons for the troupe's demise. First, as the success of the PLA in the Civil War brought new territories into Communist rule, the party transferred many cadres, instructors, and "drama troupe backbones" to newly conquered territories. Second, after land reform, many troupe members turned their attention to economic production; Sun Ying attributed this to the need for production to support the Civil War, but in light of the many years that the border region government had pushed production, the reason amateur actors focused on farming after receiving their own land was more likely personal in nature. In the end, Sun admitted, the biggest threat to the Dongyang Village Drama Troupe was local culture. With Japan finally defeated, old-style *xibanzi* troupes returned in droves, bringing high-quality traditional "big shows" back to rural stages. As traditional operas with expensive staging drew ever-larger crowds, amateur troupes found their audiences rapidly diminishing. Seeing the crowds and the money that these traditional shows were bringing in, talented amateurs rushed to turn professional. In neighboring Ding County, a "*yangge*" troupe sprang into existence, but this was a for-profit *xibanzi* outfit. As this phenomenon spread across the countryside, those amateur troupes that could not turn professional simply stepped off stage.[88] Despite Zhu Muzhi's claim that peasants who had experienced *fanshen* would prefer new-style *jutuan* troupes over traditional *xibanzi* outfits, Sun Ying's experiences proved the exact opposite to be true.

In examining the issues and trends that marked the push for village drama troupes during the early 1940s, the persistence of local culture thus looms large. Communist Party dramatists drew from the North China countryside's rich heritage of local opera in their creations, but local cultural traditions were as much a threat as they were a source of inspiration. Even as Man Qing heralded the rise of village troupes in 1946, he admitted that traditional dramas were still widespread. Some local cadres, meanwhile, had simply accepted the fact that the masses did

---

[87] Sun Ying, "Chunyu guohou baihua kai – jieshao dongyangzhuang cunjutuan" [After the spring rain one hundred flowers bloom – introducing the Dongyangzhuang Village Drama Troupe] JCJX (1986), 383.

[88] Ibid., 382–383.

not like the modern dramas that the party so relentlessly promoted.[89] Forced to compete with traditional *xibanzi* performers, village troupes often imitated their rivals and moved towards professional status. Repeated calls for village troupes to keep shows simple and to avoid unneeded expenditures reveal this to be a common problem in the Communists' cultural army.[90] This "problem" of the draw of professionalism, moreover, would plague cultural leaders throughout the Maoist era.

Some villages, of course, were able to establish and develop high-quality amateur drama troupes. In explaining the success of model troupes, cultural observers were quick to point to the importance of leadership and organization. To be sure, the faith in the power of drama that was shared by artists and the Communist Party's elite found little counterpart among most local cadres. Surveying the rural cultural scene in 1945, Feng Suhai and Hou Jinjing found a host of issues stemming from deficient leadership. Some village leaders only paid attention to amateur drama troupes during the holiday season. Mid-level cadres paid lip service to cultural work, but ignored the difficult details of managing the campaigns.[91] With village cadres often ignoring cultural work, it fell on professional and military drama troupes to organize and train amateur performers, but these troupes were far too rare to offer much help. The High Street Village Drama Troupe had in fact benefited from training with a military drama troupe during the early days of its existence, but few village troupes had such an opportunity.[92] In addition to this training, the High Street players also had a local patron in the cadre who ran their village co-op; known as a "co-op hero," his management skills meant that the troupe enjoyed sufficient funding despite its "amateur" status.[93] Even before the troupe was singled out as a model for emulation, High Street Village dramatists held advantages that were simply unavailable in the vast majority of North China villages.

Yet even the limited formation of amateur drama troupes within North China villages posed no small challenge to traditional culture. Open to female membership, the existence of amateur troupes was troublesome for patriarchal norms. As Wang Lin emphasized, the mixture of men and women in drama troupes, long assumed to be hotbeds of immorality, caused consternation within rural society. Some cadres, Wang noted,

---

[89] Man Qing, "Ji-Jin qu yi nian lai de xiangyi yundong," 358.

[90] Jin-Cha-Ji bianqu juxie fenhui, "1942 niandu wei chuangzuo mofan cun jutuan er douzheng," 326.

[91] Feng Suhai and Hou Jinjing, "Dui muqian xiangcun wenyi yundong de ji dian yijian," 335.

[92] "Yanzhe *Qiongren le* de fangxiang, fazhan qunzhong wenyi yundong," 320.

[93] Wang Lin, "Wei Jizhong cun jutuan jiang yi yan" 338.

had attempted to solve this problem by simply keeping women out of drama troupes. In response, Wang insisted that drama troupes be open to both men and women, even noting that a free marriage between troupe members was not only permissible, but ideal, as the union of two talented artists was to be lauded. Wang's warning that troupe members refrain from affairs, however, serves as a reminder that even amateur drama troupes were held in suspicion. In part, this was simply because of their role as agents of change. Kang Zhuo, in his glowing account of the Chaizhuang Village Drama Troupe, argued that villagers accepted actors because of their simple style. When one dared to part his hair (*liu fentou*) in imitation of the urbane members of a professional PLA drama troupe that had visited the village, an old villager ridiculed him by shouting: "Hey! He looks like he is from the Firing Line Drama Troupe!"[94] Properly chastised, the young actor un-parted his hair. Clearly, this was a change that Chaizhuang Village was not ready for.

Conclusion: nineteen days of drama

In early 1945, the fight against Japan, while showing progress, did not have a clear end in sight. Yet the Communists made sure to find time for drama. That February, cultural worker Zhi Hua found out just how important drama was for the Communists' cause. When his district held a Mass Hero Meeting (*qunying dahui*), nine drama troupes came together to stage forty-eight shows over the course of nineteen days. These shows largely focused on supporting the war effort, promoting production, and raising educational standards. While the range of topics was noteworthy, the different styles that these nine drama troupes staged were truly exceptional. Some troupes performed *yangge* dramas, mixing dialogue, singing, and *kuaiban* "wooden clapper" performances. Simple shows that did not even need a curtain, Zhi Hua found that these shows were best suited to amateur troupes.

Others staged *geju* operas; according to Zhi Hua, these shows combined *yangge* style singing with *huaju* spoken drama scene structures and movements. More realistic and accomplished than *yangge* shows, these *geju* operas were more expensive and difficult to stage. Some troupes staged *huaju* spoken dramas, and while many in the audience complained about the lack of theatricality of these shows, Zhi Hua argued that these inexpensive shows were ideal for telling stories. Yet another artistic form staged over the nineteen days was the revolutionary historical drama

---

[94] Kang Zhuo, "Chaizhuang jutuan" [The Chaizhuang Village Drama Troupe] JCJX (1949), 320.

(*geming lishiju*), which proved quite popular, although Zhi Hua noted that these needed expensive props and a talented troupe. The same could be said for "modern" shows that used the structure and styles of these historical shows.[95] As might be expected from this description, the nine troupes that entertained the Mass Hero Meeting represented a diverse lot. Some, such as the government troupes, were professionals that had left agricultural work. There were also semi-professional troupes, which returned to agricultural production during the busy seasons. And, finally, there were village drama troupes, who only performed during holidays and the winter slack season.[96]

As evidenced by the wide variety of dramas staged during these nine-teen days, Communist leaders devoted much time and attention to its cultural army during the Sino-Japanese War. As this chapter has detailed, the Communist Party dealt with a wide variety of drama troupes, from "big drama troupes" that served the party and its armed forces, to professionals who had to balance the need to earn a living with the dictates of the party, to amateurs who struggled to find the resources to perform for their neighbors. The Communist Party had assembled its long-desired cultural army, but as cultural warriors in the battle against Japan, these actors and musicians proved an unruly force.

The reason was partly simple economics. With the cultural army receiving scant financial support from the Communists, traditional dra-matic performances that eschewed political messages proved lucrative. One mid-1946 report noted that while amateur troupes were expected to perform for free, or at the most for a meal if they were outside the village, that was not the case with *xibanzi* opera troupes, which could expect substantial fees in exchange for their performances of traditional opera.[97] In mid-1947, another report on an amateur drama troupe from Dongbao Village was upfront about the difficulties the troupe had faced from its competition. The troupe was performing short *yangge* dramas, but had been essentially pushed off stage by the craze for old shows, which were being staged by other local troupes. After almost giving up, the troupe retooled its repertoire, adding more music and costumes to better match traditional shows.[98]

---

[95] Zhi Hua, "Kan xi shijiu tian" [Watching dramas for nineteen days] SGWZ (1945), 242–243.

[96] Ibid., 243–244.

[97] Xia Qing, "'Bu gang qiang de duiwu' – Taiyue yangcheng gulongcun nongcun jutuan jieshao" ["An army that does not carry guns" – an introduction to the Taiyue Yangcheng Gulong Village Rural Drama Troupe] SGWZ (1946), 493.

[98] Hua Han, "Jieshao wuxiang dongbaocun jiefang jutuan" [An introduction to the Wuxiang Dongbao Village Drama Troupe] SGWZ (1947), 481.

Finally, while the Communists viewed drama as one of the most effective methods of mass mobilization, they tended to direct this cultural weapon at soldiers at war or villagers working in the fields. Drama was seldom used in the process of rural revolution during the Sino-Japanese War. Dramatists and actors made for ideal work team members to carry out the revolution, but they were valued for their literacy and political acumen, not for artistic skills. The Taihang Mountains Drama Troupe, for example, was too busy with political work to perform dramas as they helped establish the Eighth Prefecture. Similarly, when Yuan Chenglong led a team of cultural workers to carry out "Double Reduction" work in Shandong's Linshu County, they were organized as a "work team" (*gongzuotuan*) and not a "cultural work team" (*wengongtuan*). Mostly from Beijing and Shanghai, team members faced the usual period of acclimation to village life, with those with Western haircuts shaving their heads. But despite being in Linshu for over half of a year, their work remained focused on mundane political tasks, save for a few songs at "struggle" meetings.[99] Only with the arrival of Civil War and land reform would the Communists bring drama into the actual process of rural revolution, synchronizing cultural and political performances. It is to this moment that this study now turns.

[99] Yuan Chenglong, "'Shuangjian' gongzuotuan zai Linshu" ["Double reduction" work team in Linshu], in *Hongse Jiyi* [Red Recollections] (Beijing: Zhonggong dangshi chubanshe, 2009), 252–254.

3   Playing soldiers and peasants
Civil War and agrarian reform

In light of his "bandit" origins, He Long may have originally seemed an unlikely patron of the arts. But by the time the long expected Civil War finally erupted in 1946, Commander He, then stationed in the Jin-Sui Military Region, had a well-established commitment to fielding drama troupes on the battlefield. With a combination of a villager's love for folk art and a Communist's fervent belief in the power of drama, He Long's drive to expand his division of Mao's cultural army proved relentless. When the Jin-Sui branch of the People's Anti-Japanese Military and Political University left for the Northeast front at the start of the Civil War, He Long made sure to retain its cultural work teams, reorganizing these amateur players into a new unit, the Combat Dramatic Propaganda Team.[1] And his penchant for artistic criticism remained ever vigilant, as Chen Bo, one of the team's leaders, discovered after receiving a stern lecture from He Long for daring to look down on Shanxi opera.

The Civil War was an eventful era for Commander He's leading drama troupe, the Combat Dramatic Society. During their first clash at the Battle of Suibao, troupe members found themselves tending to the wounded, and soon the troupe perfected the art of dividing into small performance teams to entertain soldiers on the frontlines. "Mass work" remained equally important, especially after the 1946 May 4th Directive launched all-out agrarian revolution. When troupe members first took part in the earliest rounds of land reform in northern Shanxi, however, their roles remained entirely political in nature: actors, dispersed into work teams, never had a chance to perform. The troupe did, however, collect material for future creations, most notably *Land Returns Home* (Tudi hui laojia), first staged on New Year's Day, 1947. While very specific about the details of speaking bitterness, settling accounts, and dividing landholdings, the show still failed to satisfy He Long, who demanded a greater

---

[1] This newly created propaganda team would eventually be absorbed by the Combat Dramatic Society, as always He Long's most elite performance unit.

focus on the suffering of peasants, specifically calling for a greater imitation of *The White-Haired Girl*.[2]

For the Combat Dramatic Society, the double burden of serving the military and overseeing mass work in the countryside continued throughout the Civil War years as the troupe followed its patrons He Long and Peng Dehuai from the Jin-Sui Military Region to the Northwest Field Army. Peng also proved a passionate drama critic, exploding in anger when one of his officers requested a traditional show of dubious content.[3] During the Civil War, the troupe endured long marches and pitched combat, with its service at the Battle of the Huanglong Mountains earning special recognition. Yet military service was not enough, for as He Long made clear in Jin-Sui, cultural workers had to take part in the actual process of land reform and also create new works dealing with agrarian revolution.[4] For the Combat Dramatic Society, this meant regular participation in land reform. In Xin County, for example, the troupe led land reform as regular work team members, but also performed a special three set program to support the campaign. And the troupe found time to create – most notably *Liu Hulan*, the number that cemented the troupe's legacy. The troupe even staged propaganda-heavy dramas in urban areas, performing with local troupes and students in Linfen City after its "liberation."[5]

As the troupe's experiences demonstrate, the late 1940s was an era profoundly marked by Civil War and land reform. These massive and violent campaigns culminated in the Communists' takeover of China's cities, and all three processes demanded drama troupe involvement. In the aftermath of the Sino-Japanese War, Mao's cultural army underwent rapid expansion as the Communist Party transferred large numbers of cultural workers to new areas, including a huge mobilization of cultural talent to the Northeast at the outset of the conflict.[6] At this stage, propaganda teams and professional drama troupes attached to the PLA and

---

[2] Chen Bo, "Zhandou jushe zhandou zai xibei zhanchang" [The Combat Dramatic Society battles in the Northwest front] JZSQ (ca. 1980s), 15–21.

[3] Ibid., 28.

[4] He Long "Dui Jin-Sui wenhua gongzuozhe de jianghua" [Lecture to Jin-Sui cultural workers] JZSQ (ca. 1940s), 7.

[5] Chen Bo, "Zhandou jushe zhandou zai xibei zhanchang," 21–23.

[6] According to one Liaoning gazetteer, beyond staging a wide variety of cultural forms, everything from large-scale operas to simple puppet shows, the newly created drama troupe infrastructure in the Northeast "created a large number of cultural festivals and cultivated many literature and arts activists; many propaganda team members also participated in land reform and the construction of local governments." *Liaoning shengzhi: wenhua zhi* [Liaoning provincial gazetteer: cultural gazetteer] (Shenyang: Liaoning kexue jishu chubanshe, 1999), 129.

Communist regional governments formed the mainstay of Mao's cultural army. While amateur rural drama troupes continued to perform, three factors limited the ability of the Communists to rely on amateurs. First, local cadres and cultural workers were in short supply as military success drew experienced party members towards newly "liberated" areas. Second, new rural campaigns, particularly the time-consuming implementation of land reform, left little time for villages to organize cultural performances. Finally, as seen in Chapter 2, because popular culture evidenced a strong preference for traditional performances, without oversight by local cadres or cultural workers, villagers tended to shy away from staging modern works. During the Civil War, the Communists' message was thus typically spread by propaganda teams attached to the ever-growing PLA in tandem with professional drama troupes working in conjunction with the similarly expanding border region governments, with many performance organizations using both propaganda team and drama troupe designations.

As might be expected, PLA troupes focused on the needs of their military comrades, performing works designed to spur fighting units to victory. Open-air shows, however, allowed drama troupes to exploit the protean nature of revolutionary operas, which were typically designed to influence villagers and soldiers alike. As the PLA advanced out of the base areas, villagers living in newly captured territories were exposed to Communist ideology as they watched operas alongside soldiers.[7] When the Northwest Literary and Art Work Team performed *The White-Haired Girl* for military units, for example, soldiers in the audience angrily shouted their intention to avenge the deaths of the peasant characters.[8] Villagers in the audience, meanwhile, received a powerful lesson in the Maoist conception of rural society. By performing for both military battle and land reform, propaganda teams and drama troupes made solid contributions to the Communist cause, culminating in the takeover of China's cities. As Westad notes in his study of this era, the success of the Communists at the local level was "dependent on their propaganda skills. By portraying opponents as enemies of all groups of Chinese – poor and rich, peasant and bourgeois, man and woman – and itself as defender of the nation," the Communist Party "skillfully managed to increase its support."[9]

As the PLA and the base areas rapidly expanded over the course of the latter half of the 1940s, the Communists constantly created, renamed,

---

[7] *Shaanxi sheng xiju zhi: shengzhi juan* [Shaanxi Provincial Drama Gazetteer: Provincial Edition] (Xian: Sanqin chubanshe, 2003), 51.
[8] Ibid., 521.   [9] Westad, *Decisive Encounters*, 10.

reorganized, transferred, and dispersed their performance organizations. Given this turnover, it is impractical to follow individual troupes as had been possible in earlier eras. Instead, this chapter draws on a mixture of memoirs, party documents, and local gazetteers to highlight broad trends in drama troupe performances during the Civil War period in three related realms: fighting the Guomindang in the Civil War, carrying out land reform in the countryside, and promoting the new regime during the urban takeover. Generally among the most talented political workers available to the Communist cause, troupe members played many roles in these three realms. Within the context of Civil War, military conflict typically required actors to devote most of their efforts to rear-line support. Yet troupes found ways to stage dramas during even the most chaotic moments of battle, with their performances for "captive" audiences particularly important for the war effort. During agrarian reform, drama troupe and propaganda team members regularly found their way into land reform work teams. On these work teams, artists did not always have an opportunity to perform, but land reform provided inspiration for the artistic creations heavy in Maoist rhetoric and ritual that would help drive land reform and the revolution to completion. The urban takeover, finally, presented an entirely new set of opportunities and challenges to propaganda teams and drama troupes. In newly "liberated" cities, cultural workers found audiences hungry for information about the new regime. But when actors exchanged open-air performances for "modern" theatres, they often found urban audiences difficult to tame.

Military revolution: propaganda teams and drama troupes at war

Few drama troupes performing in the Yan'an region during the Sino-Japanese War received as much praise as the Popular Masses Drama Troupe, founded in 1938.[10] A 1946 *Liberation Daily* article, for example,

---

[10] Like many drama troupes discussed in this chapter, the Popular Masses Drama Troupe went by more than one name. In 1947, the troupe was split into two units, the first of which was attached to the military, while the second was to focus on the countryside. In June, 1949, the first unit became the First Field Army Political Department Propaganda Unit, only to change its name again that September to the First Field Army Political Department Cultural Work Team. At the same time, the second unit of the Popular Masses Drama Troupe became the Shaan-Gan-Ning Border Area Popular Masses Drama Troupe, yet changed its name again in February, 1950, to the Northwest Popular Masses Drama Troupe. In 1952, the troupe got its final name change, becoming the Shaanxi Provincial Drama Research Center. See *Shaanxi sheng xiju zhi*, 43–64.

praised the troupe for spending three out of every eight days touring in rural areas. Under the direction of Ke Zhongping and Ma Jianling, the troupe traveled throughout the border area, claiming to have performed 14,750 times, an average of once every two days, with a total audience of over 2,600,000.[11] Yet despite its status as one of the most renowned drama troupes of the Yan'an era, the early Civil War period found the troupe struggling to survive. After the fall of Yan'an to the Guomindang, the troupe was ordered to quietly cross the Yellow River and regroup. With around eighty members, only four of whom were women, the troupe wandered about with its four draft animals lugging its costumes, gas lights, and other theatrical equipment. According to artist Lei Feng, while the troupe initially drew large crowds, as the military situation deteriorated actors started to outnumber their audience. Growing desperate, the troupe sought out the Northwest Field Army, traveling to Peng Dehuai's headquarters and requesting to enlist in the army, officially becoming the First Field Army Political Department Cultural Work Team in April 1947.[12] The troupe, previously known for touring the countryside and performing for rural audiences, was now dispatched to the frontlines. When not entertaining Peng Dehuai and other PLA leaders, their primary responsibility would be to motivate soldiers to kill their enemies.

The experiences of the Popular Masses Drama Troupe were far from unique. During the chaos of the Civil War era, many troupes sought affiliation with the PLA or border region governments.[13] The Communists, meanwhile, desperately needed artists to promote their latest war against the Guomindang, with educating and mobilizing soldiers a top concern. Xiao Xiangrong, head of the Department of Propaganda in the Northeast Bureau, made the primacy of serving soldiers explicit, insisting that cultural workers "write about soldiers, perform as soldiers, and

---

[11] Ibid., 47.
[12] Lei Feng, "Cong Shaan-Gan-Ning bianqu minzhong jutuan dao yi ye zhengzhibu wengongtuan" [From the Shaan-Gan-Ning Border Region Minzhong Drama Troupe to the First Field Army Political Department Cultural Work Team] JZSQ (1987), 44–46.
[13] The similarly named Huaibei Popular Masses Drama Cultural Work Team, for example, collectively joined the PLA in 1948. Founded in 1944, the troupe had been taking part in military operations as rear-line support even before formally becoming the East China Field Army Fifth Cultural Work Team. After an influx of new members and reorganizing into drama, music, and fine arts divisions, the troupe followed its new military comrades into Shandong. There the troupe periodically divided into work teams to perform quick shows for army units, regrouping for large-scale shows such as *The White-Haired Girl* or *Returning to the Army* (Gui dui), an original creation about a soldier who goes AWOL only to have his disappointed wife send him back to the PLA. Song Guoxian and Wang Yonghong, "Cong Huaibei dazhong wengongtuan dao huaye wengongtuan wudui" [From the Huaibei Masses Cultural Work Team to the East China Field Army Fifth Cultural Work Team] JZSQ (1987), 255–256.

perform for soldiers."[14] PLA cultural workers should still take part in the "mass literature and arts movement," but Xiao suggested limiting this participation to the simple posting of "wall newspapers" (*qiangbao*).[15] Dramas were best reserved for military audiences. While Xiao Xiangrong was explicitly addressing PLA cultural workers, the Communists moved to mobilize their entire cultural army to serve the military needs of the Civil War.

As the Communists sought to expand their cultural army, the tradition of the "child stars" of Red Drama proved highly influential. At a time when able-bodied men were needed for military service and agricultural production, children represented an untapped talent source. And while parents might object to having their children taken to the frontlines to perform for soldiers, not all children had such careful guardianship. Thus, one cultural work team from Liu Bocheng and Deng Xiaoping's Central Plains Field Army simply sent a recruiter to the Xiangyang Third Hubei Orphanage. Announcing the "liberation" of Xiangyang, the recruiter called on the young students to join him as revolutionary intellectuals. According to Li Ping, then a young girl, dozens of orphans found themselves immediately thrust into a forced march to southern Henan. Along the way, the children, whose ages ranged from eleven to fifteen, developed blisters on their feet, while their backs bled after their heavy backpacks broke through their skin. After getting fitted for uniforms, the orphans studied politics and then the arts, starting with revolutionary songs before graduating to supporting roles for the "big shows" *A Hatred of Blood and Tears* (Xue lei chou) and *The White-Haired Girl*. Li Ping took great pride in her revolutionary service during the Civil War, which culminated in playing the titular martyr in *Liu Hulan*. But the descriptions of the horrors of war that fill her memoir suggest the difficulties of serving as a child actor during the Civil War.[16]

The PLA found child actors from other sources as well: "child stars" were often "liberated" from the Guomindang.[17] Take, for example, the Children's Drama Troupe. Originally formed in 1944 in Henan as a

---

[14] Xiao Xiangrong, "Budui de wenyi gongzuo yinggai wei bing fuwu" [Army cultural work should serve soldiers] JZSQ (1947), 474.

[15] Ibid., 475–476.

[16] Li, for example, recalled how she had witnessed a bound and humiliated captive, her fears of the slowly tightening Guomindang encirclement, and her shock at the unexpected arrival of enemy tanks. Li Ping, "Cong E xibei dao da Xi'nan – huiyi er ye liu zongdui wengongtuan di yi duan shenghuo" [From Northwest Hubei to the great Southwest – recollecting a period in the life of the Second Field Army Sixth Column Cultural Work Team] JZSQ (ca. 1980s), 172–179.

[17] Ping Bo, "Huadong yezhanjun shier zong wengongtuan gaikuang" [General situation of the East China Field Army 12th Corps Cultural Work Team] JZSQ (1987), 369.

Peking opera troupe, Wang Jingwei's "puppet" regime had taken control of the troupe, renaming the outfit the National Construction Drama Troupe, with all the students taking new names containing the character for "construction" (*jian*). During the chaos following Japan's surrender, a defecting general "liberated" these child performers, and soon the troupe, colloquially known as the Children's Drama Troupe, was performing for PLA units in Jiangsu. The troupe's traditional performances proved incredibly popular with audiences, and the children were one of the most popular performing groups attached to the East China Field Army Political Department, staging works in a number of regional operatic styles in front of audiences that included Zhu De and other top Communist leaders.[18]

The Guomindang thus inadvertently helped relieve the shortage of cultural workers in the PLA. The Communists especially valued the Guomindang's skilled musicians and their hard-to-find instruments. The East China Field Army Military Band, one of many bands staffed with "liberated" artists, started with a group of nineteen musicians and one conductor, who all claimed to have been "tricked" into serving the Guomindang. By the end of the Huaihai Campaign, the band had grown to over four hundred members, almost all of them captives culled from Guomindang military bands. The East China Field Army Military Band played an appropriately contradictory mix of imported songs and folk tunes, all with Western instruments.[19] In a move that must have been particularly upsetting to Jiang Jieshi, the Advanced Position Drama Troupe, a Communist-directed unit that had originally been a local government troupe before joining the PLA, absorbed the Long Live China Drama Troupe, which had been attached to Jiang's presidential compound in Chongqing.[20]

Mao Zedong had once complained about allowing Red Army deserters on propaganda teams, but during the Civil War the PLA went even further and put enemy captives on stage. In 1947, for example, dramatist Sun Mu was assigned to work with "liberated" Guomindang officers,

[18] Chen Wenyuan, Lu Jianrong, and Zhang Wei, "'Wawa jutuan' shi kuanggai lue" [Outline of the historical situation of the "Children's Drama Troupe"] JZSQ (1988), 403–411.

[19] This huge band proved unwieldy, so the musicians were divided into branches and distributed through the army. Luo Xin, "Geming junyue, guwu zhanshimen fenyong qianjin – ji huadong yezhanjun junyuedui" [The Revolutionary Army Band, inspiring soldiers to bravely advance – remembering the East China Field Army Band] JZSQ (ca. 1980s), 295–298.

[20] Chen Xiao et al., "Qianshao jutuan chicheng zai jiefang zhanchang – qianshao jutuan tuanshi jielu" [Advanced Position Drama Troupe gallops onto the battlefield of liberation – a history of the Advanced Position Drama Troupe] JZSQ (ca. 1980s), 170.

a task that included giving them a "cultural education." Under Sun's direction, the captured officers created and acted in their own dramas, eventually forming a propaganda team with about thirty members. According to Sun, having Guomindang officers acting out pro-Communist messages on stage gave these shows a powerful resonance. Having the team stage *Pressganged Solider* (Zhua zhuang ding), however, must have seemed particularly poetic.[21] These officers proved loyal actors, but other Guomindang performers resisted their Communist directors. After capturing some "cultured male comrades" south of the Yangtze, the Central Plains Drama Troupe gave the men starring roles, only to have them flee to Nanjing right before show time.[22] But despite Mao's anger over the poor quality of propagandists in the late 1920s, the dictates of war meant that anyone capable of entertaining soldiers, even Guomindang officers, might be invited on to Communist stages. One Hainan troupe even drafted a "talented" monkey to help them draw crowds.[23]

The Communists' ever-growing cultural army accompanied the PLA as it rapidly advanced, first into North China and the Northeast at the end of the Sino-Japanese War, and then south as the PLA pushed back against failed Guomindang offensives. At times, marches provided effective forums for political work. In early 1948, for example, a cultural work team marched across the East China Field Army's frontlines, disseminating propaganda along the way. Marching for over two weeks, the work team put on fourteen *wanhui* evening variety shows for an audience estimated at some 16,500. The team also distributed leaflets and posted 689 slogans, 210 poems, and 57 cartoons.[24] But this march was essentially a planned tour. Typically marches were time consuming and dangerous, if not potentially deadly. Team member Ma Xuan, for example, did not find this early 1948 marching tour worthy of inclusion in her recollections the Civil War. Instead, she highlighted painful barefoot marches in pouring rain, avoiding enemy bombs, and a near death experience when a flash-flood interrupted a dangerous river crossing.[25]

---

[21] Sun Mu, "Teshu de wenyi gongzuo dui" [A special literature and arts work team] JZSQ (ca. 1980s), 68–70.
[22] Liu Zhen, "Jiefang zhanzheng zhong wo suo zhi" [What I know from the War of Liberation] JZSQ (ca. 1980s), 128.
[23] Wang Kun, "Hainan dao huoxian shang de wenyidui" [Literature and arts team in the Hainan island firing line] JZSQ (ca. 1980s), 445.
[24] Chen Hong, "Huadong yezhanjun zhengzhibu wenyi gongzuotuan de jiben qingkuang he jingyan" [The basic situation and experiences of the East China Field Army Political Department Literature and Arts Work Team] JZSQ (ca. 1980s), 209.
[25] Ma Xuan, "Yi ge wengongtuan yuan de huiyi" [A cultural work team member's recollections] JZSQ (ca. 1980s), 288–289.

Dan Min, another female actor, similarly recalled dangerous long marches with her work team, attached to the New Fourth Army. According to Dan, many of her fellow work team members would simply disappear on marches, assumed to have been captured or killed.[26]

Accounts of long and dangerous marches fill artist recollections of the late 1940s. Propaganda teams under Liu Bocheng and Deng Xiaoping, for example, had to endure a two-month march to the Dabie Mountains.[27] Ill or injured team members were simply left behind, often never to be heard from again; one drama troupe lost nearly half of its actors in the Dabie Mountains, including all of its female actors.[28] Marches were in fact particularly difficult for women, often in ways that escaped the notice of their male comrades. In her recollections of the hardships female cultural workers faced during the late 1940s, Liang Quan noted how the six women in her troupe all stopped menstruating. At first, the women were happy, thinking that the absence of their monthly "situation" (*qingkuang*) would make marching easier. Male troupe leaders were concerned but clueless as to what should be done, although the women eventually found a treatment from a local doctor.[29] Any accounting of the activities of drama troupes in the late 1940s must consider the toll that constant marching had on the health and vitality of troupe members, to say nothing of the time that was given over to these treks.

Of course, as seen in the two-week marching tour of the East China Field Army's cultural work team, the line between marching and performing was not always clear. The Vanguard Drama Troupe, to cite another example, performed during a deadly crossing of the Yellow River in a manner reminiscent of Long March *gudongpeng* agitation stations.[30] Directives from PLA leaders frequently reminded propaganda teams and drama troupes to prioritize performing in support of the war effort with shows before, during, and after battles, including frontline performances.

---

[26] Dan Min, "Zai xiaoyan zhong change, zai xiaoyan zhong chengzhang – yi xinsijun wu shi shisan lü wengongdui de zhandou shenghuo" [Singing in gun smoke, growing up in gun smoke – remembering the New Fourth Army Fifth Division Thirteenth Brigade Cultural Work Team's life of battle] JZSQ (1982), 312–313.

[27] Wang Derong, "Cong yi zong xuanchuandui dao shiliu jun wengongtuan" [From the First Army Propaganda Team to the Sixteenth Army Cultural Work Team] JZSQ (1978), 148.

[28] Liu Zhen, "Jiefang zhanzheng zhong wo suo zhi," 128.

[29] Liang Quan, "Wenyi nübing qinli ji" [Remembering the personal experiences of female literature and arts soldiers] JZSQ (1987), 392.

[30] Cao Xin, "Jinxing zai kaige sheng zhong – ji jiefang zhanzheng zhong de xianfeng jutuan" [Progressing amid a triumphant sound – remembering the Vanguard Drama Troupe in the War of Liberation] JZSQ (ca. 1980s), 114.

Organizing frontline shows, however, presented real challenges. According to Mo Yan of the National Defense Drama Troupe, the Huaihai Campaign left no time for frontline shows; instead, the troupe did rear-line support work, including shows for resting soldiers.[31]

Gu Baozhang similarly recalled how his troupe initially only performed for the army before and after battles, with army leadership always sure to move the troupe to safety before any engagements with enemy forces. As a result, soldiers complained about having to march long distances to and from these shows. After reading Mao's "Talks at the Yan'an Forum" during its 1947 rectification, the troupe began to split up and visit the frontlines during battles, although military leaders still feared for their safety.[32] In moving to small frontline units, Gu Baozhang's troupe followed the example set by He Long's Combat Dramatic Society, which excelled at frontline mobilization, breaking up into smaller units that took their names from the number of actors in the small group. In his account of the Seven Person Drama Troupe, organized in the summer of 1946, Yan Jizhou detailed how he and six of his comrades traveled to the front armed with one violin, one harmonica, one eyebrow pencil, four rifles, five grenades, and one pistol. With many PLA soldiers confused as to why they were again at war in 1946 after fighting so long against Japan, Yan and his comrades performed short dramas blaming Jiang Jieshi for the Civil War, as well as works praising heroic soldiers. After hearing that soldiers were not following the PLA's rules of discipline, the Seven Person Drama Troupe also created and performed a short *yangge* opera about the importance of following rules. According to Yan, while only active for a few days, the troupe staged six shows for an audience of some eight hundred soldiers.[33]

While performing on the frontlines was always challenging, female actors faced additional hardship. James Gao, for example, has noted the frustration that came when women joined the revolution, especially when they served as nurses or propagandists. These "dream girls" were relentlessly pursued by PLA officers and soldiers, most of whom were bachelors who "wanted a wife like that."[34] Their desirability made women popular performers, but many propaganda teams and drama troupes balked at sending women to the frontlines. The Advanced Position Drama

---

[31] Mo Yan, "Zai na zhan huo fenfei de niandai" [Those years in the flames of war] JZSQ (1987), 229.

[32] Gu Baozhang, "Yi ci nan yi wangque de 'jianghua' xuexi" [A hard to forget study of the "Talks"] JZSQ (1982), 421–423.

[33] Yan Jizhou, "Xiju zai huoxian shang" [Drama on the firing line] JZSQ (ca. 1980s), 52–54.

[34] Gao, *The Communist Takeover of Hangzhou*, 189.

Troupe, for example, divided its ranks by gender. Female actors carried out support work in relative safety, while male troupe members performed on the frontlines, their shows typically featuring male actors in drag, a throwback to the days of Red Drama. According to the recollections of several troupe members, the men of the Advanced Position Drama Troupe quickly mastered frontline shows, traveling light and building wooden stages from lumber or wooden rods. After experimenting with rapid stage building and alternative lighting sources, the men were able to stage two shows per day, mixing *huaju* spoken dramas with shows that drew on local operatic styles.[35]

But given the central role of women in the Communists' drama troupes, it was difficult to keep female actors off the frontlines. Liang Quan recalled how she "conspired" with male troupe members to travel to the Huaihai front for a set of performances.[36] Ma Xuan, who described barefoot marches and dangerous river crossing above, also took part in frontline performances during the pivotal Huaihai Campaign. According to Ma, her four-person unit sang for PLA forces and even took the surrender of Guomindang soldiers, despite the fact that the team was only armed with a violin.[37] Similarly, in He Jieming's account of a small drama troupe performing on the frontline during the Battle of Suiqi near Kaifeng, women accounted for two of the group's six members. After a performance that included song, dance, and *kuaiban* "wooden clapper" performances, soldiers and actors endured a Guomindang bombing raid together. According to He Jieming, the presence of the two female actors, singing as the bombs fell, provided extra motivation for the PLA soldiers, who vowed to keep the two women safe.[38]

As this suggests, frontline performances required bravery, talent, and extreme creativity. As members of the Liangguang Army Cultural Work Team recalled of the Huaihai Campaign, the only time for creation and rehearsing was during marches. Most difficult, however, was finding the time for shows. The team would often construct its stage and prepare makeup and costumes only to have its show canceled by an order to move out. The focus on extreme mobility, moreover, required the utmost creativity in terms of stage props: a PLA uniform turned inside out became a Guomindang costume, while actors pantomimed a "car"

---

[35] Chen Xiao *et al.*, "Qianshao jutuan chicheng zai jiefang zhanchang – qianshao jutuan tuanshi jielu," 161–162.
[36] Liang Quan, "Wenyi nübing qinli ji," 400.
[37] Ma Xuan, "Yi ge wengongtuan yuan de huiyi," 292.
[38] He Jieming, "Huoxian shang de wenyi bing – suiqi zhanyi de riri yeye" [Literature and arts soldiers on the frontline – days and nights of the Battle of Suiqi] JZSQ (1980), 300–307.

using kaoliang stalks attached to drawings of circles.[39] While the performance of revolutionary drama had never been easy, all-out civil war clearly presented new challenges.

These creative problems, of course, paled in comparison to the danger of performing for the PLA during wartime. While troupes only staged shows in moments of relative calm, save the occasional projectiles thrown on stage by irate audience members, peril was everywhere. Drama troupe members might make the simple but fatal mistake of stepping on a landmine.[40] Chen Jie, who played the lead role of Xi'er in her troupe's productions of *The White-Haired Girl*, was killed while attempting to rescue wounded comrades.[41] And as seen by the experiences of the New Peace Traveling Drama Troupe, fatalities could occur far from the battlefield. Sent to perform for wounded soldiers, one child actor mishandled a "prop" gun that accidently fired, killing a fellow troupe member. Eventually troupe leaders realized that while child actors had been ideal performers of anti-Japanese propaganda in Guomindang areas, the dictates of war required adaptation. The troupe thus spun off its child actors so that the remaining adult members could focus on frontline work for military units.[42]

While performing for PLA soldiers was the explicit first duty of drama troupes, there were other ways to serve the military. Just as important were the myriad duties troupes performed in support of the Civil War. Intimately related to shows for fighting troops was rear-line support work, which was essential for the overall war effort. As seen above, the PLA often moved highly valued artists, especially female actors, away from the frontlines to conduct support work. In the defense of Yan'an, for example, the Red Star Dramatic Society focused on transporting and tending to the wounded.[43] The First Army Propaganda Team, then called the Warrior Dramatic Society, actually spent much of the early Civil War far from the battlefront. While half of the team conducted mass

---

[39] Li Zhao *et al.*, "Liangguang zongdui wengongtuan zai huaihai zhanyi zhong de huaju yanchu huodong" [Liangguang Army Cultural Work Team spoken drama performance activities during the Battle of Huaihai] JZSQ (ca. 1980s), 428–429.

[40] Song Guoxian and Wang Yonghong, "Cong Huaibei dazhong wengongtuan dao huaye wengongtuan wudui," 257.

[41] Zhang Chengyang, "Chunqiu si huo – ji nü wengongtuan yuan Chen Jie" [Spring and autumn like fire – remembering female cultural work team member Chen Jie] JZSQ (ca. 1980s), 324–326.

[42] Da Peng, "'Xinlü' zai jiefang zhanzheng zhong qianjin" ["Xinlü" advances in the War of Liberation] JZSQ (ca. 1980s), 272–276.

[43] Li Jing and Su An, "Wang shi ru yan – yi jiaodao lü hongxing jushe" [Past events vanish like smoke – remembering instructing the Traveling Red Star Drama Club] JZSQ (1987), 77.

work in villages, the other half roamed the countryside requisitioning grain.[44] Rear-line work was still quite dangerous, as one East China Field Army cultural work team discovered during a pitched battle in July 1946. The team worked as medics and transporters in the rear-lines, but the battle still claimed the life of the team's young lead musician and wounded two others. According to Zhu Jing, while most of the team acted bravely, one *huaju* spoken drama specialist simply fled in terror.[45]

Frontline performances and rear-line support work are the most well-known duties of Communist propaganda teams and drama troupes during the Civil War. But perhaps their most important role was working with recently captured enemy soldiers. As the PLA racked up military victories over its increasingly hapless Guomindang foes, the Communists captured huge numbers of soldiers – more than fifty thousand following the capture of Jinan alone – and the rapid conversion of surrendered soldiers proved one of the keys to winning the Civil War.[46] The PLA assigned propaganda teams and drama troupes the task of reeducating and rehabilitating these prisoners of war, many of whom had heard shocking rumors regarding the Communists. In an attempt to win over the massive numbers of Guomindang soldiers captured during the Huaihai Campaign, the National Defense Drama Troupe used drama to directly refute the oft-told tale that the Communists buried Guomindang captives alive. The troupe turned this horrific rumor into a comedy, in which a recent captive is commanded to dig an air raid shelter but mistakenly believes he is being asked to dig his own grave. The on-stage confusion created when the captive is told to get into the ditch to see if it is deep enough inspired howls of laughter among the offstage prisoners of war. According to Mo Yan, this one comedy scene effectively dispelled the ghastly rumor.[47] Yet other members of the troupe recalled that not all shows for Guomindang captives went well. According to Sun Xiyue, these prisoners of war could be quite ill-mannered, disrupting shows and verbally abusing the troupe's female actors.[48]

Despite such difficulties, the PLA clearly believed drama to be the quickest way to indoctrinate prisoners of war. New works designed for Guomindang soldiers, such as the 1947 drama *Oppressive Officials Drive*

[44] Wang Derong, "Cong yi zong xuanchuandui dao shiliu jun wengongtuan," 142.
[45] Zhu Zijing, "Zai zhanhuo zhong zhilian – huadong yezhanjun zhengzhibu wengongtuan chengli chuqi" [Through the battle fires – establishment and early era Huadong Field Army Political Department Cultural Work Team] JZSQ (1987), 348.
[46] Westad, *Decisive Encounters*, 201.
[47] Mo Yan, "Zai na zhan huo fenfei de niandai," 231–232.
[48] Sun Xiyue,"Jiefang zhanzheng shiqi de guofang jutuan" [The National Defense Drama Troupe during the War of Liberation] JZSQ (1988), 238–239.

the People to Rebellion (Guan bi min fan), formed an essential part of the repertoire of revolutionary drama troupes. This opera told the story of a peasant pressganged into the Guomindang army by his village head. While serving in the army, the village head's "running dog" (*zougou*, a person who is paid to do evil things) sexually assaults the peasant's wife and further accuses her of collaborating with the Communists. The unlucky peasant finally returns home, only to be thrown in jail until he is rescued by the PLA, which properly punished the village head and his "running dog."[49] With a skillful mixture of entertainment and emotionally charged content, the PLA promoted shows such as the *Oppressive Officials Drive the People to Rebellion* as the surest way to reach out to captured soldiers. Between battles, Peng Dehuai had his Northwest Field Army Cultural Work Team perform for captured soldiers, even personally picking out a program that began with *The White-Haired Girl*.[50] According to troupe member Lei Feng, Peng Dehuai described shows staged for captured Guomindang soldiers as a form of "speaking bitterness education" (*suku jiaoyu*), which could help in the subsequent "speaking of bitterness."[51] Peng's assessment is particularly accurate: captives not only saw examples of how the Guomindang exploited soldiers, they also saw the actual process of "speaking bitterness," an important Communist ritual that captive soldiers had to perform in real life.

The Communists, in fact, mobilized all PLA soldiers to perform "speaking bitterness," or *suku*. While the practice of *suku* has correctly been understood as a central component of the land reform process, *suku* was first developed through PLA mass campaigns during the Civil War before the Communists exported this ritual to villages throughout China.[52] Propaganda teams and drama troupes played important roles in three campaigns using *suku* to ensure loyalty and ideological purity in the ever-expanding ranks of the PLA: the Three Checks and Three Rectifications Campaign, the Wang Keqin Campaign, and the Speaking Bitterness Movement. In 1949, Zhou Enlai, speaking to cultural workers, would point to *suku* and other forms of ideological reform (*sixiang*

---

[49] Ke Ding, "Ji ershisi jun wengongtuan zai jiefang zhanzheng zhong de chuangzuo he yanchu huodong" [Remembering the creations and performance activities of the Twenty-fourth Army Cultural Work Team during the War of Liberation] JZSQ (ca. 1980s), 383–384.

[50] Wang Yongnian, "Wei baowei Yan'an, jiefang da xibei de zhanzheng fuwu – ji xibei yezhanjun wengongtuan" [Serving the battle to defend Yan'an and liberate the great Northwest – remembering the "Northwest Field Army Cultural Work Team"] JZSQ (ca. 1980s), 41.

[51] Lei Feng, "Cong Shaan-Gan-Ning bianqu minzhong jutuan dao yi ye zhengzhibu wengongtuan," 48.

[52] For a discussion of *suku* in land reform, see Anagnost, *National Past-Times*, Chapter 1.

gaizao) among PLA soldiers, including captured Guomindang soldiers, as perhaps the single most important factor in the Communist victory.[53] All three of these campaigns hinged on soldiers' ability to perform rituals featuring the practice of *suku*, and PLA cultural workers playing soldiers on stage took the lead in teaching the art of speaking bitterness through cultural performance.

The Three Checks and Three Rectifications Campaign, launched in late 1947 and running until autumn 1948, primarily affected soldiers in the Shandong region, although it soon spread to Central Hebei and other military regions. Designed as a form of class education, soldiers were asked to use the political performance of *suku* to "check" class, work, and fighting spirit, while party organizations were to "rectify" ideology, organization, and work styles.[54] Drama troupes and propaganda teams taking part in the campaign staged *The White-Haired Girl* and other dramas with a strong focus on class exploitation to inform political performances in the PLA. In 1948, Mo Yan and the National Defense Drama Troupe, directed to create new works to promote the campaign, quickly created and staged *Blind Granny* (Xia laoma). During one performance of this opera, Mo Yan even inspired a solider to rise up and shout his intention to kill Mo's evil landlord character. Onlookers wrestled away the soldier's rifle, but he still charged onto the stage, causing Mo Yan to flee and hide under the troupe's makeshift makeup table until the irate solider could be calmed down and reminded that this was only a show.[55] Once again, the lines between drama and revolution blurred dangerously close.

The Wang Keqin Campaign, meanwhile, aimed to encourage soldiers to emulate Wang Keqin, a PLA officer in the Jin-Ji-Lu-Yu Field Army, a predecessor to the Central Plains Field Army. Pressganged into the Guomindang army, Wang was eventually "liberated" and joined the PLA, where he became a squad leader and party member. Quickly martyred in battle, Wang Keqin served as a selfless, loyal, and conveniently dead role

---

[53] Zhou Enlai, "Zai zhonghua quanguo wenxue yishu gongzuozhe daibiao dahui shang de zhengzhi baogao" [Political report for the All-China Literature and Arts Worker Representative Congress] ZWGD (1949), 22.

[54] As party organizations, propaganda teams and Communist drama troupes also had to undergo the "three checks" and "three rectifications." For example, in what was later called a "leftist deviation" the Firing Line Dramatic Society carried out the campaign in late 1947, promoting the slogan "poor peasants and hired hands in charge" (*pin gu nong dangjia*) and criticizing troupe members from rich peasant and landlord backgrounds. Chang Zheng, "Jizhong junqu huoxian jushe dashi ji, 1945–1945" [A record of important events for the Central Hebei Military Region Firing Line Dramatic Society] JZSQ (1985), 815.

[55] Mo Yan, "Zai na zhan huo fenfei de niandai," 228.

model. Liu Bocheng and Deng Xiaoping heavily promoted Wang Keqin, urging PLA soldiers to emulate his commitment to the revolutionary cause, particularly his bravery on the battlefield. In order to develop the campaign, the Jin-Ji-Lu-Yu Field Army's Political Department called in its Sixth Army Cultural Work Team to create a drama based on the martyr. The resulting opera, *Wang Keqin's Squad* (Wang Keqin ban), was quickly mastered by other performance units in the PLA, especially those under Liu Bocheng and Deng Xiaoping.[56] While the Wang Keqin model was promoted in newspapers and other forms of media, dramatists insisted that live performances were particularly effective in spreading the message of soldiers supporting soldiers and hating class enemies. Notably, because Wang Keqin's character performs "speaking bitterness" during the show, *Wang Keqin's Squad* was said to be of great benefit to the "Speaking Bitterness Movement" as well as in motivating soldiers for battle.[57] Drama troupes, as they would do again during the pivotal moments of rural revolution, were providing models for the performances needed in offstage Maoist ritual.

As suggested by the centrality of the performance of *suku* in the "three checks and three rectifications" and Wang Keqin campaigns, these movements blended into the larger Speaking Bitterness Movement that swept through the PLA during the first half of the Civil War. The movement started in the Northeast in 1947 under propaganda team originator Luo Ronghuan, now Lin Biao's political commissar in the Northeast Field Army, with Mao granting his approval in late September of that same year. With both this movement and the concurrent land reform campaign relying on inciting class hatred, propaganda teams and drama troupes staged *The White-Haired Girl* and similar works in rural hamlet and military camp alike. One drama troupe found this Yan'an land reform opera incredibly effective, to the point that no matter how many times the troupe explained that this was simply a show and its actors were revolutionaries, not class enemies, it was "unavoidable" to have some soldiers hurl rocks at villainous characters.[58] New shows were also created specifically for this moment, with PLA dramatist Yu Ji crafting one of the most famous military *suku* works. Yu Ji had already penned several works to educate soldiers, including the 1946 *Zhang*

[56] Jiang Tao, "*Wang Keqin Ban* chuangzuo, yanchu qianhou" [Before and after the creation and performance of Wang Keqin's Squad] JZSQ (1988), 136.

[57] Ma Hongwen, "Zhandou li chengzhang de shier jun wengongtuan" [The Twelfth Army Cultural Work Team develops in battle] JZSQ (ca. 1980s), 155–156.

[58] Ruan Ruoshan and Shan Wen, "Jiefang zhanzheng zhong de liaodong junqu zhengzhibu wenyi gongzuotuan" [Liaodong Military Region Political Department Literature and Arts Work Team during the War of Liberation] JZSQ (ca. 1980s), 618.

Debao Returns to the Army (Zhang Debao gui dui), designed to encourage soldiers to remain in the PLA. In 1948, Yu Ji created *Three Generations of Hatred* (San shi chou) to promote the *suku* movement. This opera carefully depicted three generations of peasant suffering, which not surprisingly resulted from the machinations of an evil landlord and his "running dogs."[59] Thus, while *Three Generations of Hatred* and other *suku* shows were created with the education of PLA fighters in mind, they also perfectly served the Communists' efforts to carry out land reform during the war.

Civilian rural revolution: drama troupes in land reform

The PLA's successes on the battlefield were intimately related to the Communists' ability to win over rural China through land reform.[60] But because land reform required villagers to accept class labels and violently overthrow village elites, the campaign could not succeed without first carefully educating and preparing villagers. For the Communists, drama and other forms of popular entertainment continued to represent one of the surest ways to reach rural audiences. A May 1947 directive from the Jin-Cha-Ji Central Bureau, for example, demanded cultural workers to create works "reflecting" land reform, "an event that has never occurred before in Chinese history."[61] As Westad noted in his study of the Civil War, these shows "could lead to direct political action and even violence."[62] Communist cultural leaders frequently reminded cultural workers to focus on military matters, but the importance of land reform ensured this campaign became a creative concern. Thus, while military topics tended to dominate the stage during the Sino-Japanese War, in the late 1940s drama troupes increasingly staged shows concerning agrarian reform and rural class struggle.[63]

For cultural workers, however, the significance of land reform transcended the creative realm. The rapid expansion of Communist controlled

---

[59] Wang Shaoyan, "Yi Yu Ji tongzhi zai jiefang zhanzheng de suiyue li" [Recollecting Comrade Yu Ji during the era of the War of Liberation] JZSQ (1987), 244.

[60] The relationship between land reform and the Civil War effort is discussed in Levine, *The Anvil of Victory: The Communist Revolution in Manchuria, 1945–1948* (New York: University of Columbia Press, 1987), 11.

[61] "Zhonggong Jin-Cha-Ji zhongyangju guanyu wenyi gongzuo de san ge jueding" [Three decisions concerning literature and arts work by the Chinese Communist Party Jin-Cha-Ji Central Bureau] JZSQ (1947), 695.

[62] Westad, *Decisive Encounters*, 132.

[63] Hu Ke, "Shijian zhong xueshi de shi nian – dui kangdi jushe xiju chuangzuo huodong de huiyi" [Studying through ten years of practice – remembering the creation activities of the Resist the Enemy Dramatic Society] JZSQ (ca. 1980s), 718.

territory generated an insatiable demand for land reform work team members to lead agrarian reform at the village level. In the Northeast, for example, Steven Levine has argued that land reform was severely hampered by a lack of veteran cadres to serve in work teams; the result was substandard land reform, with one county only able to field one work team member for every 1,441 county residents.[64] As repeated calls for cultural workers to create for land reform and serve in land reform demonstrate, the education and authority of propaganda team and drama troupe members made them perfect candidates to help lead land reform. Drama troupes did create and perform shows to support Civil War era land reform, but when artists did take part in the campaigns, they often did so as members of land reform work teams as opposed to propaganda teams or drama troupes.

Members of the Northwest Field Army Cultural Work Team, for example, took part in land reform from late 1947 to early 1948. Organized into land reform work teams by He Long and dispatched from Yan'an to Sai'an in Suide County, troupe members served as work team leaders, with each troupe member in charge of an administrative village (*xiang*). Carrying out the campaign proved challenging, with most troupe members falling ill and needing hospitalization during their time in the countryside. But even if troupe members remained healthy, they were often too dispersed to stage dramatic performances.[65] In fall 1946, the New Peace Traveling Drama Troupe similarly spent a month in Liuxiaozi Village, carrying out land reform. While the New Peace troupe did not perform, its creative team did find inspiration for *Fanshen*, a *huaju* spoken drama. As seen in these recollections, cultural workers excelled in political work and would continue to play key roles in land reform work teams throughout the campaigns.[66]

But perhaps the finest example of drama troupe performance in Civil War era land reform comes from the Commander He's Combat Dramatic Society. When conducting land reform in Lin County over the winter of 1947, troupe members played two roles, serving as members of both a land reform work team and their own "propaganda team." Yan Jizhou served on one such propaganda team, a unit with around ten musicians and thirty actors of both genders, which locals nicknamed the Fanshen Drama Troupe. According to Yan Jizhou, because Lin County was

---

[64] Steven Levine, "Mobilizing for War: Rural Revolution in Manchuria as an Instrument for War," in Kathleen J. Hartford and Steven M. Goldstein, eds., *Single Sparks: Chinas Rural Revolutions* (New York: M.E. Sharpe, 1987), 158–159.

[65] Wang Yongnian, "Wei baowei Yan'an, jiefang da xibei de zhanzheng fuwu – ji xibei yezhanjun wengongtuan," 39.

[66] Da Peng, "'Xinlü' zai jiefang zhanzheng zhong qianjin," 276.

sparsely populated, his propaganda team might have to walk up to eighteen miles before arriving at its designated village, banging drums and gongs to signal the team's arrival. If the target village did not have temple stage, actors and musicians would set up a simple stage that mainly functioned to hide the band from view. The team performed both day and night, with evening shows illuminated by gas lanterns or simple oil lights. Audiences in market towns numbered over one thousand, while smaller villages might only attract a few dozen spectators, with Yan recalling times when actors outnumbered their observers.[67]

Playing peasants and landlords on stage, Yan Jizhou's Fanshen Drama Troupe performed short *yangge* style shows that directly focused on land reform. *Entering a Tiled Roof* (Jin wafang) concerned the joys of taking possession of a new house after the redistribution of landlord property. The *End of the Road for Zhang Yushan* (Zhang Yushan de molu) told the story of landlords attempting to wreck land reform. And *Pretending to be Poor* (Zhuang qiong) was a satirical comedy about a landlord trying to trick his way out of land reform. According to Yan, the team, by carrying out quick investigations after entering target villages, tailored set lists and even shows to fit local conditions. This allowed the Fanshen Drama Troupe to make concrete contributions to land reform with dramas heavy in the rhetoric and rituals of the campaign. Thus, residents of Guojiagou Village watched a show that helped explain the new class categories that were being introduced during the land reform; as these villagers told the actors, one viewing of a drama was more effective than ten readings of the *Outline Land Law*. In Magu Village, meanwhile, the team discovered that activists had kicked two households out of the village in order to secure a greater share of the fruits of the class struggle. In response to what they saw as a clear mistake, the team staged *Outside Households* (Wai lai hu), which convinced the Magu villagers to welcome back their former neighbors.[68]

Drama troupe members thus often found a balance between the political leadership of land reform and cultural performance in support of the campaigns. In the Northeast, for example, some 4,300 cultural workers created and staged multiple works for land reform, including the operas *The Land is Ours* (Tudi shi women de) and *Tending Our Own Land* (Shinong ziji de di).[69] While these shows were staged throughout the Northeast countryside, artists also carried out political work as land reform work team

---

[67] Yan Jizhou, "Ji tugai xuanchuandui" [Remembering a Land Reform Propaganda Team] JZSQ (1987), 71–72.
[68] Ibid., 72–73.
[69] Cultural workers also created *huaju* spoken dramas, such as *Land Returns Home* (Tudi huan jia). Wang Dikang, "Dongbei budui wenyi gongzuo gaishu" [General description of literature and arts work in the Northeast Army] JZSQ (1987), 481–486.

members, although at times agrarian reform left no time for performing in the countryside. When members of the Northeast Field Army Artillery Cultural Work Team joined land reform work teams in November 1947, for example, they did so not as artists but as urban intellectuals well versed in Communist Party policy.[70] The demands of instigating land reform kept these actors from performing, but another Northeast team, stocked with PLA propagandists, staged selections from *The White-Haired Girl* to prepare villagers for land reform in Wuchang County, encouraging audiences to see the connections between local landlords and the opera's villain. This troupe would later create its own land reform opera with the familiar title of *Land Returns Home* (Tudi huan jia), which it then staged for soldiers and villagers to promote land reform and class struggle.[71]

Land reform, however, did not always go smoothly. This was especially true prior to 1948, when the party finally halted land reform in areas not firmly under Communist control.[72]

These areas were not secure militarily, meaning villagers had to deal with the constant fear of landlord and Guomindang reprisals. The lack of established activists, meanwhile, meant that work teams had to often rely on self-interested individuals whose bravery in standing up to traditional village leaders was often coupled with impure motivations. The result was a particularly violent round of land reform. As Deng Xiaoping would later chillingly summarize his experience leading the movement in western Anhui:

The masses would hate a few landlords and want them killed, so according to the wishes of the masses we would have these landlords killed. Afterwards, the masses would fear reprisals from those who had ties to those we had just killed, and would draw up an even bigger list of names, saying if these people were also killed, everything would be alright. So once again, according to the wishes of the masses, we would have these people killed as well. After we killed these people, the masses felt that even more people wanted revenge for these deaths, and would draw up an even bigger list of names. So once again, according to the wishes of the masses, we killed these people. We kept on killing, and the masses felt more and more insecure. The masses were frightened, scared, and took flight. The result was that over two hundred people were killed, and work in twelve administrative villages (*xiang*) was ruined.[73]

[70] Zhao Yiwu, "Si ye paobing wengongtuan tuanshi" [Team history of the Fourth Field Army Artillery Cultural Work Team] JZSQ (1987), 521–524.
[71] Qiu Song, "Zhanhuo zhong de wenyi bing – ji sanshiba jun wengongtuan" [Literature and arts soldiers in the heat of battle – remembering the 38th Army Cultural Work Team] JZSQ (ca. 1980s), 576–578.
[72] Pepper, *Civil War in China*, 309.
[73] Luo Pinghan, *Tudi gaige yundong shi* [A History of the Land Reform Movement] (Fuzhou: Fujian renmin chubanshe, 2005), 273.

As Deng's cultural workers learned first-hand when they attempted to carry out land reform in the "newly liberated" Yu-Wan-Su[74] Border Region, a lack of military security invited reprisals.

The Advanced Position Drama Troupe, for example, took part in a 1947 round of land reform in West Anhui's Qianshan County. Splitting up into four work teams, troupe members dispersed into the countryside and quickly carried out the basic steps of land reform, starting with "visiting the poor to ask of their bitterness" (*fangpin wenku*) and the formation of peasant associations. As several artists would later recall, this was a rushed and forced land reform that frightened middle peasants, hurt rich peasants, and simply scared off landlords. And while these "deviations" were later corrected, enemy attacks in the spring of 1948 utterly destroyed their work. Cadres were captured, activists killed, and work teams fled, only surviving by relying on the skills some of them had honed during guerilla warfare in the Taihang Mountains.[75]

Ma Xuan and Zhu Zijing's work team similarly carried out land reform in Yu-Wan-Su villages that suffered reprisals from Guomindang forces or militias organized by ousted landlords, commonly known as "return to the village corps" (*huanxiang tuan*). Implementing the *Outline Land Law* in Anhui's Jieshou County, their troupe split into two teams, visiting villagers to determine class status and organizing poor peasants to attack their landlord neighbors. But as Zhu Zijing noted, these peasants, fearful of their landlords returning, proved difficult to organize. After wasting over a week without making any progress, the team members instituted a "three together" policy. While living, eating, and working with villagers allowed some advances to be made, land reform proved difficult. Jieshou County, still recovering from massive flooding after the Guomindang smashed the Yellow River's dikes in an attempt to slow the Japanese advance, was an unforgiving region. Many troupe members fell ill after subsisting on "four eyed soup," a gruel so thin as to be reflective.[76] But there were fates worse than drinking "four eyed soup": four of Ma Xuan and Zhu Zijing's fellow team members were murdered and dismembered while traveling to the county seat.[77] Performing as peasants and landlords could be just as dangerous as playing soldiers.

In the late 1940s, drama troupes and propaganda teams performed land reform dramas on stage and directed land reform campaigns in the

---

[74] Henan-Anhui-Jiangsu.
[75] Chen Xiao *et al.*, "Qianshao jutuan chicheng zai jiefang zhanchang – qianshao jutuan tuanshi jielu," 165–166.
[76] Zhu Zijing, "Zai zhanhuo zhong zhilian – huadong yezhanjun zhengzhibu wengongtuan chengli chuqi," 352–353.
[77] Ma Xuan, "Yi ge wengongtuan yuan de huiyi," 290–291.

field. Many artists would follow the lead of the Resist the Enemy Dramatic Society and take part in multiple rounds of agrarian revolution.[78] But while actors were essential players in land reform, leading rural revolution required enduring hardship and dangers. Sometimes troupe members created their own problems: one artist from the Central Plains Drama Troupe ran off with a landlord's daughter, leaving his comrades to deal with this "political accident."[79] But overall the experiences of drama troupes in land reform during the Civil War reflect the land reform campaigns of that era, which were violent affairs characterized by wild swings in policy. Troupe members performed important roles in land reform, staging shows laced with land reform rhetoric and ritual while also overseeing land reform at the village level. This rural work, however, was soon balanced by new urban responsibilities.

Urban revolution: drama troupes and the urban takeover

The success of military and land reform campaigns signaled the beginning of the end of the Civil War. With Communist power in the countryside increasingly secure, it was time to bring the revolution to China's cities. The arrival of Mao's cultural army created a heady atmosphere of hope mixed with fear as urban populations prepared themselves for life in "New China."[80] While the urban takeover has traditionally received scant academic attention, James Gao's recent monograph on the arrival

---

[78] Hu Ke, "Shijian zhong xueshi de shi nian – dui kangdi jushe xiju chuangzuo huodong de huiyi," 718.

[79] Liu Zhen, "Jiefang zhanzheng zhong wo suo zhi," 127.

[80] For case studies of the urban takeover, see Kenneth Lieberthal, *Revolution and Tradition in Tientsin, 1949–1952* (Standford, CA: Stanford University Press, 1980); Ezra F. Vogel, *Canton Under Communism: Programs and Politics in a Provincial Capital, 1949–1968* (Cambridge, MA: Harvard University Press, 1980). For a comparison of urban and rural areas during the early days of the PRC, see Jeremy Brown, *City Versus Countryside in Mao's China: Negotiating the Divide* (New York: Cambridge University Press, 2012). A few scholars mention the role of culture during the process of the urban takeover, starting with Chang-tai Hung, who quotes Derk Bodde on the use of *yangge* dancing as the "Red Army" marched into Beijing on February 3, 1949. See Hung, *Mao's New World*, 77. Several chapters in a recent collection edited by Jeremy Brown and Paul Pickowicz, finally, touch on the cultural realm: Fredrik Wakeman notes the role of singing and *yangge* as the Communists first entered Shanghai; Christian Hess shows that the Communists used cultural forms in an attempt to reach out to foreigners in Dalian; Perry Link, in his discussion of *xiangsheng*, discusses the lives of artists, mostly in Beijing; and Paul Pickowicz highlights how private-sector filmmaking was transformed as the Communists set up shop in Shanghai. See Jeremy Brown and Paul G. Pickowicz, eds. *Dilemmas of Victory: The Early Years of the People's Republic of China* (Cambridge, MA: Harvard University Press, 2010).

Communist power in Hangzhou is particularly helpful in illuminating the basic problems faced by cultural workers as they moved from the countryside to cities. As recreated by Gao, a severe shortage of political workers hampered political work; despite calls for the rapid recruitment of "revolutionary intellectuals," the Communist Party failed to train enough political workers and as a result peasant cadres were the main force overseeing the urban takeover.[81]

In light of this shortage, PLA cultural workers assumed critical roles, both explaining Communist policies and signing up urban intellectuals to serve the new regime. In Hangzhou, for example, cultural workers staged street corner dramas during PLA parades, with attractive young women playing prominent roles and drawing large crowds.[82] Communist recruiters, meanwhile, capitalized on the popularity of the song "Go with Mao Zedong" to find students for Huadong University, a cadre training school with branches in Jinan, Nanjing, and Suzhou.[83] During the urban takeover, the party faced a severe shortage of political workers and desperately needed skilled cultural workers to spread the Communist message and oversee recruiting drives. Propaganda teams and drama troupes, having already aided the Civil War and land reform efforts, were called on again to explain the party's policies and pacify an anxious urban population. While troupe members attempted to adjust to urban life and perform works promoting the Communist Party, city residents offered a mixed reaction. Some were genuinely pleased by the arrival of the Communists' cultural army, devouring performances. But, as might be expected, not all urban residents welcomed these outsiders and the political movement they represented, and offered what resistance they could. Most urbanites wavered between hope and fear; for them, these first interactions with propaganda teams and drama troupes would help shape their attitudes towards the emerging PRC regime.

Mao famously insisted on avoiding the disastrous mistakes of Li Zicheng, the rebel who neglected to fully pacify the countryside before taking Beijing at the close of the Ming dynasty. But the Communists did in fact move too quickly to take urban centers. Immediately following Japan's surrender, Communist forces made temporary advances in the Northeast, giving Communist propaganda teams and drama troupes an early opportunity to stage urban shows. After the city of Zhangjiakou was "liberated" by the Eighth Route Army in August 1945, for example, the Resist the Enemy Dramatic Society built makeshift stages on top of army

---

[81] Gao, *The Communist Takeover of Hangzhou*, 19.
[82] Ibid., 73.   [83] Ibid., 52.

trucks and performed single act plays for its urban audiences.[84] Soon troupes were staging the *huaju* spoken drama *The King Li Zicheng* (Li chuang wang), a morality tale concerning the ultimate failure of Li Zicheng's "peasant rebellion," in Harbin and other Northeast cities. Operas, especially *A Hatred of Blood and Tears* and *The White-Haired Girl*, meanwhile, explained the rationale behind the Communists' radical rural reforms.[85]

As seen in Kaifeng, however, the subsequent forced departure of the Communists undercut the power of these performances. The June 1948 entry of East China Field Army and its Fifth Cultural Work Team into Kaifeng's south gate signaled the city's first "liberation." This team, which included the female actor Ma Xuan, spent the night at a local school before braving the Guomindang bombardment to cover the city in slogans, conduct street corner propaganda, and establish a recruiting station to process the hundreds of urban youths who came forth to join the revolutionary cause.[86] The team's creative group even crafted a special *yaogu* "waist drum" number, *Kaifeng Liberation Yaogu* (Kaifeng jiefang yaogu), updating an older production with new lyrics explaining the rules of PLA discipline. But a Guomindang counterattack forced the Communists to hastily leave the city. In order to explain their departure, the team created another work, *A Message to the People of Kaifeng* (Gao Kaifeng renmin shu), which sagely claimed that the PLA had in fact invited this counterattack.[87]

The Kaifeng debacle reinforced the importance of fully pacifying the countryside before occupying cities. China's most important cities did not fall to the PLA until late in the Civil War, with Beiping and Tianjin only captured after the conclusion of the pivotal Pingjin Campaign in January, 1949. PLA drama troupes staged revolutionary dramas and carried out other forms of propaganda in both cities, and by the time Xi'an, a symbolic seat of power in close proximity to Yan'an, fell to the Northwest Field Army that spring, cultural workers were well prepared for urban work.[88] The Popular Masses Drama Troupe, which had joined the Northwest Field Army after the fall of Yan'an, would fittingly play

---

[84] Hu Ke, "Shijian zhong xueshi de shi nian – dui kangdi jushe xiju chuangzuo huodong de huiyi," 709.
[85] Wang Dikang, "Dongbei budui wenyi gongzuo gaishu," 483.
[86] Ma Xuan, "Yi ge wengongtuan yuan de huiyi," 291.
[87] Song Guoxian and Wang Yonghong, "Cong Huaibei dazhong wengongtuan dao huaye wengongtuan wudui," 260.
[88] For revolutionary drama in Beiping, see Dai Bixiang, "Women zai wei jiefang zhanzheng de shengli fuwu – ji Dongbei yezhanjun qi zong xuanchuandui" [Our service in the victory of the War of Liberation – remembering the Northeast Field Army Seventh Column Propaganda Team] JZSQ (ca. 1980s), 544. For Tianjin, see Li Zhao *et al.*, "Liangguang zongdui wengongtuan zai huaihai zhanyi zhong de huaju yanchu huodong," 430.

a leading role in the Communist takeover of Xi'an. As troupe leader Lei Feng later recalled, the smaller cities and towns that fell to the PLA as it approached the ancient capital gave troupe members ample opportunity to practice delivering speeches from street corners and trucks, as well as avoiding the bricks and rocks that were sometimes thrown at them by less than enthusiastic crowds.[89] While the Popular Masses Drama Troupe survived Xi'an unscathed, its truck flipped on the way to Lanzhou, seriously injuring most of the troupe.

Also taking part in the Xi'an takeover was the Northwest Military Region Propaganda Department Drama Troupe. Having rehearsed *The People's City* (Renmin chengshi) and other *huaju* spoken dramas in preparation for urban work, these performers were among the first Communists to enter the city, arriving through the city's north gate and staying, in the classic drama troupe tradition, at a local temple. But the rapid departure of their PLA escort, as the Northwest Field Army continued to pursue Guomindang forces, left a sense of uncertainty in the city. According to troupe member Ren Ping, "spies" filled Xi'an, creating a palpable sense that the city might fall back into Guomindang hands. Rumors that the Communists would soon depart spread rapidly, and the few shops that stayed open refused the new *renminbi* currency, insisting on payments in silver. In light of this situation, Ren Ping and his comrades took to the streets to announce PLA movements and victories, hoping to ensure residents that the Communists were in Xi'an to stay, while confusing potential spies with misdirection.[90] Combined with parades and performances of *The People's City*, a sense of normalcy returned to Xi'an, especially once the PLA returned. Soon the troupe welcomed an influx of new students and created the *August 1st Song and Dance* (Bayi gewu), an instant history that dramatized the entirety of the revolution, from the Autumn Harvest Uprising to the "liberation" of Xi'an.[91]

As the economically developed cities along the Yangtze River fell to the PLA during the spring and summer of 1949, Communist drama troupes came into contact with modern cities on a scale that put Xi'an to shame. What they discovered often surprised troupe members. Entering Hankou, Liu Zhen and the Central Plains Drama Troupe found that their competitors for public attention included a "freak show" (*guai ren tuan*) featuring a number of grotesque children, a dwarf, a tiger,

---

[89] Lei Feng, "Cong Shaan-Gan-Ning bianqu minzhong jutuan dao yi ye zhengzhibu wengongtuan," 49.
[90] Ren Ping, "Lianzheng Xuanchuandui zai baowei Yan'an de rizi li" [Joint Defense Propaganda Team in defense of Yan'an] JZSQ (1987), 102.
[91] Wang Yongnian, "Wei baowei Yan'an, jiefang da xibei de zhanzheng fuwu – ji xibei yezhanjun wengongtuan," 42–43.

and "wild chickens" (*ye ji*), a euphemism for young prostitutes.[92] But given its size and cultural infamy, Shanghai represented the most important East China destination for Communist drama troupes. PLA general and future Shanghai mayor, Chen Yi, thus gathered propaganda teams and drama troupes in Yangzhou, where he continually stressed the importance of cultural work for the imminent takeover of Shanghai.[93]

Chen Yi, his forces entering Shanghai in late May, had planned well. As captured in Wei Ming's recollections, crowds cheered cultural workers as they performed "lightning" (*shandian*) style shows in factories and schools throughout Shanghai, their welcome cemented when famous movie stars joined Communist actors on stage.[94] Street corners, public squares, factories, and schools all hosted shows by the newly arrived Communists, the cultural offensive culminating in a massive PLA parade on July 6th featuring *yangge* and *yaogu* dancing. Following the directives of Chen Yi, cultural workers trained *yaogu* dance teams inside the city, a difficult task given the lack of authentic *yaogu* "waist drums" in the Shanghai area.[95] The National Defense Drama Troupe, just one of many troupes to visit the city, performed *Fair Deal* (Gongping maimai), *Big Yangge of Liberation* (Jiefang da yangge), and *Wu Mengqiang Gifts a Chicken* (Wu Mengqiang song ji) for Shanghai audiences. Yet even in "modern" Shanghai the troupe forbid its male actors from parting their hair.[96]

With the capture of Shanghai, the former Guomindang capitals of Nanjing and Chongqing remained the final set of symbolically important cities not yet under Communist control. Given the size and importance of these cities, the Communists deployed multiple drama troupes and propaganda teams to disseminate urban policy and calm city residents. For most cultural workers, performing in Nanjing was a smooth process, with some even enjoying a stay at Jiang Jieshi's former presidential compound.[97] But the experiences of the Central Plains Drama Troupe hint at the tensions that lay under the surface of the urban takeover. Staging performances of Communist shows that included the Yan'an classics *Brother and Sister Open Wasteland* (Xiong mei kai huang) and

[92] Liu Zhen, "Jiefang zhanzheng zhong wo suo zhi," 128–129.
[93] Xu Shi, "Fenghuo zhong yansheng de yi ge zhandou jiti – ji shanda jutuan dao huadong junqu wengongtuan" [A battling organization born in flames – remembering the Shanda Drama Troupe becoming the Huadong Military Region Cultural Work Team] JZSQ (ca. 1980s), 365.
[94] Wei Ming, "Huaihai juezhan qianhou de san ye wengongtuan yi tuan" [The Third Field Cultural Work Team First Team before and after the Decisive Battle of Huaihai] JZSQ (1987), 381–382.
[95] Da Peng, "'Xinlü' zai jiefang zhanzheng zhong qianjin," 281–283.
[96] Sun Xiyue, "Jiefang zhanzheng shiqi de guofang jutuan," 236.
[97] Wei Ming, "Huaihai juezhan qianhou de san ye wengongtuan yi tuan," 382.

Figure 6 PLA propagandists entering Shanghai

The White-Haired Girl at Nanjing's Central University, one troupe member
instigated an "incident." According to Liu Zhen, Li Qingxiu, of peasant
background, got into an argument while setting up the stage in the university's auditorium and publically announced that all of the university's
teachers and students were in fact "captives" (*fulu*).[98] The troupe quickly
disciplined Li Qingxiu, but his outburst illuminates the rural–urban
tension that marked the urban takeover.

[98] Liu Zhen, "Jiefang zhanzheng zhong wo suo zhi," 128.

Propaganda teams and drama troupes, well versed in creating the powerful symbolic moments that heralded the arrival of Mao's "New China," brought their experiences to bear on the streets of Chongqing, one of the last major Chinese cities to fall to the PLA. After Chongqing opened its gates to the PLA, Ma Hongwen and his cultural work team solemnly paraded into the city alongside soldiers, hoisting portraits of Chairman Mao and Zhu De, while *yaogu* dance teams and red flag bearers led the way. This was just the opening salvo of a month of propaganda. Before the team departed with the army to "suppress bandits," Chongqing residents were treated to a full lineup of revolutionary dramas that included *The White-Haired Girl, Liu Hulan, A Hatred of Blood and Tears, Fair Trade, Brother and Sister Open Wasteland,* and *Wang Keqin's Squad.*[99] Li Ping, selected to play the lead role in her troupe's rendition of *Liu Hulan,* noted with pride that her troupe performed in one of Chongqing's modern theaters, attracting great interest among the city's residents, especially youths seeking to join the troupe.[100]

For the orphan Li Ping, who had earlier endured a long forced march after joining the revolution in Xiangyang, the chance to play the lead role in one of the most famous and powerful land reform operas had already represented an accomplishment. To play Liu Hulan in Chongqing on a modern stage was, of course, even more of a professional honor. Much like Li Ping, Communist cultural workers had come a long way during the turbulent 1940s. Granted, not all shows during the early days of the urban take over went perfectly, especially when linguistic issues arose as troupes traveled far from their places of origin. This was generally not an insurmountable problem in North China, but troupes traveling from the south had to quickly learn standard Chinese (*putonghua*) to prevent audiences from thinking that actors were performing in a foreign language.[101] But having survived combat during the Civil War, braved agrarian revolution during land reform, and triumphantly returned to China's urban spaces with the imminent establishment of the PRC, what would be next for Communist cultural workers?

Conclusion: revolutionary drama in 1949

As the Civil War ended in victory for the Communists, cultural workers were at a crossroads. The end of all out military conflict drastically

---

[99] Ma Hongwen, "Zhandou li chengzhang de shier jun wengongtuan," 155–156.
[100] Li Ping, "Cong E xibei dao da Xi'nan – huiyi er ye liu zongdui wengongtuan di yi duan shenghuo," 177–178.
[101] Li Zhao, "Yi liangguang zongdui wengongtuan" [Remembering the Liangguang Army Cultural Work Team] JZSQ (1987), 448.

reduced the need for military propaganda teams and drama troupes. This trend was reflected in the reform of PLA propaganda teams in late 1951, when the military slashed the number of cultural workers from 64,000 to 6,972.[102] The PLA demobilized massive numbers of propagandists, but unlike the PLA rank and file, who found themselves unwelcome in urban areas after leaving the army, demobilized troupe members were seldom forced to return to the countryside.[103] Some drama troupes easily located new urban patrons at the end of the conflict. The Children's Drama Troupe, for example, became the East China Experimental Peking Opera Troupe, remaining in Shanghai under new mayor Chen Yi. Other cultural workers found new employment opportunities, including jobs in the film industry.[104] To be sure, the formal proclamation of the PRC in October 1949 did not eliminate the need for military action and military propaganda teams. Now, however, the field of battle moved to China's peripheries, with military troupes transferred to Lanzhou, Xinjiang, and other points far west.[105] Ma Hongwen's troupe, meanwhile, was one of many dispatched to Korea in late 1950.[106] In Korea, the military would follow the Civil War precedent, and press cultural workers into service as stretcher bearers and medical staff.[107]

But as Chen Bo and the rest of the Combat Dramatic Society discovered, 1949 brought real and substantial change to cultural work. With the chaos of the Civil War era receding, cultural workers could finally bring order to the dramatic realm. As He Long informed the troupe in March 1949, the Communists planned a series of national representative

---

[102] Deng Bangyu, ed., *Jiefangjun xiju shi*, 208. The propaganda unit system was largely restored over the following several years.

[103] Diamant, Neil J., *Embattled Glory: Veterans, Military Families, and the Politics of Patriotism in China, 1949–2007* (Lanham, MD: Rowman & Littlefield Publishers, 2009), 71.

[104] Xu Shi, "Fenghuo zhong yansheng de yi ge zhandou jiti – ji shanda jutuan dao huadong junqu wengongtuan," 367.

[105] For example, two of He Long's propaganda teams, the Popular Masses Drama Troupe and the Northwest Military Region Propaganda Department Drama Troupe, were combined into a new unit that would henceforth be headquartered in distant Lanzhou. Liu Ruzhou's propaganda team, specializing in *pingju* opera style, was one of many teams dispatched to Xinjiang, which would become its long-term home base. Wang Yongnian, "Wei baowei Yan'an, jiefang da xibei de zhanzheng fuwu – ji xibei yezhanjun wengongtuan," 43. Liu Ruzhou, "Pingjutuan shang Yan'an" [Ping opera troupe goes to Yan'an] JZSQ (1987), 66.

[106] Ma Hongwen, "Zhandou li chengzhang de shier jun wengongtuan," 155.

[107] Allied Translator & Interpreter Section (ATIS) Interrogation Report No. KG 087, July 17, 1951; Interrogation Reports KG 0001-KG 0154, File 461.01, Box 55; General Correspondence, 1951; Assistant Chief of Staff, G-2, Theater Intelligence Division; Records of the U.S. Army Military District of Washington, 1942–1991, Record Group 554, Entry 17A (General Headquarters, Far East Command, Supreme Command for Allied Powers, and United Nations Command); National Archives at College Park, Md. (NACP), 4.

meetings in the newly "liberated" Beiping, including one for China's fragmented cultural world. As the creators of one of the most famous land reform operas, the Combat Dramatic Society would have the honor of performing *Liu Hulan* during the upcoming cultural Congress. For some in the troupe, this was a return to urban life and sophisticated audiences demanding high-quality *huaju* spoken drama and refined Peking opera. For these artists, performing on stages in modern theaters marked the end of their long rural sojourn. But for most of the Combat Dramatic Society, this was the first time in a city of any size; during a stopover in Shijiazhuang, for example, many troupe members, seeing a stoplight for the first time, had to be taught the meaning of red and green lights.[108]

The troupe hurried to Beiping, arriving in May and quickly taking to the stage. In an inspired decision, the troupe brought Liu Ailan, the martyr's younger sister, to Beiping to introduce *Liu Hulan* before each performance. The troupe performed for over two weeks in front of full-capacity audiences that included cultural luminaries such as the Marxist theorist Zhou Yang and the famous playwright Tian Han. All of this was mere preparation for its performance during the All-China National Cultural Worker Congress in early July, where Zhou Enlai and other top Communist Party leaders sat in attendance. The troupe stayed in Beiping long enough to expand its ranks, leaving the city with some three hundred students.[109] Journeying to the Southwest to reunite with He Long, the troupe would return to its military roots. But the Congress at which the troupe had just performed heralded a new era in cultural work for the PRC. The first hurdle of this new era remained the completion of land reform, which required the largest mass mobilization ever attempted under the Communists. During land reform and in everyday life in the PRC, villagers would be expected to perform new roles as socialist peasants. With the ties between cultural and political performances growing ever stronger, drama troupes would remain an essential element of land reform and rural revolution. Before turning to the PRC era, however, the following chapter explores why land reform operas proved so powerful in the Chinese countryside.

---

[108] Huang Qinghe, "Ji jian nanwang de wangshi" [A few unforgettable events] JZSQ (ca. 1980s), 107.
[109] Chen Bo, "Zhandou jushe zhandou zai xibei zhanchang," 32–33.

4 Staging rural revolution
Land reform operas

On March 7, 1947, Jack Belden became one of the few Westerners to observe Mao's cultural army in the field. Reporting on the Chinese revolution during the height of the Civil War, Belden caught a performance of *The White-Haired Girl*, the Communists' most famous "land reform opera." Belden estimated the show's audience at over two thousand, the crowd seemingly oblivious to the freezing North China night. Here Belden describes the audience's reaction to the opera's depiction of a "Speaking Bitterness Meeting," during which characters debate the fate of Huang Shiren, their villainous landlord:

At this juncture, to my utter surprise, many members of the audience stood up in great excitement, shouting, "Sha! Sha! Kill him! Kill him!" ... At several points in the play, I saw women, old and young, peasant and intellectual, wiping tears from their eyes with the sleeves of their jackets. One old lady near me wept loudly though nearly the whole play... As a matter of fact, the Communists' whole theatrical effort was extremely impressive.[1]

Belden's account highlights the ability of land reform operas to draw massive crowds and powerfully affect audiences. What made these shows so powerful? And were audiences really so easily drawn to and affected by revolutionary drama?

By the time Belden saw *The White-Haired Girl*, Communist-affiliated artists had decades of experience in dramatic creation. The Yan'an years had seen heated debates over the proper use of dramatic forms, but the process of "rectification" firmly established the ideal of mixing elements of Western cultural structures with Chinese folk art. During the Sino-Japanese War, co-opting local musical styles in *"yangge* operas" offered Communist cultural workers the chance to compete with for-profit *xibanzi* opera troupes. By the land reform era, dramatists had developed *yangge* further, crafting *geju* operas, a mixture of Western spoken drama,

---

[1] Jack Belden, *China Shakes the World* (New York: Monthly Review Press, 1970), 210.

local opera, and dance.[2] With its increasing professionalism and ever-greater use of Western musical instruments, *geju* represented the next stage in the evolution of *yangge*.

Cultural workers used the hybrid formats of *yangge* and *geju* operas as carriers of provocative narratives, designed to evoke emotional responses from audiences. During land reform, this meant inspiring hatred towards landlords and other newly labeled class enemies. As one Communist cultural worker insisted, drama served education, not entertainment. Thus, while rural audiences may have been primarily interested in an entertaining show, from the Communists' perspective the performance of *The White-Haired Girl* was to "spark class hatred and encourage the spirit of struggle."[3] Land reform operas provided the political culture, practical cultural tools such as the concept of class status and the rhetoric of class struggle that newly created peasants needed to master in order to successfully implement land reform. Operas such as *Liu Hulan*, purporting to represent a true story, provided villagers with new concepts, new identities, and new modes of behavior.

While any drama performed within the context of agrarian revolution might be considered a "land reform opera," works that centered on rural class struggle proved most useful in the field. The most influential "land reform opera," *The White-Haired Girl*, does not even mention agrarian reform. But while not all land reform operas transmitted content specific to the actual campaign, such as the staging of a "struggle" session, they all adhered to the Maoist worldview that informed land reform and attempted to represent village life in a "realistic" manner that promoted the campaigns. The most successful productions, meanwhile, drew on traditional operatic practices, both in the move to local opera styles and in the co-opting of rural drama troupes. These concessions to local traditions gave land reform operas a chance to compete against traditional works, which still drew large audiences in the countryside.

This study is largely concerned with drama troupe performance in the field, but the success of Communists' cultural army was dependent on creation. Dramatists had to create shows that were not only powerful, but entertaining as well. As Perry Link has demonstrated with Communist literature, entertainment was a crucial, if "unofficial," aspect of propaganda.[4] After exploring the creation of the three most influential land

[2] Shi Man, Tian Benxiang, and Zhang Zhiqiang, *Kangzhan xiju* [War of resistance drama] (Kaifeng: Henan daxue chubanshe, 2005), 142.
[3] Sun Lin, *Nongcun jutuan zenyang bianju he paiju* [Playwriting and production for village drama troupes] (Shandong: Shandong renmin chubanshe, 1951), 1.
[4] Link, *The Uses of Literature*, 300–301.

reform operas (*The White-Haired Girl, Liu Hulan,* and *Red Leaf River*), this chapter analyzes their plot structures and character archetypes to explain why these operas were such potent instruments in rural revolution. But because drama troupes and audiences ultimately determined the success or failure of revolutionary dramas, this chapter also considers the performance and reception of land reform operas. Accounts of land reform opera performances uniformly praise these shows for their ability to captivate audiences and direct political action. This chapter, however, uses archival sources to reveal the true story behind the single most famous staging of a land reform opera: the 1948 performance of *Red Leaf River* in Longbow Village, recorded by William Hinton in *Fanshen*.

The party school paradigm: the creation of *The White-Haired Girl*

Home to the vast majority of party intellectuals and artists, it is no surprise that the most famous and influential land reform opera, *The White-Haired Girl*, was created in the Communist wartime capital of Yan'an. This foundational opera tells the story of Xi'er, a young peasant woman whose beauty attracts the attention of Huang Shiren, her villainous landlord. Huang tricks Yang Bailao, Xi'er's father, into selling her to the Huang household as a servant girl. Yang kills himself in remorse, leaving Xi'er to suffer abuse at the hands of the Huang family. Wang Dachun, a peasant and Xi'er's love interest, unsuccessfully challenges the landlord's power and flees the village. After raping Xi'er, Huang Shiren plans to sell the now pregnant girl to avoid potential complications. Learning of this plot, Xi'er escapes to the mountains, where she lives for years until her hair turns white, leading superstitious villagers to mistake her for a ghost. But eventually Dachun returns to the village with the Eighth Route Army and rescues Xi'er, allowing the young woman to return home and play a lead role in the "struggling" of her former tormentor.

Produced by a creation team at Luyi, *The White-Haired Girl* represented the attempt of elite party of artists to answer the challenges set forth by Mao's 1942 "Talks at the Yan'an Forum." Mao's championing of "national" cultural forms helped create a craze for *yangge* dancing and other traditional folk arts, which posed a dilemma for the artists at Luyi. Most Luyi artists preferred Western style works, which in terms of drama meant the increasingly scorned form of *huaju* spoken drama. To spur the development of *yangge* operas, the school formed the Luyi Work Team in late

Figure 7 A student performance of *The White-Haired Girl*, 1946

1943.[5] Team members initially struggled with the shift to traditional rural artistic forms, but eventually found a formula for success by liberally fusing elements of local traditions with Communist ideology and Western narrative structures.

---

[5] The team quickly produced *The Hardened Bandit Zhou Zishan* (Guanfei Zhou Zishan), a five-act *yangge* opera. This opera "showed how it was necessary for the Communist Party to transform the subjective world while it was transforming the objective world." Huang Renke, *Luyi ren: hongse yishujiamen* [Luyi people: Red artists] (Beijing: Zhonggong zhongyang dangxiao chubanshe: 2001), 137.

The team, for example, decided to use the northern Hebei folk tale "The White Haired Female Immortal" as the basis for a new opera.[6] Shao Zinan led the creation of the opera's first draft, entitled *The White-Haired Fairy* (Bai mao xiannü). During rehearsals, the head of Luyi, Zhou Yang, displeased with the team's results, demanded a rewrite and recruited He Jingzhi and Ding Yi from the school's Literature Department to oversee a new draft.[7] This began a three-month writing process, lasting from January to April of 1944, during which the new authors focused on ideological concerns, eschewing a simple anti-superstition tale. According to He Jingzhi, the writers wanted to "show the difference between two societies [the feudal past versus life under the Communists] as well as demonstrate the *fanshen* of the people."[8] He and Ding accomplished this goal by crafting a villainous landlord who preyed on innocent peasants until the arrival of the Communist Party, a formula that other operas would closely follow.

Composing a musical score that would appeal to local audiences, however, proved the greatest challenge for the creators of *The White-Haired Girl*. Zhang Geng, head of Luyi's Drama Department, repeatedly rejected the work team's compositions. Not until Zhang Lu, the only student composer on the team, had a late-night revelation to simply use the popular folk tune "Little Cabbage" (Xiao baicai) as the music for Xi'er's opening song "The North Wind Blows" did the team begin to uncover an appropriate method to write the musical score for the opera.[9] In what would prove to be the standard for land reform operas, the Luyi team wrote the musical score for *The White-Haired Girl* with a mishmash of local styles adapted for new purposes. Composers lifted tunes from Hebei, Shanxi, and Shaanxi folk traditions, altering some songs but leaving others intact.[10] The use of local music in *The White-Haired Girl* and other land reform operas helped create a bridge between cultural workers and artists, providing a template of combining folk traditions with Western narrative structures and Communist ideology.

---

[6] The plot of this folk tale was similar to that of the opera, but with some key differences: in the original story, there was no romance between the female character and a young peasant, nor was there a final struggle session against a landlord. The time period of the story was also altered. He Jingzhi, "*Bai mao nü* de chuangzuo yu yanchu" [The creation and performance of *The White-Haired Girl*] (1946), in He Jingzhi and Ding Yi, *Baimao nü* [The White-Haired Girl] (Beijing: Renmin wenxue chubanshe, 1952), 249–251.

[7] Huang Renke, *Luyi ren*, 138.

[8] He Jingzhi, "*Bai mao nü* de chuangzuo yu yanchu," 253.

[9] Huang Renke, *Luyi ren*, 141–142.

[10] Ma Ke, Zhang Lu, and Qu Wei, "Guanyu *Bai mao nü* de yinyue" [Regarding the music of *The White-Haired Girl*] (1945), in He Jingzhi and Ding Yi, *Baimao nü* [The White-Haired Girl] (Beijing: Renmin wenxue chubanshe, 1952), 262.

The White-Haired Girl premiered in Yan'an on April 28, 1944 with a special performance for the Communists' Seventh Party Conference. Party luminaries in attendance included Zhu De, Liu Shaoqi, and Zhou Enlai. Mao Zedong arrived fashionably late. Following the performance, Zhou Enlai and other party members broke with tradition by visiting backstage to congratulate cast and crew.[11] The opera was an immediate success, enjoying a first run of more than thirty performances, and soon other Shaanxi drama troupes were studying and performing the opera, allowing *The White-Haired Girl* to spread throughout the base areas, grabbing the attention and imagination of rural audiences.[12] He Jingzhi, for example, noted how villagers called the show's actors by their stage names, while young children even cursed the actors playing villainous roles, blurring the lines between on-stage performance and everyday life.[13]

The Luyi creation team continuously revised their emerging master-piece, with one major change quickly following the show's premiere; party leaders sent a note suggesting that despite official policy, the landlord character should be executed at the end of the opera, a change that immediately proved popular with audiences.[14] The opera's first major revision, designed to make the show a more forceful tool in the promotion of rural revolution, occurred in October 1945. Dramatists strengthened the personality of Xi'er after the third act, while also adding a scene where the elderly peasant Uncle Zhao talks about the Eighth Route Army to demonstrate "the hope buried in the hearts of peasants in the old society."[15] While the Luyi team further revised the opera, these early changes resulted in a much stronger emphasis on class struggle.[16] The opera's coupling of Communist ideology with local operatic forms

---

[11] Huang Renke, *Luyi ren*, 147.

[12] The Northwest Literary and Art Work Team was the first troupe to stage its own performance, with the Suide Area Cultural Work Team following suit in late 1945, its efforts greatly aided by a chance encounter with the Luyi performers that led to a spirited discussion about the opera's characters. See *Shaanxi sheng xiju zhi: shengzhi juan*, 44–45.

[13] He Jingzhi, "*Bai mao nü* de chuangzuo yu yanchu," 155.

[14] This note, which implied that class issues would be at the forefront of Communist Party policy following the Sino-Japanese War, represented the views of Liu Shaoqi. Huang Renke, *Luyi ren*, 148.

[15] Dramatists also added a scene where poor peasants Dachun and Dasuo resist rent-dunning "running dogs." He Jingzhi, "*Bai mao nü* de chuangzuo yu yanchu," 256–257.

[16] Other, stylistic changes were also made, especially in rewriting clumsy dialogue at the end of the play. The end of the play remained unsatisfactory despite revisions in 1947 (in the Northeast) and 1949 (in Beijing). Not until the fifth and "final" revision (also in Beijing) was the problem solved by combining the fifth and sixth acts, while eliminating much of the description Xi'er's life on the mountain. See He Jingzhi, "Qianyan" [Forward] (1950), in He Jingzhi and Ding Yi, *Baimao nü* [*The White-Haired Girl*] (Beijing: Renmin wenxue chubanshe, 1952), 2.

represented the Communists' best hope of reaching and affecting rural audiences. This formula, moreover, proved highly malleable.

The PLA's land reform opera: the creation of *Liu Hulan*

Created by He Long's Combat Dramatic Society, *Liu Hulan* tells the story of a young peasant woman who is tireless in her support of the Communist cause. Liu Hulan leads her local Women's Association, helping organize peasants to make shoes and donate grain to the PLA, even taking in and hiding an injured PLA soldier. Yet Liu Hulan's activism inspires the hatred of Shi Sanhai, her village landlord. Refusing to submit to the new village order created through land reform, Shi Sanhai keeps a record of Liu Hulan's deeds and conspires to bring enemy soldiers to the village to punish the young peasant activist. These "bandit" soldiers led by Company Commander Xu, the notorious "Big Beard," occupy the village, but Liu Hulan refuses to renounce the Communists. Infuriated, Company Commander Xu forces peasants to beat Liu Hulan before having her executed. At the end of the narrative, Communist forces avenge her death by killing Xu.

Figure 8 A performance of *Liu Hulan*, 1947

This brutal drama was directly based on the real-life execution of Liu Hulan, a young female activist from Yunzhouxi Village. In February 1947, shortly after the *Jin-Sui Daily* published an article about Liu Hulan's recent martyrdom, Wei Feng and the Combat Dramatic Society happened to be marching through Daxiang, a town situated less than two miles away from Yunzhouxi. Armed with a letter of introduction from the county head, Wei Feng made his way to the village, only to find residents unwilling to speak with an outsider. Working with a local cadre, Wei tracked down and interviewed Liu Hulan's mother, who proved an enthusiastic subject. Talking with Wei for two hours, she walked him through the sequence of events at the execution ground and even gave Wei her daughter's tiger balm box and handkerchief. The troupe used these "real-life" items as actual props, a testament to the importance of realism in land reform operas.[17]

Wei Feng collaborated with troupe leader Zhu Dan to produce the drama's first draft in less than a week. As originally created, *Liu Hulan* was a four-act *huaju* spoken drama, its successive acts detailing the plot against Liu Hulan, her capture, her martyrdom, and the memorial held by PLA soldiers to eulogize her death. Thus, the original version of the opera did not show the death of Company Commander Xu, yet according to Wei Feng, the show was nevertheless extremely effective.[18] While Wei insisted on the power of this *huaju* version of *Liu Hulan*, other troupe members focused on its deficiencies. Liu Lianchi, a collaborator on the drama's second draft, dismissed the original version of *Liu Hulan* as only concerned with the titular character's moral courage (*qijie*) during her execution, ignoring the larger story of Liu Hulan's life. According to Liu Lianchi, the show was still powerful and caused soldiers to cry out and fire their weapons at the actors playing evil characters, but viewers disliked its limited focus. As Liu Lianchi emphasized, Mao Zedong had indeed praised Liu Hulan's "glorious death" (*si de guangrong*), but he also extolled her "great life" (*sheng de weida*).[19]

Chen Bo's memoirs uncover the most immediate factor leading the troupe to convert the show into a *geju* opera. While Wei Feng had simply noted that the show was converted into a *geju* opera to mimic *The White-Haired Girl*, Chen details a revealing joint performance that the Combat Dramatic Society held with a *pingju* opera troupe, a *xibanzi* outfit that

---

[17] Wei Feng, "Yongfang guangmang de mingzi – Liu Hulan" [A name that shines eternal – Liu Hulan] JZSQ (1986), 55–57.

[18] Wei Feng, "Yongfang guangmang de mingzi – Liu Hulan," 58.

[19] Liu Lianchi, "Xie zai *Liu Hulan* qianmian" [Forward to Liu Hulan] (1948), in Xibei zhandou jushe, [Northwest Combat Dramatic Society], *Liu Hulan* (Beijing: Renmin wenxue chubanshe: 1952), 2.

had only recently joined the PLA. Performing *Du Shiniang* and other traditional shows, this *pingju* troupe drew huge crowds, but the Combat Dramatic Society's shows failed to impress, its audience largely composed of dozing soldiers. Feeling "humiliated" the troupe decided to convert *Liu Hulan* into a *geju* opera; in Chen's recollections, only after revision did their audience attack the stage.[20]

The recreation of *Liu Hulan* as a *geju* opera took place in the spring of 1948, after the troupe reunited after one of its many rounds of land reform. Wei Feng, joined by Liu Lianchi, Yan Jizhou, and Dong Xiaowu in a creation group, spearheaded the effort to overhaul *Liu Hulan* into an opera. Because the team continued to revise the drama after getting feedback from other members of the Combat Dramatic Society and its "brother" troupes in the Northwest, Liu Lianchi could insist that the new *geju* version of *Liu Hulan* was a "collective creation." The show's ending, however, emerged as a point of contention amongst its many creators. The *huaju* version had ended without properly punishing Liu Hulan's tormenters, and the *geju* revision had followed this precedent by closing the show with a solemn memorial service (*zhuidaohui*). This proved entirely unacceptable to audiences. Many villagers refused to disperse until the show concluded properly. Ascribing these new demands to the improved military position of the PLA *vis-à-vis* the Guomindang, Liu Lianchi and his fellow dramatists rewrote the end of the opera to ensure audiences saw "Big Beard" get his proper comeuppance.[21]

The demands of the crowd, however, also reflected audience expectations resulting from the use of folk traditions. Following the example of *The White-Haired Girl*, the composers drew heavily on folk tunes for songs, for example adapting the Hebei ditty "Jumping Bamboo Horse" (Tiao zhu ma) for the duet between two female activists. For reactionary characters, the troupe turned to local opera, using both Shanxi and Peking opera tunes traditionally associated with painted face (*hualian*) male roles, many of whom are evil or crafty.[22] Musical accompaniment was carried out throughout the show, heightening the emotional impact of dialogue and action. In the words of Yan Jizhou, the band would play "sneaky and treacherous" music as spies entered Yunzhouxi Village, peaceful music as Liu Hulan stood guard at night, and frightful music as villains beat villagers.[23] Despite the liberal use of folk traditions, composer Huang Qinghe would still lament that the score still had a bit of a "foreign

---

[20] Chen Bo, "Zhandou jushe zhandou zai xibei zhanchang," 24.
[21] Liu Lianchi, "Xie zai *Liu Hulan* qianmian," 3–5.
[22] Huang Qinghe, "Ji jian nanwang de wangshi," 170.
[23] Yan Jizhou, "Ji tugai Xuanchuandui," 167.

flavor" (*yang weidao*).[24] But there were other traces of Western influence in the show, including a mixture of *huaju* realism and operatic symbolism. Thus, while most props were real, building entrances were imaginary, so that actors pantomimed opening and closing doors; movements, meanwhile, were often exaggerated and dance-like, particularly when accompanied by music.[25]

After its revision, *Liu Hulan* rapidly spread throughout Communist base areas, performed by both military and local drama troupes.[26] Peng Dehuai ordered all army troupes under his command to stage the show, and by the end of the year even the *pingju* troupe that had "humiliated" the Combat Dramatic Society was now staging its own version of *Liu Hulan*. One member of that *pingju* troupe would even claim that while audiences were sometimes dissatisfied with the telling of a modern story in a traditional form, overall the *pingju* version of the show proved even more effective than the *geju* opera performed by the Combat Dramatic Society.[27] Still, it was the Combat Dramatic Society that staged *Liu Hulan* as its keynote performance during the All-China Cultural Worker Representative Congress in the summer of 1949. Performing before China's most distinguished artists, the troupe received a tremendous amount of feedback, leading Liu Lianchi to oversee another revision in 1950. While the alterations in this revision did little to modify the show's plot, one slight linguistic change hints at the perils of realism on stage. According to Liu Lianchi, during the execution scene, the script had originally called for "fresh blood flying, head rolling on the ground" (*xianxue fenfei, rentou luodi*). Liu now admitted this phrasing was wrong (*you maobing*), as it led some drama troupes to stage excessively bloody execution scenes.[28] The desire for realism, in the end, did have limits.

Penned by a party intellectual: the creation of *Red Leaf River*

While *The White-Haired Girl* and *Liu Hulan* were both collective productions, *Red Leaf River* was the product of a single party intellectual. A tale of class exploitation, *Red Leaf River* dramatized the suffering of the Wang clan under its landlord Lu Chengshu and his "running dog" Qiu Gui. Lu

[24] Huang Qinghe, "Ji jian nanwang de wangshi," 170.
[25] Yan Jizhou, "Ji tugai Xuanchuandui," 166–167.
[26] *Shanxi tongzhi di sishi juan: wenhua yishu zhi*, 157.
[27] Liu Ruzhou, "Pingjutuan shang Yan'an," 64–65.
[28] Liu Lianchi, "Guanyu xiudingben shuoming" [An explanation of revision] (1952), in Xibei zhandou jushe [Northwest Combat Dramatic Society], *Liu Hulan* (Beijing: Renmin wenxue chubanshe: 1952), 9.

Chengshu extorts and impoverishes Wang Dafu and his son Wang Hezi before raping Yan Yan, Wang Hezi's young wife. After Yan Yan's subsequent suicide, Wang Hezi flees the village in a helpless rage, leaving his father to fall ever further into poverty. The scattered family, however, reunites when a destitute Wang Hezi returns after the PLA "liberates" his home village. Unlike *The White-Haired Girl* and *Liu Hulan*, this land reform opera actually showed the process of agrarian reform on stage, making *Red Leaf River* the most potent expression of land reform ritual in the arsenal of the Communists' cultural army. First staged during a high tide of land reform in 1947, *Red Leaf River* quickly spread throughout North China and beyond. According to one local gazetteer, following its release "many drama troupes vied to put it on stage" so that the opera "provided an important mobilization function during the War of Liberation, especially in land reform in the New Liberated Areas."[29]

While eventually staged by a multitude of drama troupes and propaganda teams, *Red Leaf River* had a singular creative voice in Ruan Zhangjing. Introduced in Chapter 2 as the demanding artistic director of the Taihang Mountains Drama Troupe, Ruan now headed the Jin-Ji-Lu-Yu Cultural Federation's drama division. Because Ruan Zhangjing had overseen political organization in the real-life *Red Leaf River* village during the summer of 1945, he followed the lead of other dramatists and insisted on the factual basis for his work.[30] Reflecting on his motivations for creating his opera, Ruan focused on wanting to change perceptions of fate, noting that many peasants believed ownership of land resulted from preordained forces. But Ruan also wanted to give voice to an old peasant, who had told him a sorrowful tale of landlord oppression that had torn his family asunder.[31]

Ruan's work progressed slowly, a fact he later attributed to defects in his creative and theoretical abilities, although his duties within the Jin-Ji-Lu-Yu Border Region were certainly to blame. Yet Ruan Zhangjing found himself pressed to finish this creation after promising a new opera for the Xiangyuan Rural Drama Troupe, introduced in Chapter 2 as a professional troupe that the party elevated to model status after its actors finally gave up opium and embraced reform.[32] Ruan finished

---

[29] *Shanxi tongzhi di sishi juan: wenhua yishu zhi*, 158.   [30] Ibid., 158.

[31] Ruan Zhangjing, "Houji" [Afterword] (1949), in Ruan Zhangjing, *Chi ye he* [*Red Leaf River*] (Beijing: Xinhua shudian, 1950), 113.

[32] After a number of administrative transfers and name changes, the troupe was now called the Taihang People's Drama Troupe (Taihang renmin jutuan). To avoid confusion with the Taihang Mountains Drama Troupe, this chapter keeps their traditional name. Changzhi shi wenhua ju, *Changzhi shi yishu biaoyan tuanti shigao* [Draft history of Changzhi City's performing organizations] (Changzhi: Changzhi shi wenhua ju, 1993), 182.

his first draft during the summer of 1947, but before the work could be staged the opera needed its all-important musical score. Having no expertise in musical composition, Ruan had simply planned for *Red Leaf River* to be adapted into a variety of operatic forms. For the show's first production, he assigned the creation of the score to his colleagues in the Xiangyuan Rural Drama Troupe.[33]

As described by troupe member, Gao Jieyun, the music of *Red Leaf River* evolved through a process of trial and error. Geng Jiang, a blind Wuxiang County musician, provided most of the music for the first version of the opera. Working under a tight deadline, Gao did his best to match folk ditties to the opera's lyrics, not changing some tunes, adapting others to the best of his ability, and even creating a few new numbers. Realizing that he simply did not have enough music to score the opera and encouraged by Ruan Zhangjing's promotion of experimentation, some songs were performed in the "a cappella *yangge*" (*ganban yangge*) style. But audiences disparaged the opera's music as chaotic, disparate, or obviously copied from other works.[34] Critics also charged Ruan Zhangjing with clinging to the "middle peasant line" in his portrayal of the relative wealth of the Wang family; this wealth, he later insisted, only emphasized the family's eventual suffering at the hands of their landlord.[35]

A first revision helped overcome these problems, and as his new opera spread throughout the Jin-Ji-Lu-Yu Border Region and beyond, Ruan Zhangjing and the Xiangyuan Rural Drama Troupe completed a second revision in September 1948 in Shijiazhuang.[36] Advised by Zhou Yang, Ke Zhongping, and other cultural leaders grouped at North China University in the city's suburbs, Ruan streamlined the show but kept a controversial subplot portraying a village cadre as an opportunist in cahoots with class enemies.[37] Gao Jieyun, meanwhile, worked with composer Liang Hanguang and other members of the prestigious North China University People's Cultural Work Team, which would perform the revised show in Shijiazhuang. With help from the talented Liang Hanguang, Gao gave the opera a more natural and consistent score.[38]

As drama troupes and propaganda teams studied and staged *Red Leaf River*, the show continued to evolve, with dramatists free to make minor

---

[33] Ruan Zhangjing, "Houji," 115–116.

[34] Gao Jieyun, "Guanyu yinyue chuangzuo de jingguo" [Regarding the process of the musical creation] (1949), in Ruan Zhangjing, *Chi ye he* [*Red Leaf River*] (Beijing: Xinhua shudian, 1950), 127–129.

[35] Ruan Zhangjing, "Houji," 118.   [36] Then called Shimen.

[37] This subplot is discussed in Hinton, *Fanshen*, 315.   [38] Gao Jieyun, 127–129.

alterations to the show as they saw fit.[39] And in order to ensure the work's popularity, regional drama troupes adapted Ruan's masterpiece into a multitude of local styles. But after *Red Leaf River* premiered in Beiping in 1949, Ruan Zhangjing received a host of "opinions" regarding the controversial cadre subplot. Some found it a realistic and important part of the larger story, but others found it an unnecessary distraction. Ruan finally cut the subplot during the course of a third revision, later stating he had realized that "the success of the earthshaking people's *fanshen* movement derived from the leadership of the Communist Party."[40] This last revision, of course, moved the show closer to the Communists' version of reality. When staging land reform operas, actors performed as suffering peasants, militant activists, and villainous landlords. Bad cadres were simply not welcome on Communist stages.

Character archetypes in land reform operas

While many characters populate land reform operas, the centrality of young female roles has led one PRC study of land reform to suggest that these dramas were primarily aimed at women, a misguided take that obscures how dramatists used gender as a potent metaphor for power relations.[41] Because the staging of evil landlords preying on helpless women proved highly effective in generating audience passion and anger, dramatists relied on these and other stock character types. Young females suffered in "feudal" villages until the arrival of Communist power transformed them into heroines. Young men, as a corollary, were portrayed as emasculated and powerless until linking up with the Communist Party to exact revenge. For peasant men, the main force of the PLA, this proved a powerful message. The elder generation of peasants, meanwhile, was typically pathetic and helpless; tellingly, they were often simply absent from the plotline. These tales of abuse and suffering were only possible because of the creation of a "feudal" landlord class, portrayed on stage as evil and perverse. The focus on the villainy and eventual overthrow of landlords and their nefarious allies allowed dramatists to stage shows heavy in the rhetoric and rituals that were instrumental for the successful completion of rural revolution.

Character archetype 1: the abused peasant girl

All three land reform operas in question star a young female peasant who suffers at the hands of the "feudal" elements assumed to control China's

---

[39] Ruan Zhangjing, "Guanyu *Chi ye he* de san ci zhong gaixie" [Regarding the three revisions of *Red Leaf River*] (1950), in Ruan Zhangjing, *Chi ye he* [*Red Leaf River*] (Beijing: Xinhua shudian, 1950), 124.
[40] Ruan Zhangjing, "Houji," 122.   [41] Du Runsheng, ed., *Zhongguo de tudigaige*, 197.

"old society." Even when this female is not explicitly the lead character, her tale of woe drives the opera's narrative. This character archetype follows the pattern set in *The White-Haired Girl*, which centers on the agony and redemption of Xi'er, a young peasant woman living in poverty with her father. Her mother having passed away when she was just a young girl, the attractive Xi'er becomes the object of lust for the local landlord Huang Shiren. Through Huang Shiren's schemes, Xi'er is sold into the Huang household, a turn of events that leads to the suicide of her loving father. Once inside the household, the Huang matriarch physically abuses Xi'er and Huang Shiren eventually rapes her. As Xi'er laments: "Why are the poor so bitter? Why are the rich so cruel?"[42] Learning that the Huang clan plans to sell her to avoid any potential embarrassment arising from her pregnancy, Xi'er manages to escape to the nearby mountains, where she lives in a cave for three years until her hair turns white and she questions her very humanity.

Yan Yan, the female lead of *Red Leaf River*, lost both of her parents at an early age but found happiness by marrying into the Wang family, peasants poised to break out of a multi-generation battle with poverty. This optimistic future shatters when their landlord Lu Chengshu schemes to put the Wang family into serious debt. Because wedding costs account for part of this debt, Yan Yan's husband unfairly blames her for the family's plight; this is one sign that Ruan Zhangjing, party intellectual, dared to subtly criticize peasants. After the very same landlord rapes her, Yan Yan's husband blames her for the attack.[43] Overcome with shame, the young peasant girl sings out in lament:

> Twenty years have passed like a dream,
> and now only the wind and rain accompany me at the end.[44]

Yan Yan then ends her sorrows by throwing herself into the opera's titular river.[45]

The pattern of young peasant women suffering whenever they lacked the protection of the Communists continues in *Liu Hulan*. At the outset of this opera, Liu Hulan lives in a "liberated" village, enjoying political and social freedoms. After enemy forces occupy the village at the behest

---

[42] He Jingzhi and Ding Yi, *Baimao nü* [*The White-Haired Girl*] (Beijing: Renmin wenxue chubanshe, 1952), 56.

[43] From the script it is unclear if Lu Chengshu actually rapes Yan Yan, but descriptions of the show affirm that the sexual assault did occur. See Hinton, *Fanshen*, 315.

[44] Ruan Zhangjing, *Chi ye he* [*Red Leaf River*] (Beijing: Xinhua Shudian, 1950), 65.

[45] Because the staging of the opera did not explicitly depict the death of Yan Yan, some viewers expressed hope that Yan Yan had escaped the village, but as Ruan Zhangjing noted elsewhere, she indeed committed suicide. Ruan Zhangjing, "Houji," 117.

of a local landlord, however, her fortunes take a sudden turn for the worse. "Big Beard," the evil Company Commander Xu, first interrogates and threatens Liu Hulan. After refusing to betray the Communists, she is taken to the village threshing grounds, where her captors force peasants to beat her. Her suffering is perhaps best encapsulated when she urges her own sister to beat her, yelling "Beat me! Beat me!" until her teary-eyed sister complies.[46] Afterwards, enemy soldiers brutally execute Liu Hulan with a hay chopper. That the Combat Dramatic Society would often bring Liu Hulan's real-life sister on stage before its shows only increased the power of this plotline.

Character archetype 2: the emasculated young peasant male

Unable to protect village females from the predations of "feudal" forces, the emasculated and frustrated peasant male character serves as the corollary to the abused peasant girl. Usually linked romantically to the abused female lead, these peasant youths find themselves helpless against powerful and nefarious enemies until the arrival of Communist power creates a dramatic reversal of fortunes. Once again *The White-Haired Girl* provided the prototypes for these characters through Wang Dachun and Dasuo. At the outset of the opera, Wang Dachun expects to take Xi'er as his bride, only to see the landlord Huang Shiren force the young girl into his household. Unable to prevent the landlord's running dogs from taking Xi'er, Dachun's humiliation continues throughout the first half of the opera. His situation reaches its nadir when the running dog Cheng Renzhi mocks him by noting how his former future wife was now the servant girl of Huang Shiren. Dachun's close friend Dasuo shares in his helplessness, unable to prevent the abduction of Xi'er; like Dachun, he also suffers as running dogs confiscate grain from his mother. Having taken their share of abuse, the two youths attempt to ambush and murder Cheng Renzhi, but fail in the face of the running dog's superior weaponry. Dachun flees the village, while Dasuo is captured and imprisoned in the local yamen.

Wang Hezi, a leading character in *Red Leaf River*, shares more than a surname with Wang Dachun. Hot-tempered from the outset of the opera, he continually butts heads with Lu Chengshu's running dog Qiu Gui over attempts to extract wealth from his family; in one instance, Wang Hezi fumes as Qiu Gui forces the Wang family to purchase opium for the landlord. Later, Qiu Gui mocks Wang after a failed attempt to

---

[46] Xibei zhandou jushe [Northwest Combat Dramatic Society], *Liu Hulan* (Beijing: Renmin wenxue chubanshe: 1952), 87.

wrestle away Qiu's account books, a symbol of landlord power. "Do you want to die?" Qiu asks him, before breaking into verse:

> Look at you, you stupid child,
> you do not understand and dare to act wild,
> for whether your family is to live or die,
> is all in the hands of the Lu clan.[47]

Wang Hezi's financial problems, epitomized by an episode where Qiu Gui mocks him for being too poor to fulfill his dream of raising pigs, is only the start of Wang's humiliations. Already upset about the financial burden created by his marriage, Wang returns home one day to find his wife together with his hated landlord. Chased off by a gun-toting Lu Chengshu and mistakenly suspecting that Yan Yan had willingly given herself to Lu, Wang flees the village, vowing to join the Communists, only to end up a beggar. When Wang finds his way home years later, he is such a thin and pallid figure as to be unrecognizable even to his own father.

Chen Wuzi, the only important young peasant male character in *Liu Hulan*, differs from the above characters in that his relationship with Liu Hulan is not explicitly romantic. But as troupe member Chen Bo noted, Wang Zhen, his commander in the Northwest Field Army, had suggested that the dramatists explore the possibility of a romance between Chen Wuzi and Liu Hulan.[48] Liu Lianchi, one of the creators of the *geju* opera version of the show, also noted that in real-life Liu Hulan had a fiancé, who they chose to not include in their script.[49] Regardless, the connections between Liu Hulan and Chen Wuzi are quite suggestive. At the outset of the story, Chen Wuzi is on the run, having escaped conscription by military forces under Yan Xishan, the Shanxi warlord turned Guomindang general. During his absence, Liu Hulan supports Chen Wuzi's mother, acting like a filial daughter-in-law. Yet when enemy troops approach the village, it is not Chen Wuzi who saves Liu Hulan, but just the opposite. Liu gives Chen Wuzi the last of her grain so that he can flee to safety. The young man, though nominally a soldier, is unable to protect Liu Hulan from the machinations of the landlord class and its allies.

Character archetype 3: helpless or absent peasant elders

The young peasant men portrayed in land reform operas typically vented their frustrations through attempted violence or running off to join the

---

[47] Ruan Zhangjing, *Chi ye he*, 45.
[48] Chen Bo, "Zhandou jushe zhandou zai xibei zhanchang," 24.
[49] Liu Lianchi, "Guanyu xiudingben shuoming," 9.

army. Elder peasants, in contrast, were portrayed as helpless in the face of feudal oppression and resigned to their fate. Even more striking is the outright absence of peasant parents in many land reform operas. Peasant elders were of such little use in protecting their children from feudal forces that dramatists often omitted them from their stories. As represented in land reform operas, these elders have left their children orphaned and unprotected, creating a crisis solved only by the arrival of Communist power.

The White-Haired Girl encapsulates the different ways dramatists portrayed the elder generation as ineffectual against feudal power. Xi'er's mother died when she was only a young girl and does not appear in the opera. Her father Yang Bailao, meanwhile, lives in fear of his landlord, fleeing the village every year before Spring Festival to avoid paying his debts. When he finally faces his landlord, the mere act of entering the Huang family compound causes Yang to lose his wits. Pressed into selling his only child, Yang Bailao is overcome with grief yet unable to save Xi'er, pathetically taking his own life rather than have to face the day when she is to be taken away. His friend Old Zhao, while often appearing optimistic about the future, cannot alleviate his own poverty. As he confides to the youth of the village: "we old people are useless."[50] Later in the opera he turns to superstition, hoping that the "White-Haired Immortal," believed to be haunting the local temple, will avenge Xi'er and Yang Bailao.

After working in the countryside, Ruan Zhangjing came to view the peasantry under the old regime as essentially "tragic" (*beican*).[51] It is thus of little surprise that a mix of absent and helpless elders inhabit *Red Leaf River*, starting with the long-dead parents of Yan Yan. Wang Hezi's mother is similarly absent, leaving his father Wang Dafu as the sole parental figure. While he never commits suicide, his helplessness is strikingly similar to that of Yang Bailao, starting with his inability to break his family out of a three-generation cycle of debt. Besides paying rent and interest on old loans, Wang Dafu must help pay for repairs to the Lu clan ancestral temple as well as fund Lu Chengshu's opium addiction. A typical helpless peasant elder, Wang Dafu curses his son for attempting to stand up to their landlord and his running dog. Reduced to begging after his son flees the village, Wang Dafu gives up even the slightest hope for change. Wang Dafu's good friend Old Song, despite a love of sarcastic songs attacking the wealthy, is similarly helpless. For example, after hearing a landlord comment on fate he

---

[50] He Jingzhi and Ding Yi, *Baimao nü*, 38.
[51] Ruan Zhangjing, "Houji," 117.

remarks: "Landlords [here *caizhu,* meaning a rich person] all say that kind of baloney [*guihua*]. In my 58 years, I have forded rivers, crossed mountains, herded sheep, and lived and worked with landlords, but I have never once met one that was any good."[52] Yet Old Song often ran away when he saw a running dog. And during land reform he refuses to accept any land and avoids village meetings, hoping his son will do the same.

In *Liu Hulan,* portrayals of village elders emphasize absence over helplessness. While the creators of *The White-Haired Girl* jumpstarted their narrative plot with the death of Yang Bailao, in *Liu Hulan* the titular character's father is entirely absent from the narrative. This was a creative choice. In Wei Feng's memoirs, the lead creator of the show notes that he met Liu Hulan's father while visiting the dead girl's village; he was quiet and let his wife do the talking, but he was very much alive.[53] As portrayed in the drama, Liu Hulan's mother is supportive of her daughter's political activism, but cannot save Liu Hulan from the arrival of "bandit" troops. *Liu Hulan* thus follows its fellow land reform operas in treating parental figures as either helpless or absent in order to emphasize how only the Communists could protect peasants.

Character archetype 4: the evil landlord

Free from the ideological constraints binding revolutionary heroes, landlord characters such as Huang Shiren, the unadulterated force of evil in *The White-Haired Girl*, were the most vivid and dynamic characters in land reform operas. At the outset of the opera, villagers refer to Huang Shiren as a "money bags" (*caizhu*); not until the arrival of the Communist Party does he take on the class label "landlord" (*dizhu*). This simple example perfectly illuminates how land reform operas successfully spread land reform rhetoric. Onstage, fictional villagers made the linguistic shift from the value-neutral "money bags" to the Maoist and pejorative "landlord," just as audiences would do in their own offstage performances of land reform. And not only were audiences introduced to the term "landlord," but they were given a particularly reprehensible example of a "landlord" to help give this new social category real meaning.

Huang Shiren,[54] for example, cleverly masterminds the abduction of Xi'er, brazenly singing of his love of debauchery and his lecherous plans

---

[52] Ruan Zhangjing, *Chi ye he,* 10.

[53] Wei Feng, "Yongfang guangmang de mingzi – Liu Hulan," 57.

[54] Barbara Mittler has noted that Huang's name is ironic, meaning "one who has practiced the Confucian virtue of humanity for generations." Mittler, *A Continuous Revolution,* 58.

for the peasant girl. In an early monologue, in which the landlord boasts of his extensive landholdings, Huang positions himself as a villain worthy of hatred:

I, Huang Shiren, have certainly not wasted this life ... Ever since I was a youth I studied how to maximize earnings by minimizing expenditures and employing the capable, and as a result our family wealth is growing and growing. Last year my wife died and now my mother wants me to remarry, but being without a wife provides a bit more freedom. What are women, if not just like muddy bricks on a wall, piled up layer after layer? If I wanted anyone, like this one here tonight [referring to Xi'er], what could be easier![55]

The fact that many poor peasant males in the audience were lifelong bachelors made this speech particularly powerful. Calling in his loans on the eve of Spring Festival, Huang forces Yang Bailao to sign over his daughter to the Huang household, an act that leads to the old peasant's suicide. After bringing Xi'er into his household, he spends months trying to pry the girl away from the service of his mother; during this time, he drunkenly roams the family compound, commenting on his evil intentions. After Huang rapes Xi'er, he moves to sell off the now pregnant peasant in order to avoid any potential embarrassment that might affect his upcoming nuptials. To keep Xi'er from doing anything rash, he cruelly tricks her into thinking it is she that he will marry. It is little wonder that audiences wished this landlord character dead.

Much like Huang Shiren, Lu Chengshu of *Red Leaf River* is notable for both his love of cheating the peasantry and his predilection for sexual assault. Hardly limiting himself to collecting rent and interest, the landlord finds a surprising variety of ways to extract wealth from the peasantry. A sexual predator, Lu Chengshu sets his sights on Yan Yan, roaming the village in search of the young peasant girl just as Huang Shiren had wandered in search of Xi'er. After stalking and attempting to rape Yan Yan, Lu Chengshu again seeks her out and confronts her, proclaiming:

> Whose sky is above your head?
> Whose earth is beneath your feet?
> If you know what is good for you, you better submit,
> in this valley, life and death are decided by me![56]

He later rapes Yan Yan, an act that directly leads to her suicide. Unlike Huang Shiren, who remained silent during his "struggle" session, Lu Chengshu vocally defies the new regime to the very end, reciting these memorable verses:

[55] He Jingzhi and Ding Yi, *Baimao nü*, 15.   [56] Ruan Zhangjing, *Chi ye he*, 59.

Dragons are born to stir the nine rivers,
pigs are born to eat coarse grain!
How can you, born poor,
dare to curse me for being rich![57]

Lu's defiant attitude makes him an entertaining villain, but just as important his refusal to submit to the Communists allows the show's peasant characters to stage a lengthy "struggle" session. Viewers of *Red Leaf River* were treated to a full-length example of this all important land reform ritual of class struggle, which they would then re-perform on their own village stages with their own freshly labeled "landlords."

Shi Sanhai, the landlord of *Liu Hulan*, does not display any sexual deviancy, a fact that reflects the "real-life" nature of the show. Yet he certainly finds pleasure in bringing harm to peasant women. A Guomindang member and former petty official, Shi Sanhai now lives in a "liberated" village, a situation he finds utterly intolerable. Despite being given a place in village society after land reform, Shi Sanhai is intent on doing everything in his power to bring about the downfall of the new regime and bring harm to those who had targeted him during land reform, particularly Liu Hulan. As he explains in verse, his "restoration records" (*biantian zhang*) lists those who will receive retribution:

Open the "restoration records" and take a close look,
it is impossible for me not to feel hatred in my heart.
Liu Hulan led the village poor,
helping them *fanshen*, settle accounts, and divide my property.[58]

Delivering this list of village activists to the "bandit" Company Commander Xu, Shi Sanhai seals the fate of Liu Hulan. Before her execution, Liu Hulan asks the landlord how he can be so cruel when the village had forgiven him for his past economic crimes. Interestingly, at the end of the drama Shi Sanhai escapes punishment by fleeing to Guomindang-controlled territories.

Character archetype 5: the revolutionary woman

While staging the abuse of young women encouraged hatred towards a newly defined landlord class, land reform operas also contained positive portrayals of peasant women, suggesting the new identities available in revolutionary villages. Xi'er, for example, transformed into a fiery revolutionary through her hatred of Huang Shiren, a process that begins when she realizes that her tormentor will not marry her: "Huang Shiren

---

[57] Ibid., 105.   [58] Xibei zhandou jushe, *Liu Hulan*, 36.

is my enemy, if he had married me I would still have to live in bitterness and misery (*shouku shouzui*)."[59] She escapes, vowing revenge: "Move forward and do not look back; I have enmity, I have hatred; they hurt my father, and then they hurt me; even when my bones are rotten I will remember this enmity!"[60] And in the opera's dénouement, Xi'er takes a leading role in accusing Huang Shiren, forcefully detailing her family's suffering at the hands of the landlord and his running dog, whipping the crowd into such a frenzy that peasants attending the meeting begin beating the two villains before she could even finish her accusations. After she concludes her story, the two are beaten again and taken away to await trial and execution. As they are led away, the show's peasant characters sing in joy: "Those who have suffered bitterness for countless generations, today they *fanshen!*"[61] Audience members, of course, could use this revolutionary performance as a model for local rural revolutions.

Liu Hulan was another character notable for her political awareness, although her activism is present throughout the drama. Living in a "liberated" village, Liu Hulan is an exemplar of political activism, leading the local Women's Association, donating supplies to the PLA, and taking a leading role in land reform. Her activism wins her the respect and admiration of her fellow villagers, and even her enemies grant her grudging respect – after her capture, Company Commander Xu repeatedly attempts to recruit her. Tortured because of her unwillingness to depart the village and her political work, Liu Hulan's devotion to the Communist Party is striking. Having previously learnt how to properly face death from a PLA solider, she bravely accepts her fate, singing a defiant song before being summarily dispatched with a hay chopper.

Taken together, the characters of Xi'er and Liu Hulan represented powerful role models for peasant women across China, and they were of course joined on stage by male peasant activists.[62] Land reform operas, building on decades of Communist-directed dramatic creation, featured performances for rural audiences to both hate and emulate. Actors, performing as "peasants" and "landlords," gave meaning to these roles. Performances of land reform rituals such as "speaking bitterness" and

---

[59] He Jingzhi and Ding Yi, *Baimao nü*, 67.

[60] Ibid., 75.   [61] Ibid., 120.

[62] Reality, in terms of women's ability to exercise greater political and social roles, most certainly did not match the ideals represented in the worlds of these three heroines; Yan Yunxiang, for example, noted that while women took part in land reform, they generally did so separately from male villagers. Yan Yunxiang, *Private Life Under Socialism: Love, Intimacy, and Family Change in a Chinese Village* (Standford, CA: Stanford University Press, 2003), 49.

the public "struggling" of landlords, meanwhile, offered villagers a script for their own offstage performances, both in mass campaigns and everyday life. Yet the power of these performances did not, ultimately, lie in the hands of their creators. Ruan Zhangjing, for example, had crafted a moving tale of class oppression featuring the rhetoric and ritual the villagers would need to become Maoist peasants and create the Communists' "New China." But because *Red Leaf River* required audiences to willingly digest its message, the ability of Communist directed drama troupes to successfully draw and affect villagers assumed critical importance.

Never captive: audience autonomy and land reform operas

Understanding how vast and largely illiterate rural audiences received land reform operas is an impossible undertaking. As historian Kenneth Ruoff has noted, gauging reception is "the ogre of researching cultural history," and here the problem is compounded by the lack of audience reports and the massive scale of land reform.[63] But unpacking the most famous land reform opera performance, the epic four hour staging of *Red Leaf River* described by William Hinton, reveals much about the relationship between drama troupes and their audiences during the heyday of land reform operas. As captured in *Fanshen*, his seminal account of rural revolution, Hinton described this spring 1948 show as an archetypical land reform opera performance, one that had an intense and visceral effect on its viewers, much to the benefit of the Communist Party.

But drama troupe histories and county archival documents reveal a rich backstage drama that profoundly complicates any idealized view of audience reception of revolutionary drama in rural China. This is not to discount Hinton, for as was often the case during his time in Longbow Village he proved a keen observer. From his description of the troupe's rapidly constructed stage of "long pine poles bound together with rice straw rope and overlaid with boards" to his detailed recreation of the production's realistic special effects, which included "singing birds, croaking frogs, chirping crickets, pattering rain, and howling wind," Hinton vividly captured the experiences of watching a land reform opera in Longbow during the height of Civil War and agrarian reform.[64]

[63] Kenneth J. Ruoff, *Imperial Japan at Its Zenith: The Wartime Celebration of the Empires 2,600th Anniversary* (Ithaca, NY: Cornell University Press, 2010), 14.
[64] Hinton, *Fanshen*, 312–316.

As recorded in *Fanshen*, during the afternoon of its visit the "Lucheng County Drama Corps" staged three one-act shows, at least two of which were modern shows with didactic messages. Hinton's failure to describe the plot of the third show suggests this may have been a traditional number that he found uninteresting. Between these one-act shows, child actors performed *kuaiban* "wooden clapper" numbers explaining party policies. The troupe's evening performance of *Red Leaf River*, which drew a massive audience that Hinton estimated in the thousands, provided the highlight of the troupe's visit to Longbow. In Hinton's view, the power of *Red Leaf River* stemmed from how the audience drew parallels between the show and their own lives. Looking around him, he found the audience totally captivated by the drama:

> As the tragedy of this poor peasant's family unfolded, the women around me wept openly and unashamedly. On every side, as I turned to look, tears were coursing down their faces. No one sobbed, no one cried out, but all wept together in silence. The agony on the stage seemed to have unlocked a thousand painful memories, a bottomless reservoir of suffering that no one could control.[65]

Soon Hinton and male audience members were crying as well.

Hinton found the second act a jarring tonal shift, as the plot jumped ahead to the survival of the landlord after "liberation," made possible by a corrupted village head, a plotline that Ruan Zhangjing would eventually cut from his revolutionary masterpiece. The audience found this part of the show much more humorous and uplifting, and in fact preferred it to the first half, which Hinton praised as "undoubtedly superior." In Hinton's view, Longbow peasants had been moved by the first half because of their own experiences, yet at the same time the story proved "too close to their own bitter lives of such a short time ago." As a result, the peasant audience "did not enjoy the tragedy."[66] Hinton's insistence that the audience reaction was directly related to their past experiences may be questionable, but his account demonstrates that villagers flocked to this modern show and enjoyed the performance.

William Hinton, to be sure, provides one of the most vivid descriptions of a land reform opera performance. But from his vantage point in the audience, Hinton could offer little information about the troupe, which he identified as the semi-professional Lucheng County Drama Corps. According to Hinton, the troupe was "composed of 50 members, most of whom had been poor professional actors until they received their land in the great distribution of 1946." These actors now engaged in agriculture for half of the year, with the other half dedicated to performing in support

---

[65] Ibid., 315   [66] Ibid., 316

of the revolution. In Hinton's telling, these Lucheng players continued to perform not for financial gain but only out of love for acting and revolutionary fervor. As he emphasized, troupe members received no pay except for millet tickets to pay for room, board, and incidentals.[67]

In Hinton's depiction of the staging of *Red Leaf River* in Longbow, rural drama troupes were happy and effective soldiers in Mao's cultural army. Village audiences, furthermore, seem to have totally accepted land reform operas and other modern shows. But Hinton's gaze, cut off from the behind the scenes drama that was part of life in any such troupe, missed the very real difficulties these actors faced in bringing *Red Leaf River* and other modern operas to rural stages. Troupe histories and archival documents demonstrate that Hinton's brief reading of the inner workings of this troupe, actually the Lucheng County Popular Drama Troupe (Dazhong jutuan), misses the mark on many counts. Very few actors, for example, engaged in farming if they could support themselves professionally. Hinton was certainly correct in linking this troupe with its local government. But while these actors performed modern shows in exchange for grain tickets and perhaps even engaged in some farming, their livelihood ultimately depended on their ability to compete in a cultural market that strongly preferred traditional opera over its modern counterpart.

The troupe's own history, collected in the *Draft History of Changzhi City's Performing Organizations*, presents the outfit as a fully professional organization with clear ties to the Lucheng County government. According to the *Draft History*, the troupe was founded in the fall of 1944 as a district-level troupe with a core of professional actors trained in traditional *luozi* opera, most notably the talented Hu Yuzhen. With close government supervision and the addition of a group of younger actors skilled in revolutionary drama, the troupe made a partial shift to modern shows and political work, changes that vexed traditionally trained actors. Formally attached to Lucheng County in 1945, the troupe staged traditional operas and new historical dramas, but the troupe's active involvement in land reform and other mass campaigns made modern shows a key part of the troupe's repertoire. As the *Draft History* notes, their staging of a modern show caused Hinton to give the troupe a "thumbs up" in Longbow. But with a good portion of the troupe made up of old-style artists, the Popular Drama Troupe continued to stage traditional numbers.[68]

---

[67] Ibid., 313

[68] Changzhi shi wenhua ju, *Changzhi shi yishu biaoyan tuanti shigao*, 103–105. This text misidentifies the show performed in Longbow. For more on the troupe as a mixture of

Archival documents from Lucheng further reveal that despite the staging of *Red Leaf River* in Longbow, modern shows were getting pushed off county stages. In a directive concerning drama troupes dated November 20, 1948, the Lucheng's People's Education Center (Minzhong jiaoyu guan, or Minjiaoguan) explicitly addressed the problems plaguing the county's nascent cultural army. According to Lucheng's cultural authorities, because local troupes emphasized entertainment over propaganda, very few modern shows found their way to local stages. This resulted in the widespread performance of traditional shows, complete with "feudal" and "superstitious" content. Sensing that only government action could combat this trend, the People's Education Center issued a series of regulations designed to promote modern shows. All troupes visiting Lucheng, for example, had to submit playlists for approval before performances. And in a clear break with past practices, troupes had to reserve their coveted nighttime slot for modern shows, with traditional shows relegated to the daytime. The People's Education Center, moreover, required drama troupes to limit the number and length of performances in order to devote more time to political and artistic study. Henceforth, instead of the traditional three shows a day, troupes could only stage two shows for no more than nine hours. Traditional operas, finally, were sorted into three categories: those that could be staged, those that should be staged less, and those that were banned.[69]

These directives directly contravened popular demand for traditional shows and troupe practices, leaving drama troupes caught between government policy and audience expectations. Archival materials on the Popular Drama Troupe from late 1948 reveal that despite Hinton's casting of the troupe as capable revolutionaries, the troupe labored to find an acceptable balance between modern and traditional shows. To be sure, a county investigation into the troupe confirms much of Hinton's detailed description, as actors had accepted party leadership and delved into rehearsing *Red Leaf River*, with traditionally trained actors such as Hu Yuzhen taking leading roles. Led by Hu, the troupe rehearsed *Red Leaf River* in just ten days before touring in support of party rectification (*zhengdang*) and land reform. After arriving in host villages, the troupe borrowed props as well as poles and ropes to construct its stage. Daytime shows were for new historical dramas, with modern big shows,

modern and traditional actors, see Guo Tongzai, ed., *Changzhi geming laoqu* [Changzhi's old revolutionary base areas] (Taiyuan: Shanxi renmin chubanshe, 2007), 206.

[69] Lucheng xian wenjiaoting, "Lucheng xian zhengfu guanyu jutuan chuyan wenti de zhishi" [Lucheng County government directive concerning drama troupe performance issues], LCA A1–1–1380 (November 20, 1948), 2.

including *Clarifying Class* (Mingque jieji), *Wang Gui and Li Xiangxiang*, and *Red Leaf River*, exclusively staged at night. These evening performances would typically end after midnight, and after a few hours of sleep the troupe moved on to the next village. The county report presented actors as happy revolutionaries, echoing Hinton's assessment: "Ideologically, members think that eating bitterness is happiness and not earning money is joy; all members think that their work is very useful in promoting cultural propaganda and education."[70]

But even if actors willingly bent to the government's will, rural audiences proved reluctant to abandon their cherished traditions and resisted the troupe's new repertoire. Villagers, for example, often demanded traditional shows, leading to confrontations between artists and audience. During one such instance, troupe member Zhao Antang insisted that with new historical dramas, traditional shows were not needed, but such words failed to convince audiences. The strong draw of tradition crystalized during an April 15, 1948 drama fair, which forced the troupe to back away from the county-mandated focus on modern shows. During this drama festival, the Taiyue Region Drama Troupe, performing traditional shows three times a day, drew the largest crowds. Audiences, thrilled by what was essentially an old-style *xibanzi* opera outfit, did not shy away from using Maoist rhetoric to argue against revolutionary drama. Insisting that the Popular Drama Troupe had to follow the wishes of the masses, audiences successfully pushed the troupe to return to traditional shows and three performances per day.[71] Just weeks after Hinton watched the troupe perform *Red Leaf River*, audiences had struck modern shows from its playlist.

With traditional shows once again dominating the stage, vicious factionalism tore the troupe apart. Older actors trained in traditional opera reveled in their revived popularity. Using their power with audiences as a bargaining chip, these actors skipped political study and ignored party leadership. Some even mocked their teenage counterparts, who specialized in modern shows. With modern shows shunned by audiences and pushed off stage, these young actors saw no future in drama and considered leaving the troupe. But just as the troupe was reverting to an old-style *xibanzi* opera outfit, the county government dispatched its chief propagandist to lead the troupe through ideological rectification (*sixiang*

---

[70] Lucheng xian wenjiaoting, "Lucheng xian dazhong jutuan yi nian lai gongzuo zongbao" [General report on last year's work by the Lucheng County Popular Drama Troupe], LCA A1–1–1379 (December 22, 1948), 2.

[71] Ibid., 3.

zhengdun). Rectification succeeded in getting modern shows back on stage as well as a return to the two shows per day policy, but even the county had to recognize the autonomous power of audiences. Traditional shows continued to make up a significant part of the troupe's repertoire and dominated nighttime performances. Rectification, furthermore, failed to solve the troupe's factional divide between younger and older actors. Now it was the young actors' turn to inflate their self-worth, neglect their studies, act rudely to older actors, and disobey troupe leadership.[72]

Hinton's account of the staging of *Red Leaf River* demonstrates that audiences did turn out in droves for the troupe's modern shows, but no government decree could make villagers prefer these shows over their traditional favorites. And while state intervention had saved modern shows, archival sources reveal that audiences were far from passive and engaged with performances in surprising ways. Take, for example, the troupe's staging of *Clarifying Class* in Manliuhe, located in Lucheng's Third District. Here the show was perhaps too effective, sparking one peasant family to cancel a marriage contract with the daughter of a local "landlord." Yet the response in nearby Heshe proved quite different. A Heshe woman from a recently "struggled" landlord family, having recently married a village leader, refused to accept the show's message and instead sought out the troupe and pushed for a more nuanced treatment of the landlord class. Unsurprisingly given its later revisions, the troupe's staging of *Red Leaf River* proved especially divisive. The show's controversial portrayal of dishonest cadres found a welcome audience among peasants. But when the troupe sought out opinions from village cadres, they would only meekly say that the show was "alright" (*keyi keyi*).[73]

While *Red Leaf River* and *Clarifying Class* worked well with land reform and party rectification, the shows were not without fault. The county government criticized both shows, for example, for being out of touch with current policies that called for the elimination of landlords as an economic class, but not the physical extermination of landlords. These shows were thus censured for portraying landlords as fundamentally evil, as opposed to highlighting how landlords acted evil. *Red Leaf River* was further criticized for following the "poor peasant line." These problems, of course, could be solved with a rewrite. The real issue vexing the troupe was that these land reform operas simply failed to satisfy the entertainment demands of village audiences. Audiences first wanted

---

[72] Ibid., 4–5.   [73] Ibid., 6.

more shows. With the Taiyue Region Drama Troupe and other area troupes still heeding popular demand for the traditional three shows a day, the troupe found itself isolated (*guli*) due to its two show a day policy.

Audiences, furthermore, insisted on traditional shows at night and even pushed the troupe away from party policy by requesting shows with "lewd" and "feudal" content. And as seen in the troupe's visit to Kanshang in neighboring Changzhi County, village cadres tended to side with audiences in conflicts over performances. In Kanshang, for example, a cadre pressed the troupe to do "bad" operas. When the troupe refused, the audience cursed actors for "putting on airs." When the troupe attempted to stage a modern show, several attempts to explain its importance could not stop the audience from hurling further insults at the troupe. With actors on stage and the memory of land reform fresh, the audience boldly took to the stage and began to "struggle" the actors as if they were landlords, only relenting when the troupe agreed to perform a traditional show.[74] The troupe may have fancied itself a modern *jutuan* drama troupe, but to villagers it was still a *xibanzi* opera outfit. And audiences, now well versed in Maoist political culture thanks to *Red Leaf River* and other modern dramas, were using Mao's own rhetoric and rituals to challenge his cultural army.

Traditional shows and practices thus remained wildly popular, even during the height of land reform. Unable to resist popular demand, the Popular Drama Troupe resorted to a compromise, starting its afternoon performances early and staging multiple shows so that audiences could get enough of their beloved local operas. And despite the mandate to stage modern works at night, less than half of the troupe's evening performances were actually of the modern variety. Understanding audience reluctance to accept modern shows, the troupe attempted to improve the technical skills of these shows while always pairing them with traditional numbers to avoid audience revolts. These moves helped placate audiences, but crowds remained willing to challenge the troupe when it pushed modern shows. This was especially true when village cadres joined audiences in rejecting modern shows and the two shows a day policy. With other troupes performing traditional shows three times a day, the Lucheng players knew they would have difficulty competing in the dramatic market. As the report on the troupe admitted, if the county did not hold all troupes to the same standard, the Popular Drama Troupe would certainly become unpopular.[75]

[74] Ibid., 7.   [75] Ibid., 7.

Conclusion: creating narratives and capturing audiences

Given their function as a facilitator of class struggle, it is not surprising that the explication of evil landlords, including a stress on their sexual abuse of young peasant women, was an important element in performances staged by Mao's cultural army. A handful of land reform dramas did, however, offer interesting takes on gender and class. *Li Fengmei*, a three-act play created in 1950, a time when class struggle was briefly downplayed, starred the young daughter of the landlord Li Junshui. While the play portrays Li Junshui in a negative light, it does quite the reverse with his daughter Li Fengmei, a progressive intellectual willing to turn her back on the landlord class.[76] But if *Li Fengmei* offers the possibility of a new performance model, that of the "good landlord daughter," the drama never addressed the basic dilemma of the character: Li Fengmei sided with the peasantry, but could not escape her landlord class label.

A handful of land reform operas joined *Li Fengmei* in playing with the conventions of the genre, although none did so as spectacularly as the 1948 *The White-Haired Boy*.[77] Claiming a real-life basis, *The White-Haired Boy* dramatized the suffering created by the rich Song family as it relies on powerful connections to oppress local peasants. In this opera, the "Nine-Tailed Fox," the Song family matriarch, buries a peasant boy and girl alive alongside her dead husband "Mr. Pig Head" to serve as his "Golden Boy and Jade Maiden," the fabled attendants of Daoist immortals. In a total reversal of the usual sexual politics of land reform operas, the "Nine-Tailed Fox" then locks the boy's father in her cellar, forcing the unlucky man to live as her sexual servant. Only when land reform comes to the village fourteen years later does the man escape and reunite with his wife.[78]

While interesting outliers, *Li Fengmei* and *The White-Haired Boy* were difficult fits with standard Communist propaganda. The promise of land reform operas lay in their skillful use of gender relations to symbolize class exploitation; variations of this model could only water down the Communists' attempt to promote class struggle and spread land reform rhetoric and ritual. For dramatists, mobilizing audiences towards specific

---

[76] Xiao Ben and Qi Shun, *Li Fengmei*, in *Tugai xuanchuanju* [Land reform propaganda plays] (Hangzhou: Zhongguo ertong shudian: 1950).

[77] This was the show's popular title. The actual title of the show, *Nonggongbo*, refers to the village where the story takes place. The show was a *gewuju*, a drama featuring music, dance, and song.

[78] *Shandong shengzhi: wenhua zhi* [Shandong provincial gazetteer: cultural gazetteer] (Shandong: Shandong renmin chubanshe, 1995), 259.

Party goals always remained paramount. After viewing *Red Leaf River*, for example, Ruan Zhangjing's disappointed friends bombarded the playwright with questions: Why did Yan Yan have to die? Why not have the young male character return in triumph with the army? Ruan replied that this suffering was "realistic" and had to be shown.[79] While the "realism" of universal peasant suffering due to class exploitation is highly questionable, the experiences of Ruan and other cultural workers suggest that straightforward tales of landlord oppression of families and young women were the most effective way to affect audiences.

In creating *The White-Haired Girl, Liu Hulan,* and *Red Leaf River,* cultural workers translated the propaganda needs of the party into dramatic works that rural audiences, hungry for dramatic performance, could find entertaining and compelling. Cultural workers, moreover, continually reworked their dramas to present a "realistic" rural society profoundly shaped by Maoist conceptions of village life. Ruan Zhangjing, for example, discarded an entire subplot revolving around cadre corruption in favor of simplistic and stereotypical characters. The "bad cadre" plotline most certainly had roots in actual events, but land reform operas demanded an idealized and inspirational "reality." Cultural workers, furthermore, welded local stories and operatic traditions to this Communist sanctioned "realism," blending rural cultural practice and Communist ideology into the distinctive genre of the land reform opera. Because of cultural differences between intellectuals and rural audiences, this style of creation was exceedingly difficult; intellectuals, versed in Western culture, might still have preferred to write *huaju* spoken dramas if not for the forceful backing Mao gave to "national" cultural forms.

Intellectuals crafted operas that rural audiences found enjoyable only through negotiation with local culture. This negotiation occurred first in source material, as cultural workers borrowed local legends and drew on their own time in the countryside as the basis for characters and plotlines. The adaptation or outright plagiarism of popular tunes, meanwhile, represented a second and far more difficult negotiation with rural culture. With Zhang Lu's cribbing of the folk song "Little Cabbage," a student's predilection for plagiarism had provided the key not only for *The White-Haired Girl,* but Communist directed operas in general. With these local tunes, audiences found modern operas, even with their strong political content, surprisingly familiar.

A third negotiation lay in co-opting established rural drama troupes to bring land reform operas to village stages. Yet even after establishing

---

[79] Ruan Zhangjing, "Guanyu Chi ye he de san ci zhong gaixie," 124.

leadership over rural troupes, the Communists found themselves unable to exert control over rural audiences. First-hand reports show that land reform operas drew huge audiences. During shows, moreover, audiences cried in anguish and shouted in hatred, demonstrating that land reform operas fulfilled their goal of inciting audiences. Archival documents, however, reveal that while rural audiences turned out for modern and politically charged shows, local culture still evidenced a strong preference for traditional performances. During land reform and other rural campaigns, the highly relevant content of new works, along with their many concessions to local culture, helped land reform operas find an audience. Ultimately, however, rural audiences longed for a return to traditional *xibanzi* style performances and were even willing to use the Maoist rhetoric and ritual embedded in land reform operas to demand an end to modern shows. Because audiences, not actors, ultimately determined the success of revolutionary dramas, Mao's cultural army continued to struggle with audience preference for traditional dramas long after the Communists came to power.

5   State agents and local actors
Cultural work in the early PRC

In the aftermath of the failed First United Front, the Communist Party conducted a mass exodus from China's cities, a rural turn that would eventually draw thousands of China's educated elite into the countryside. For dramatists Li Bozhao and Ruan Zhangjing, the Communist Party's rural sojourn heralded a long divorce from urban life. By the summer of 1949, however, military victory over the Guomindang was finally at hand. As Zhou Enlai announced to China's leading artists that July, the PLA had already "liberated" 59% of China's population. Of even greater significance given the PLA's longtime rural strategy, the Communists now controlled 1,061 cities, representing some 55 percent of China's urban spaces, including the recently captured Guomindang capital Nanjing.[1] The violent spasms of the Civil War would linger on, but it was clear to all but the most fervent Jiang Jieshi loyalists that its outcome had been decided. The long rural exile of party artists was about to come to an end.

So it was that the members of the Combat Dramatic Society found themselves in Beiping, just months before the city was renamed Beijing and became the PRC capital. With the success of its land reform opera *Liu Hulan*, the troupe had made one of the most visible contributions to promoting military mobilization, land reform, and urban takeover during the Civil War. In recognition of the troupe's service, the Communist cultural authorities, then coalescing in Beiping, invited He Long's players to perform for the first All-China Literature and Arts Worker Representative Congress, here called the Beiping Cultural Congress. Dispatched by its longtime patron, the troupe arrived in Beiping in May, quickly finding a theater to perform for its latest urban audience. According to troupe member Chen Bo, by bringing along Liu Ailan, the sister forced to beat Liu Hulan shortly before her execution, the troupe made a particularly strong impression on Beiping audiences. Lured by

---

[1] Zhou Enlai, "Zai zhonghua quanguo wenxue yishu gongzuozhe daibiao dahui shang de zhengzhi baogao," 21.

high-quality new-style works offering insight into life under Communist rule, audiences packed the troupe's shows. With Liu Ailan introducing *Liu Hulan* before each performance, the troupe played sold out shows for two months, with crowds that included Zhou Yang, Tian Han, and other cultural luminaries.[2] Land reform operas were no longer simply a rural phenomenon. After performing *Liu Hulan* and a *huaju* spoken drama for the Beiping Cultural Congress, the troupe lingered in the city long enough to recruit hundreds of students before rejoining the PLA and patron He Long in the Southwest.[3] Among the artists who witnessed the troupe's performances of *Liu Hulan* in Beiping were He Jieming and He Fang, members of the Third Field Army's Second Cultural Work Team, one of the dozens of drama troupes similarly invited to the Beiping Cultural Congress. During that final Beiping summer, cultural workers flooded into the city, mingling with party leaders at the Beijing Hotel and other elite venues. Cultural workers even attended dance parties, and those unskilled in ballroom dancing were encouraged to bring *yangge* dances to a truly new stage. The Second Cultural Work Team performed in a number of modern venues, and even ventured out to the Western Hills in the city's suburbs. There the troupe staged special performances for top party leaders, most of whom had yet to move into Zhongnanhai, the Communists' new headquarters in the heart of the ancient city.[4] Feted by massive urban audiences, the Communist Party, and even the Beiping press, Mao's cultural army had finally arrived.

This "arrival" would suggest that 1949 represented a watershed for cultural work, a fundamental transformation that blends nicely with the Communist master narrative of two cultural eras, one feudal and one revolutionary. Yet previous chapters have demonstrated the ongoing interplay between traditional and revolutionary drama. Dramatists drew on local culture to make revolutionary messages popular and palatable. Drama troupes found themselves in a continual state of competition with for-profit *xibanzi* opera troupes. Change in the world of Chinese drama during the revolution, furthermore, was never a one-way street of "progress." A troupe might stage revolutionary shows for a time, only to revert to a traditional repertoire because of personal preference or, more likely, popular demand. The connective tissues binding cultural work on

[2] Chen Bo, "Zhandou jushe zhandou zai xibei zhanchang," 32.
[3] Huang Qinghe, "Ji jian nanwang de wangshi," 107–108.
[4] He Fang and He Jieming, "Guangrong de shiming, juda de guwu – san ye zhengzhibu di er wenyi gongzuotuan chuxi quanguo shou jie wen dai hui yi shi" [Glorious mission, epic encouragement: recollections on the Third Field Army Political Department Second Literature and Arts Work Team attending the First All-China Literature and Arts Worker Congress] JZSQ (ca. 1980s), 459–461.

the two sides of the 1949 divide are dense and unavoidable. The legacies of Red Drama, the Yan'an "national forms" debate, and land reform operas informed dramatic activities in the PRC era. Cultural work in the PRC continued to rely on highly trained party artists to coordinate a cultural army largely composed of amateur activists. The Communists, still fervent believers in the power of drama, would continue to push hybrid styles and draw on local cultural practices to direct political behavior and enlighten audiences.

But 1949 did represent a watershed for rural cultural work. Freed from the burden of fighting for survival, the Communists unleashed a tide of mass cultural campaigns unlike anything seen during their slow and uneven rise to power. Starting with the Beiping Cultural Congress, held a few short months before the founding of the PRC, party leaders mapped a bold course for its ever-expanding cultural army. Rural policy, previously hampered by disparate centers of control and varying levels of Communist penetration into the countryside, was now increasingly unified and implemented down to the village level. And while the Communist Party had long relied on the services of the educated elite, the party now enjoyed a near monopoly on their services. Students, academics, artists, and professionals rushed to demonstrate loyalty to the new regime. In 1929, Mao dreamt of a cultural army that would use culture as a weapon to recreate China. In 1949, with peace in the countryside and the Communist hold on "New China" ever stronger, Mao's cultural army seemed to be coming of age.

In the early years of the PRC, cultural workers fanned out throughout the countryside, aiming to develop a fully formed cultural infrastructure that would instantly and continuously propagate the Communist message. Mao's cultural army, originally firmly affixed to the Communist military, was now increasingly tied to the developing PRC state. The party, furthermore, now sought to make culture serve the actual process of rural revolution. With calls for an orderly and staged implementation of land reform in the "new liberated areas," guided by the relatively lenient *Land Reform Law of the People's Republic of China,* cultural workers made the organization of rural culture an integral part of land reform and other early PRC mass campaigns. No longer would cultural campaigns follow their political counterparts. On the contrary, the Communists would seek ever-greater synchronization between cultural and political performances.

This chapter explores the emerging world of PRC revolutionary drama, tracing the contours of the emerging cultural infrastructure, from party leaders in the capital down to lowly makeup artists in rural hamlets. But as Julia Andrews has outlined in her study of painters working under

Communist direction, the PRC cultural bureaucracy was a fundamentally unpredictable system, and this was certainly the case in the dramatic realm.[5] Although leaders of the newly established PRC aimed for an integrated and directed cultural network that would serve their propaganda needs, this chapter highlights the contradictions and complications that marked the emerging cultural order. At the national level, the divisive discourse at the 1949 Beiping Cultural Congress implicated artists and complicated mass work during this important transitional moment. Moving down to the regional level, cultural workers puzzled over "struggle" as they headed out into the countryside for land reform as newly minted agents of the PRC state. In newly "liberated" villages, finally, amateur dramatists and actors attempted to stage state culture for peasant audiences, yet were limited by shoestring budgets. No contradiction, however, would prove more difficult to overcome than the essential divide between urban cultural workers and village artists.

Cultural work at the center: Beiping, 1949

As Guomindang forces fled south throughout late 1948 and the first half of 1949, Communist elites naturally gravitated towards Beiping, China's former and future capital. With their numbers approaching a critical mass, the time had come to bring order and systematization to cultural work. Opening on July 2, the first All-China Literature and Arts Worker Representative Congress, here called the Beiping Cultural Congress, laid the cultural foundations for the emerging PRC order.[6] Featuring weeks of speeches from party luminaries and round after round of small group discussions, the Congress heralded the start of a new era of cultural work. July 19, the closing day of the Congress, saw the adoption of the constitution for the All-China Federation of Literary and Art Circles (Zhonghua quanguo wenxue yishu jie lianhehui), commonly referred to as Wenlian. Formally founded with writer Guo Moruo as its head, Wenlian provided a framework for the organization of artists and the implementation of cultural work in the PRC. While in theory a voluntary organization for professional artists, Wenlian and its artistic organizations were an extension of the Communist Party's Propaganda Department; as Andrews has

---

[5] Julia Frances Andrews, *Painters and Politics in the People's Republic of China, 1949–1979* (Berkeley, CA: University of California Press, 1994), 5.

[6] As Paul Clark notes, this was "the first cultural gathering on a national scale" since 1942, when Mao pushed cultural workers to embrace local cultural forms in Yan'an. Clark, *Chinese Cinema*, 32.

noted, this was common knowledge among Chinese artists, who rushed to join Wenlian affiliated organizations for professional reasons.[7]

PRC historian Deng Bangyu has rightly characterized the Beiping Cultural Congress as a moment of information exchange,[8] but scholars must investigate the nature and purpose of this exchange. Hung, in his study on cartoonists in the 1950s, posited that the primary purpose of the conference was to rally "the support of writers and artists,"[9] a view that dovetails with the generally held belief that the early 1950s represented a golden age for intellectuals. As succinctly stated by Hong Yung Lee, during the early PRC the Communist Party "adopted a pragmatic and lenient policy" towards China's educated elite in order to "utilize their functional expertise and political support."[10] Yet the Beiping Cultural Congress aimed to discipline cultural workers to serve the emerging PRC state, explicitly foreshadowing future conflicts between the party and artists. Speakers from "old liberated areas" used rhetorical strategies to place themselves in positions of strength *vis-à-vis* their counterparts from the "new liberated areas," which until recently had been under Guomindang control. Using a mixture of boasts and subtle threats, cultural leaders attempted to define the parameters of cultural work in the emerging PRC state. But by eliding the problem of cultural mobilization in the "old liberated areas" and casting suspicion on future cultural workers, the Beiping Cultural Congress needlessly complicated mass cultural campaigns in the early PRC era.

A highly staged event with little left to chance, the Beiping Cultural Congress came together under the guidance of its preparatory committee, formed on March 22 by a diverse set of forty-two cultural leaders, including Guo Moruo, Li Bozhao, and Hu Feng. In creating a list of representatives of leading cultural workers and artists who "opposed feudalism," the committee devised two categories of representatives, starting with the "natural representatives" (*dangran daibiao*) found in the leading figures of preexisting cultural organizations. This drew in Communist cultural leaders from all five existing regional governments,[11] as well as cultural luminaries from the All-China Literary and Art Circles Resistance Association (Zhonghua quanguo wenyijie kangdi xiehui), active in former Guomindang-held areas. "Invited representatives," the second and much larger group of delegates, included hign-ranking cultural workers, cultural

[7] Andrews, *Painters and Politics in the People's Republic of China*, 7.
[8] Deng Bangyu, ed., *Jiefangjun xiju shi*, 164.
[9] Hung, *Mao's New World*, 115.
[10] Lee, *From Revolutionary Cadres to Party Technocrats in Socialist China*, 65.
[11] North China, Northeast China, East China, Northwest China, and the Central Plains.

workers with over ten years of revolutionary experience, and accomplished artists with advanced ideologies, a final category that would allow further representation from "newly liberated" urban centers.[12] The committee vetted a total of 824 representatives, divided into eight delegations.[13]

The long list of leading artists in attendance signaled the importance of the meeting, as did the invitation of thirty-five drama troupes and fourteen music groups. Attendees could visit a special exhibition hall, catch screenings of fifteen films, or pick up a copy of *Literature and Arts Report* (Wenyi Bao), a newspaper created especially for the Congress.[14] A parade of speeches from party leaders provided additional evidence of the centrality of cultural work in Mao's "New China." Zhu De, using the militaristic phrasing now commonplace among cultural workers, instructed representatives that their most urgent responsibility was to "use literature and art weapons to mobilize all of the nation's people."[15] Dong Biwu, foreshadowing the central role of class for artists throughout the first three decades of the PRC, noted that class and its influences were inescapable, but suggested that with the *fanshen* of cultural workers they could "express the ideology and emotions of the masses."[16]

Propaganda chief Lu Dingyi praised the accomplishments of cultural workers in the "old liberated areas" and called for a massive expansion of the cultural army, citing the need for "thousands upon thousands (*chengqian chengwan*) of cultural work teams and drama troupes to disperse everywhere" to carry out propaganda work in the cities, towns, and villages that had only recently fallen under Communist control.[17] As expected, the appearance of Mao Zedong provided one of the highlights of the Congress, his arrival leading to wild applause and loud chants of "long live Chairman Mao." In his brief remarks before the assembled artists, Mao reaffirmed the importance of cultural work and cultural

---

[12] "Dahui choubei jingguo" [Preparation process for the Congress] ZWGD (1949), 126.

[13] The Beiping and Tianjin region was awarded two delegations, with one delegation each from each of the five regional Communist governments. The PLA sent its own delegation, while South-Central China was represented by two groups, which included Tian Han and other leading cultural figures from former Guomindang areas. "Zhonghua quanguo wenxue yishu gongzuozhe daibiao dahui dabiao mingdan" [Representative name list for the All-China Literature and Arts Worker Representative Congress] ZWGD (1949), 547–554.

[14] "Dahui choubei jingguo," 127.

[15] Zhu De, "Zhu zong siling jianghua" [Commander-in-chief Zhu's speech] ZWGD (1949), 6.

[16] Dong Biwu, "Dong Biwu tongzhi jianghua" [Comrade Dong Biwu's speech] ZWGD (1949), 9.

[17] Lu Dingyi, "Lu Dingyi tongzhi jianghua" [Comrade Lu Dingyi's speech] ZWGD (1949), 13.

workers, specifically emphasizing their central role in the now victorious revolution.[18]

Mao received the loudest welcome, but Zhou Enlai played the lead role in the Beiping Cultural Congress, with his "Political Report" providing its defining statement. In this wide-ranging presentation, Zhou set the tone for the Congress by drawing a clear line between cultural workers from the "old liberated areas" and artists who had been active in Guomindang-held territories. Generously estimating party affiliated cultural workers at some sixty thousand strong, Zhou pointed to their propaganda work among soldiers and villagers as one of the essential factors behind the Communist victory in the Civil War. Zhou also discussed progressive artists from Guomindang-held cities, a group he estimated to number around ten thousand.[19] Zhou praised their work, including the formation of the All-China Literary and Art Circles Resistance Association, which would quickly be rendered obsolete with the imminent formation of the national Wenlian. Yet Zhou's praise for this association carried a devastating subtext, as he noted that "only a few" association members were "reactionary."[20] By sending a clear message that some urban artists were enemies of the people, Zhou had called the loyalty of all non-party artists into question. This Congress was not their moment to shine or even stake a claim to revolutionary credentials. As the renowned author Ba Jin meekly noted, he attended the Beiping Cultural Congress not to "give a speech" but merely to "study."[21]

Zhou Enlai's bifurcation of artists into two camps, party cultural workers and questionable newcomers, became the enduring theme of the Beiping Cultural Congress. Throughout the meeting, the party's leading cultural figures took center stage in order to highlight the experiences of cultural workers in the "old liberated areas." But as they detailed their accomplishments over the previous years, the tone of the conference shifted. Zhou Enlai, for example, had given nearly half of his speech to detailing the deficiencies of cultural work in the "old liberated areas." Thus, Zhou praised party affiliated cultural workers for the time they had spent in the countryside, but he also noted that many still suffered from decidedly limited perspectives in dealing with people from different backgrounds. Zhou further questioned the effectiveness of the Communists' cultural army by drawing special attention to its size and deployment.

---

[18] Mao Zedong, "Mao zhuxi jianghua" [Chairman Mao's speech] ZWGD (July 6, 1949), 3.

[19] Zhou Enlai, "Zai zhonghua quanguo wenxue yishu gongzuozhe daibiao dahui shang de zhengzhi baogao," 27.

[20] Ibid., 19.

[21] Ba Jin, "Wo shi lai xuexi de" [I came to study] ZWGD (1949), 392.

While the party may have had tens of thousands of cultural workers, Zhou noted their uneven distribution in the PLA and the countryside, which left some counties bereft of any real cultural work.[22]

The reports given by the party's cultural elite similarly covered a wide range of themes, from the organization of base area educational institutions to the problems of dramatic work in the countryside. But the overriding message given to China's cultural world on the eve of the establishment of the PRC lacked the nuance seen in Zhou Enlai's speech. According to party cultural leaders, "old liberated area" cultural workers may have initially been hampered by class issues, but these had been decisively solved through political education, artistic training, and the process of "rectification," particularly the study of Mao's "Talks at the Yan'an Forum." Having overcome class issues and sided with the masses, these revolutionaries had mastered mass line drama by creating new content works using traditional folk forms. Cultural workers further claimed to have reformed old-style drama in the base areas, mobilized rural drama movements, and made major contributions to the revolution. By emphasizing their status as true and unproblematic revolutionaries, these cultural leaders elided the real difficulties in cultural work during their long rural exile. But with some attention, attendees could make out the defining issue that would shape drama work in the early 1950s and beyond: basic contradictions between intellectuals and local artists, two groups that would have to work in tandem to bring order to revolutionary performance in the countryside.

China's leading urban artists and new cultural workers, while ostensibly welcomed into the fold to help oversee cultural and political performances, were actually being held in distrust for their suspect class status. As a minority of the party's cultural leaders noted, class had also been an issue for "old liberated area" cultural workers. In detailing literature and arts work in the Jin-Sui region, for example, Zhou Wen correctly identified Communist dramatists as primarily composed of young urban intellectuals.[23] Reporting on the Shandong region, Zhang Linqing concurred that cultural workers, even when living and working alongside the PLA, typically had artistic views profoundly influenced by "petit bourgeois" attitudes.[24] Zhang Geng, one of the composers of *The White-Haired Girl*, reminded cultural representatives that Yan'an era

---

[22] Zhou Enlai, "Zai zhonghua quanguo wenxue yishu gongzuozhe daibiao dahui shang de zhengzhi baogao," 29–32.

[23] Zhou Wen, "Jin-Sui wenyi gongzuo gaikuang jianshu" [A brief introduction to Shanxi-Suiyuan literature and arts work] ZWGD (1949), 313.

[24] Zhang Lingqing, "Shandong wenyi gongzuo gaikuang" [A general description of literature and arts work in Shandong] ZWGD (1949), 364.

stages had once been dominated by "big shows" concerning city life such as Tian Han's *Sunrise* (Richu), with artists only focused on elevating (*tigao*) their work.[25] Sha Kefu, one of the most experienced of all party dramatists, recalled how many cultural workers, expressing a profound dislike for traditional opera, unsuccessfully attempted to force "intellectual" shows on village troupes.[26]

These brief admissions, however, were overshadowed by forceful claims that rectification and rigorous study had solved class issues among cultural workers. Discussing artistic education in the "liberated" areas, famed poet Ai Qing thus emphasized the role of political education, especially for those who had traveled from Guomindang or Japanese-held areas; by studying Mao's artistic line, they had overcome the idea that art existed for art's sake and other "bad" beliefs.[27] Detailing the successes of Shaan-Gan-Ning cultural work, Ke Zhongping reminded representatives of the post-rectification tidal wave of creation in *qinqiang* opera and other folk forms that peaked in the New *Yangge* Drama Movement.[28] Zhou Yang, however, went the furthest in overstating the credentials of Yan'an era cultural workers, declaring "old base area" cultural workers to be "essentially worker-peasants."[29]

In stark comparison to the educated elite who would write glowingly of learning from the peasantry during the imminent thought reform (*sixiang gaizao*) campaigns,[30] Zhou Yang and other cultural leaders from the "old liberated areas" felt little compulsion to overstate their ideological conversions. Having braved war and agrarian reform in the countryside, they let their work speak for itself, highlighting folk artistic creation and the mobilization of rural culture in the old base areas. Zhou Yang argued that cultural workers, by becoming one with the masses and truly understanding peasant realities, had been uniquely suited to use peasant culture and language to create new works, the vast majority of which concerned war or land reform. Zhou Yang cited *The White-Haired Girl*, *Liu Hulan*, and *A Hatred of Blood and Tears* as proof that cultural workers had not just bottled "new wine in old bottles," but had in fact created new cultural

---

[25] Zhang Geng, "Jiefangqu de xiju" [Liberated area drama] ZWGD (1949), 186.

[26] Sha Kefu, "Huabei nogncun xiju yundong he minjian yishu gaizao gongzuo" [The North China rural drama movement and folk art reform work] ZWGD (1949), 349.

[27] Ai Qing, "Jiefangqu de yishu jiaoyu" [Artistic education in the liberated areas] ZWGD (1949), 239.

[28] Ke Zhongping, "Ba women de wenyi gongzuo tigao yi bu" [Raise the level of our cultural work] ZWGD (1949), 298.

[29] Zhou Yang, "Xin de renmin de wenyi" [New people's literature and arts] ZWGD (1949), 89.

[30] Brian James DeMare, "Casting (Off) Their Stinking Airs: Chinese Intellectuals and Land Reform, 1946–1952" *The China Journal*, No. 67 (January 2012).

forms that drew on folk styles to captivate village audiences.[31] The painstaking effort and endless revisions that had been a part of these "successful" creations received no mention.

Party cultural leaders also elided the difficulties that had characterized cultural mobilization in the countryside. As seen in previous chapters, the creation of rural amateur drama troupes in North China proceeded slowly, largely because of the strong preference among villagers for traditional operas. Even when progress was made, the departure of cultural workers or cessation of war might lead to "backsliding" and the return of for-profit *xibanzi* opera troupes. Many audiences rejected model Communist dramas in favor of traditional numbers, often heavy with "feudal" content. None of this nuance was present in the discussion over base area culture in Beiping, as cultural leaders boasted of the thousands of rural drama troupes formed under their direction. In his report on the Jin-Sui region, Zhou Wen praised the rapid expansion of drama troupes, with twelve counties forming over 340 amateur troupes during the course of the Sino-Japanese War.[32] Zhang Geng claimed that the Jiaodong region of Shandong was home to over ten thousand active village drama troupes. While this number already strained credibility, he further asserted that half of these troupes had performed *The White-Haired Girl*.[33] Most revealing was Sha Kefu's depiction of the rural drama troupe movement, which in his telling was so successful that by 1943 large villages in the Taihang, Jizhong, and Beiyue regions all had drama troupes.[34] As seen in Chapter 2, most of these village troupes barely existed and rarely performed didactic works, but the Beiping Cultural Congress, intended to herald a new day in cultural work, was not a time for such subtle distinctions.

Reports from the "old liberated areas" presented at the Beiping Cultural Congress glowingly depicted rural arts in the base areas. These reports, furthermore, also praised the unique figure of the cultural worker. Far from intellectuals of questionable loyalty, cultural workers, especially dramatists whose work was seen as the purest expression of the mass line in the arts, were true revolutionaries and leading players in the Communists' rise to power. Liu Zhiming, discussing literature and arts work in the Northeast, was particularly adamant in insisting on the centrality of cultural work in the revolution. According to Liu, after Japan's surrender, cultural workers dispatched to the Northeast found the region's cities infected by a "slave culture" that the Communists

---

[31] Zhou Yang, "Xin de renmin de wenyi," 70–78.   [32] Ibid., 320.
[33] Zhang Geng, "Jiefangqu de xiju," 188.
[34] Sha Kefu, "Huabei nongcun xiju yundong he minjian yishu gaizao gongzuo," 350.

cured with performances of *A Hatred of Blood and Tears* and *The White-Haired Girl*. The Northeast countryside, which according to Liu simply lacked any real culture, had been given new life through land reform cultural work.[35] Ke Zhongping similarly praised the efforts of cultural workers during the mid to late 1940s, a time when "war and land reform were intertwined (*jiaocha de*)." During this time, cultural workers "steeled" themselves in land reform and "served the victory" of both the agrarian revolution and Civil War.[36]

The reports presented to the Beiping Cultural Congress were not, of course, merely full of boasts concerning cultural workers and their accomplishments. Representatives noted a wide range of issues that had emerged in the "old base areas," including the need to further impress the importance of cultural work on village cadres. Such concerns, however, were relatively minor when compared to a trenchant observation made by Sha Kefu in his discussion of the problem of uniting with traditional artists. With over a decade of experience in rural work, Sha Kefu noted that folk artists tended to see intellectuals such as himself as "foreign things" (*yang wanyi*), a telling observation given his time spent studying in the USSR. Intellectuals, meanwhile, saw traditional artists, so beloved in the countryside, as simple "old things" (*jiu wanyi*), relics that had no place in a modern society.[37] The result had been a basic contradiction between the two sides, an unfortunate state that hindered rural cultural work for years.

In his glorification and simplification of old base area cultural work, Sha Kefu claimed that intellectuals and local artists had overcome their differences in the "old base areas." But his description of cultural workers and local artists in extreme conflict hinted at ongoing problems for PRC mass campaigns. The new cultural order of the PRC had to take root in village China, where locals had little interest in "elite" artistic forms and even mocked actors that dared to part their hair. The Communist Party, however, would call on urban intellectuals to create this new cultural world in the countryside. The vast network of drama troupes envisioned by party cultural leaders would be organized and overseen by the urban elite, but staffed largely by traditional artists and village amateurs. If these "foreign things" and "old things" failed to work together, the entire project of synchronizing cultural and political performances in Mao's "New China" would prove unsustainable.

---

[35] Liu Zhiming, "Dongbei san nian lai wenyi gongzuo chubu zongjie" [Summary of the initial steps in literature and arts work in the Northeast over the past three years] ZWGD (1949), 323–325.

[36] Ke Zhongping, "Ba women de wenyi gongzuo tigao yi bu," 300–301.

[37] Sha Kefu, "Huabei nongcun xiju yundong he minjian yishu gaizao gongzuo," 358.

In the field: wielding cultural weapons during PRC land reform

The actor Han Bing was the rare figure whose report for the Beiping Cultural Congress doubled as an opportunity for confession. Active in urban dramatic circles before the Japanese invasion pushed her to flee to Yan'an, Han Bing quickly found new life on stage in the wartime Communist capital. Starring in *Sunrise* and other "big shows," Han Bing basked in her status as a "famous" actor until Mao's "Talks at the Yan'an Forum" forced a dramatic shift in the Communists' theatrical world. Now playing peasant women, Han Bing did her best to understand female villagers, although she admitted difficulty in this regard even as she lived in the Shaanxi countryside. For this self-described "old intellectual actor" (*jiu zhishifenzi yanyuan*), however, the real hurdles were *yangge* dance and drama. Like the many urbanites that saw *yangge* as ugly, Han Bing looked down on this folk form as low-class and crude.[38] Through "rectification" and the promotion of *yangge*, Han Bing claimed to have overcome her aversion to folk art and even starred in a number of *yangge* dramas, but her story serves as a reminder of the gulf between urban artists and rural society. Han Bing lived in Yan'an for years, going through a protracted and highly structured "rectification" program alongside her peers. Urban artists drawn to rural revolution after the founding of the PRC, in contrast, had to master the steep learning curve of working with peasants in a matter of weeks.

In the months following the Beiping Cultural Congress, the regional governments of the emerging PRC state prepared for a number of state-building campaigns. For "newly liberated" territories, state-building efforts centered on land reform, which the Communists envisioned as the lynchpin of their efforts to solidify control over the still volatile countryside. In preparation for these campaigns, the Communists recruited artistically talented intellectuals and progressive artists to ensure that culture served the process of rural revolution. Thus, in early 1950, only a matter of months after China's cultural elites first gathered in Beiping, Wuhan hosted a similar conference for cultural workers. This Zhongnan (South-Central China) Literature and Arts Work Conference, regional where the Beiping meeting had been national in scale, aimed at coordinating a mass culture campaign (*qunzhong wenhua yundong*) to serve the Zhongnan region's massive land reform campaigns.

As Xiong Fu, the head of the preparatory committee for the Zhongnan Wenlian made clear, cultural workers in the Zhongnan region would

---

[38] Han Bing, "Wo de yanju shenghuo" [My life as an actor] ZWGD (1949), 457–459.

follow the directives of national cultural leadership and focus on dissemination (*puji*) over raising standards (*tigao*). Cultural workers at the meeting were also given a host of standard platitudes and instructed to learn from peasants, reform folk artists, and create works in local styles.[39] Such vague calls, however, were of little practical value for artists aiming to use cultural weapons to aid agrarian revolution, which, as the conference made clear, formed the "basic" responsibility for Zhongnan cultural workers for at least two years. Zhongnan cultural workers were thus called on to "struggle" the landlord class alongside the peasantry, while simultaneously creating new works reflecting land reform.[40]

Despite the fact that the Civil War had ended, the implementation of land reform in Zhongnan and other "newly liberated" areas still faced significant challenges. Land reform campaigns during the Civil War, while generally successful in generating support for the Communist cause, had not gone smoothly. The party had encouraged a trial and error approach during the early stages of the campaigns, creating a wide variety of violent "deviations," mostly "leftist" in nature, which had severely disrupted village society and economy. Land reform campaigns overseen by Deng Xiaoping, most notably, had been implemented in unsecured territories, leading to round after round of executions.[41] While the Communists had eliminated many of the problems that plagued early rounds of land reform, the arrival of the campaigns in "newly liberated" territories created two new complications for land reform work teams. First, work teams now followed an entirely new set of guidelines in the 1950 *Land Reform Law of the People's Republic of China*. This new land law contained surprising policy changes, especially in its relatively lenient treatment of landlords and its call to preserve the "rich peasant economy." Second, because work teams were implementing this new land law in new social and economic terrains, the experiences gained in the "old liberated areas" proved of limited value. In light of these challenges, the Zhongnan regional government first carried out a "test point" land reform campaign within Henan province to provide experience and models for full implementation of agrarian reform in South-Central China.

Xiong Fu and other cultural leaders in the South-Central region similarly used "test point" land reform in Henan as an opportunity to

---

[39] Zhou Gangwu, *Lun qunzhong wenyi yundong* [On the mass culture movement] (Guangzhou: Xinhua shudian huanan zongfen dian, 1951), 2–7.

[40] Xiong Fu, "Weirao tudi gaige, kaizhan chuangzuo yundong" [Focus on land reform, develop the creation movement] WZCT (1950), 18.

[41] Luo Pinghan, *Tudi gaige yundong shi*, 273.

experiment with the deployment of cultural workers to the countryside. The Zhongnan Wenlian divided 150 cultural workers into two teams, where artists first underwent intensive preparation, studying land reform policies and submitting to "ideological preparation" as they endeavored to prepare themselves for class struggle. Team members also prepared for double duty: cultural workers would oversee the process of land reform while also organizing cultural performances in support of the campaign.[42]

Work teams, finally, created new land reform shows that reflected changes in land reform policies. Arriving in the Henan countryside, these two large teams of cultural workers further dispersed into smaller land reform work teams, with three to five cultural workers to a team. While this dilution hampered the ability of cultural workers to stage land reform dramas, the size of land reform, even in this limited test run, demanded dispersion; one of the two teams, dispatched to Henan's Xiping County, found themselves overseeing land reform in nine administrative villages with a population of some ninety thousand residents. When carrying out "test point" land reform, cultural workers tended to focus on the political aspects of the campaign, only performing short shows when possible. After the distribution of land deeds, however, the Henan campaign called for villages to hold "Land Returns Home Celebratory Meetings." This provided an opportunity for cultural workers to regroup and tour with larger and more complex dramas in support of the campaign.[43]

The experiences of these 150 cultural workers in Henan, while certainly important for the implementation of "test point" land reform, proved truly significant as a model for the subsequent drive to bring agrarian reform to the rest of South-Central China, a vast region that stretched from Henan to Hainan. With fifty million villagers scheduled to undertake land reform starting in the fall of 1950, Du Runsheng, general secretary of the South-Central China Bureau, called for a second Cultural Work Conference in April, with the explicit goal of linking land reform and mass cultural campaigns. As Du explained to the assembled cultural workers, land reform was as much a cultural project as an economic reform. Calling for a "cultural army" of North China cadres, newly trained cultural workers, and traditional artists to "occupy the feudal literature and arts battleground," Du Runsheng proposed a land

---

[42] "Wenyi gongzuozhe canjia Henan tugai de jingyan" [Experiences of literature and arts workers participating in Henan land reform] WZCT (1950), 55–56.

[43] "Wengongtuan (dui) ruhe canjia tugai?" [How should cultural work teams participate in land reform?] WZCT (1950), 65.

reform campaign that would lean heavily on cultural work for its success-ful completion.[44]

Addressing the seventy cultural worker representatives gathered at the conference, Du stressed that because this was a "state controlled" (*guanban*) land reform, the Communists were responsible for raising peasant aware-ness during the process of land reform in order to fully overthrow feudalism. And because of the impossibility of holding training classes for fifty million peasants before land reform, action (*xingdong*) and edu-cation (*jiaoyu*) must work in tandem during the movement. To compli-cate matters further, Du noted that raising peasant consciousness had to be accomplished by using works that reflected the party's new and increasingly lenient policies with regard to the landlord class while also criticizing the former "poor peasant line." Du also requested works that emphasized the importance of party leadership during land reform, pointing to the Boxer Uprising as an example of a mass movement that went astray without proper leadership.[45]

As Du Runsheng's comments indicate, artistic creation emerged as a serious concern during the second Zhongnan cultural work conference. Xiong Fu also addressed the meeting and repeated the claim that current land reform campaigns, conducted after the establishment of the PRC, represented a new stage of agrarian reform and thus required new works. While peasants would still "struggle" landlords, the Communists called for the curtailing of anti-landlord violence and would now allow those categorized as "rich peasants" to keep their excess property. According to Xiong Fu, land reform creation still needed to focus on class struggle, but Xiong now asked cultural workers to downplay violent struggle and instead praise peasants as both reasonable and powerful in the process of "speaking reason" with landlords.[46] Urging cultural workers to find realistic events for models, Xiong Fu advised starting with real-life char-acters and stories before adding artistic embellishments. Yet even as some Communist leaders argued that land reform classics from the "old liberated areas" were not applicable to PRC era land reform, Xiong Fu offered *Liu Hulan* as a fine example of a creation based on a "real-life" story.[47] Land reform opera classics remained the true models for PRC creative work, but this posed a challenge for cultural workers. *Liu Hulan* dramatized the horrific execution of a peasant girl by "reactionary"

---

[44] Du Runsheng, "Zai Zhongnan di er ci wenyi gongzuozhe huiyi shang guanyu tugai wenti de baogao" [Report on land reform issues at the second Zhongnan Cultural Worker Conference] WZCT (1950), 8

[45] Ibid., 9–12.

[46] Xiong Fu, "Weirao tudi gaige, kaizhan chuangzuo yundong," 25–27.

[47] Ibid., 34–35.

Guomindang forces. With the Guomindang defeated, the uncertainties of the new PRC regime represented the greatest threat facing Zhongnan villages. Cultural workers would be hard pressed to find inspiration for another *Liu Hulan*.

The experiences of cultural workers in Henan's land reform demonstrate the difficulty of creating dramas for PRC era land reform. In the field for up to three months, these cultural workers oversaw campaigns that ran both quickly and smoothly, with most villagers receiving their land within a month after the arrival of work teams. Well versed in new land reform policies, work team members found very little resistance from local landlords, resulting in a decidedly non-confrontational "struggle method" (*douzheng fangshi*). Most cultural workers found the resulting land reform "boring," a problem that especially afflicted playwrights attempting to transcribe land reform into their creations. Dramatists often found themselves having to write about peasant association meetings, which were of great importance but of little inspirational value. Complicating matters further, villages had already undergone a campaign for rent reduction and other mass campaigns. During these campaigns, peasants had already "spilled bitter water" and were anxious to finish the land reform. Expecting fierce "struggle" and the speaking of bitterness, cultural workers in Henan found land reform "uninspiring" (*pingdan*).[48] Hoping to uncover a true story that would lead to a new version of *The White-Haired Girl*, cultural workers instead created works that explained an economic system that allows some peasants to remain rich (rather than taking their wealth for redistribution). Hoping to perform as a compelling villain like Huang Shiren, actors instead portrayed reformed landlords engaging in production.

The divisive rhetoric and the dishonest appraisal of rural culture in the "old liberated areas" at the Beiping Cultural Conference had already muddied PRC cultural work. And by issuing contradictory directives regarding the role of "struggle" in new artistic creations, the Communists only further confused cultural work at the regional level. On one hand, Communist leaders instructed cultural workers to hew the new party line and depict an orderly and peaceful land reform process. Dramatists were continually reminded that the violent campaigns of the Civil War, which had demanded physical attacks on landlords and the confiscation of rich peasant property, had come to a close. Du Runsheng thus called for cultural workers to create works that taught peasants how to legally "struggle" landlords through "speaking reason." Noting that

---

[48] "Guanyu tugai chuangzuo de yi xie wenti" [Some issues concerning land reform creation] WZCT (1950), 44–48.

some cultural workers had claimed Henan land reform to be without class struggle and thus not worthy of artistic creation, Du insisted that dramatists broaden their understanding of class struggle beyond the formalistic sense of the clash between landlords and peasants to the ideological "struggle" that occurred throughout the land reform process. With this understanding of "struggle" in mind, Du asked cultural workers to fully investigate peasant life and not simply seek out the most obvious forms of "struggle,"[49] even though "speaking bitterness" and confrontational "struggle" meetings had been the mainstays of land reform dramas.

At the same time, however, Zhongnan cultural leaders pushed dramatists to uncover "struggle" in order to give their land reform creations life. Yue Ming, drawing on personal experience in Henan's "test point" land reform, contradicted Du Runsheng by advising artists to actively seek out events with good "struggle" content, such as "speaking bitterness" meetings or the struggling of landlords.[50] Or as "Experiences of Literature and Arts Workers Participating in Henan Land Reform" argued, "looking at flowers from horseback" (*pao ma kan hua*) was not an acceptable method of land reform work; cultural workers instead must take part in "real struggle" (*shiji douzheng*). While "real struggle" meant becoming one with the masses instead of standing to the side and taking notes, it also meant that cultural workers, unlike regular cadres, could choose their work locations. According to "Experiences," cultural workers should seek out sharp instances of "struggle," for example finding villages with concentrated landholdings. If their selected village proved useless for creative purposes, cultural workers might change locales, although this required agreement from leading land reform cadres.[51] Put simply, cultural workers were being pulled in two opposing directions, furthering the contradictions in cultural work that had started in Beiping.

As the South-Central region prepared for its massive rounds of land reform, Xiong Fu estimated that the Communists could mobilize some three thousand cultural workers to take part in the campaigns.[52] Yu Lin, one of the region's most experienced cultural workers, had already taken part in three distinct land reform campaigns, once in the "old base

---

[49] Du Runsheng, "Zai Zhongnan di er ci wenyi gongzuozhe huiyi shang guanyu tugai wenti de baogao," 14–15.

[50] Yue Ming, "Cong muqian wenyi chuangzuo renwu tan dao xiaxiang chuangzuo wenti" [From current literature and arts responsibilities to the problem of going to the countryside and creating] WZCT (1950), 94.

[51] "Wenyi gongzuozhe canjia Henan tugai de jingyan," 57–59.

[52] Xiong Fu, "Weirao tudi gaige, kaizhan chuangzuo yundong," 40.

areas," once in the suburbs of Shijiazhuang, and once again in Henan.[53] Yu Lin and thousands of Zhongnan cultural workers went to the country-side to take part in land reform, create land reform works, and lay the foundations for the rural cultural movement by developing cultural activists and establishing amateur drama troupes. The "literature and arts weapon" was to be put into peasant hands.[54] But the transfer of this weapon would prove difficult. In his account of Henan land reform, Yu Lin revealed that cultural workers often came into conflict with local cadres. Yu, furthermore, told the story of a female cultural worker who arrived in the countryside with great hopes for the masses, befriending a female peasant representative. After giving the peasant activist money to purchase a journal, the cultural worker was profoundly disappointed when the woman instead purchased a pair of socks.[55] In the countryside, cultural workers would face a variety of issues, from balancing their cultural and political responsibilities to finding the right formula for cultural creation in an era of relatively peaceful land reform. But as Yu Lin's anecdotes of cadre clashes and sock purchasing suggests, working with newly cast peasants represented the ultimate challenge for cultural workers.

Villagers playing peasants: amateur actors onstage

For all of the attention lavished on professional cultural workers at the start of the PRC era, this talented group represented a tiny minority of China's vast population. The huge South-Central region had called on culture to play a decisive role in the 1950 to 1951 round of land reform, but could only muster some three thousand cultural workers. Even putting aside the double burden of conducting political and cultural work during land reform, these artists could hardly hope to perform for the estimated fifty million villagers then undertaking land reform. PRC cultural leaders, following patterns set as early as the era of Red Drama, thus sought to extend their cultural infrastructure down to the village

---

[53] According to Yu Lin, during that first campaign his work team had overemphasized the mass line, pushing peasants to confiscate all landlord property, turning landlords into beggars. The second campaign outside of Shijiazhuang had erred in the other direction, with Yu Lin's comrades only pretending to let the masses run the campaign while they made all important decisions. Only in Henan were these problems solved, as party policy and the mass line worked in tandem to produce a smooth and successful land reform. Yu Lin, "Wo zai tugai zhong de yi dian jingyan" [Some of my experiences in land reform] WZCT (1950), 138–140.

[54] "Zuzhi qilai, canjia tugia, fanying tugai" [Organize and participate in land reform, reflect land reform] WZCT (1950), 2.

[55] Yu Lin, "Wo zai tugai zhong de yi dian jingyan," 143–144.

level by establishing or co-opting village amateur drama troupes. As one 1955 handbook noted, amateur drama troupes had proven their worth by "propagating party policy, enthusiastically mobilizing the masses, and implementing Communist moral education." Compared to "dead" (*si de*) cartoons or storytellers of questionable talent, drama was alive with props and costumes, to the point that audiences often forgot that they were watching a staged performance.[56]

After the establishment of the PRC, amateur drama troupes finally operated without fear of enemy reprisal, yet performing for the Communists remained difficult. Many cultural workers found peasant audiences, often said to be starved for any culture, to be harsh and demanding critics. During the Beiping Cultural Congress, Wang Congwen, a model folk artist, argued that compared to urban audiences who sat respectfully during shows and welcomed performances in a wide variety of formats, peasants refused to sit still, could not read subtitles, and insisted on excitement (*renao*) and music in their shows. If a show had too much dialogue for their tastes, peasants were liable to ignore the show and talk amongst themselves.[57]

Given the high expectations of rural audiences, local dramatists needed to be creative as well as talented. As seen in handbooks for establishing amateur troupes and staging village dramas, created by experienced cultural workers such as Sun Lin and Su Yiping, a wealth of "do it yourself" experience informed amateur production. Sun Lin's 1951 guide for the production of rural dramas, for example, served as an insightful guide to staging dramas at the local level, containing detailed information on props, lighting, and sound effects. As a handbook for performing revolutionary dramas on village stages, the guide promoted a spirit of local innovation that allowed rural drama troupes to draw on their talents and limited resources to create shows that spoke to village audiences. As Sun Lin stated at the outset of his handbook: "There are many magicians, but they all possess their own tricks."[58]

Rural ingenuity and tricks of the trade overcame many of the challenges facing amateur production, but no amount of imagination could conquer the basic problems of content, performance, and financing. In the creative realm, amateurs struggled to find suitable scripts for their shows. When producing original works, village artists found it difficult to

---

[56] *Yeyu jutuan yanxi changshi wenda* [Questions and answers concerning general knowledge of amateur drama troupe performance] (Nanjing: Jiangsu renmin chubanshe, 1955), 3.

[57] Wang Congwen, "Gaige jiuxi yundong de ji dian jingyan yu jianyi" [Some experiences and opinions on the movement to reform old drama] ZWGD (1949), 484.

[58] Sun Lin, *Nongcun jutuan zenyang bianju he paiju*, 1.

write about local conditions in a manner that did not clash with Maoist perspectives of rural society. The dictates of popular culture, meanwhile, often led troupes to stage traditional dramas, many of which contravened official policies. Turing to performance, amateurs went to extreme measures to bring stories to life in a "realistic manner," painstakingly training shy peasant actors and utilizing the latest in do-it-yourself special effects, yet were always limited by tight budgets. The problem of finances, the most serious of the issues afflicting village troupes, was in fact a creation of Communist policy. Simply put, amateur troupes did not receive enough fiscal support, a situation that the PRC state actively encouraged. In response, amateur troupes would often defy party policy and attempt to solve their fiscal burdens by making the move towards professional status. Contradictions and complications in the early PRC cultural infrastructure extended down to its lowest levels.

Amateur creation in the PRC

Su Yiping, a veteran of the Yan'an era Northwest Cultural Work Team and a leading figure in the Northwest Wenlian, wrote extensively on amateur drama troupes in the countryside. As she made clear, drama troupes needed quality scripts if they hoped to stage state-friendly shows. Inspired by Communist directed professional drama troupes, some amateurs staged the revolutionary classics that had emerged from the Civil War era. But an editorial in *The People's Daily* condemned amateurs for performing *The White-Haired Girl, Liu Hulan,* and *A Hatred of Blood and Tears,* arguing that these productions of "big shows" wasted time and money.[59] Yet attitudes towards village troupes staging these "big shows" often proved contradictory. Cultural workers in the Northwest, for example, heavily promoted a Chang'an county amateur troupe that routinely performed *The White-Haired Girl* and other large-scale shows.[60] Another handbook, meanwhile, found that "big shows" were not suitable for most amateur troupes and advised dramatists to seek approval from

[59] "Guanyu nongcun yeyu jutuan de jige wenti" [A few questions concerning amateur rural drama troupes], *Renmin ribao* [The People's Daily] (July 17, 1953), 9.

[60] This model amateur troupe, formed from the remnants of three old style *xibanzi* troupes, performed regularly and toured extensively. Ke En, Ke Qin, and Gao Qi, "Yi ge jiao hao de nongcun yeyu jutuan – Chang'an xian weibin qu di shi xiang nongmin yeyu jutuan jieshao" [A relatively good rural amateur drama troupe – introducing the Chang'an County Weibin District Tenth Village Peasant Amateur Drama Troupe], in *Mingque nongcun yeyu jutuan de fangzhen bing jiaqiang lingdao* [Clarify the direction and strengthen the leadership of rural amateur drama troupes] (Xi'an: Xibei xingzheng weiyuanhui wenhuaju, 1953), 11.

superiors before attempting any such shows.[61] Conflicting opinions regarding the performance of these shows hints at the basic contradiction at the heart of amateur performance: the Communists wanted high-quality productions at the local level, but also understood a successful troupe would have the opportunity to turn professional.

Cultural leaders also discouraged "big shows" under the belief that shorter dramas based on local events and characters held the highest value for mass campaigns in the countryside. Because many village troupes tended to perform traditional folk art, Communist cultural leaders pushed amateurs to create new works. But amateur creations often failed to impress. Su Yiping, complaining about new content shows, noted that some amateur dramatists played too loose with the presentation of "facts," such as one show about Mao Zedong that was far too creative in its portrayal of the Chairman's biography. Other "new" shows were merely old works with a few superficial changes.[62] Thus, in the creation of new dramatic works, Sun Lin emphasized the use of local stories over those taken from newspapers or other sources.[63] These local stories, he argued, were not only easier for peasants to understand, but also contained built-in interest as people were naturally drawn to tales that reflected familiar events. While taking care not to offend peasants or overemphasize their weaknesses, Sun Lin encouraged village drama troupes to take local characters and events and retell these stories in dramatic form. Sun Lin also stressed the need to tell stories in a plot-driven fashion, not simply stating the story and its moral.

This emphasis on character-driven stories and overall believability added impetus to the use of actual events and people known to villagers. At the same time, however, Sun Lin noted the importance of complications and plot twists; as not to strain credibility, complications were to be sought in the story and the characters, not merely added for the sake of a plot twist or two. Here Sun Lin's guide serves as a reminder of the importance of realism; if a drama's plot was too fantastic, rural audiences would not find the show believable as a representation of village life. Once a troupe had decided on and plotted a story, the next step was dividing the tale into acts and scenes before producing a script. According to Sun Lin, this could be the work of one troupe member, or the troupe could produce the script as a team. In the latter manner, each character would be assigned

---

[61] *Yeyu jutuan yanxi changshi wenda*, 7.

[62] Su Yiping, *Mingque nongcun yeyu jutuan de fangzhen bing jiaqiang lingdao* [Clarify the direction and strengthen the leadership of rural amateur drama troupes] (Xi'an: Xibei xingzheng weiyuanhui wenhuaju, 1953), 3.

[63] Sun Lin, *Nongcun jutuan zenyang bianju he paiju*, 3.

to an actor, with the troupe improvising the play until a formal script could be produced.

Even when carefully explained by Sun Lin, artistic creation was no easy matter. Cultural leaders, for example, admitted that many drama troupes could not create original works.[64] These troupes were advised to rely on local educational and propaganda organs for scripts, while also staging works from the folk tradition. Over the years, however, amateurs increasingly solved their creation problems by drawing on local opera. With rural amateur troupes still allowed to stage short costumed dramas, villagers were finding excuses to bring back their beloved traditional repertoire. In 1956, a handbook on rural troupes, for example, admitted that villagers still staged old shows, including operas with "feudal" content. Troupes often claimed to have revised traditional operas to match current issues, but cultural workers discovered that this was simply a ruse. Amateur troupes would simply make a few rhetorical alterations, adding key words like "liberation" to show titles or adding a "modern" character to a historical show.[65] As explored in later chapters, the Communists never developed a policy that could diminish the popularity of traditional opera in the countryside, greatly complicating their attempt to guide cultural and political performance in rural China.

Amateur performance in the PRC

Assuming an acceptable script was found, amateurs could begin rehearsals, where the organizational hierarchy of the drama troupe largely determined a show's success. As Sun Lin emphasized, a single director had to control rehearsals in order to maintain order within the troupe. Troupe leaders, furthermore, also needed to rely on their authority when casting shows. As one handbook noted, there were two basic methods for matching village actors and characters. In the first, the director assigned roles, while, in the second, actors requested roles; in both scenarios, group discussion finalized casting decisions. This was necessary because of the many problems that emerged during the distribution of parts. Actors competed for larger roles, and peasants did not hesitate to express their displeasure when given smaller roles. Young women resented playing middle-aged or elderly women for reasons of vanity. Fearing ridicule, actors also shied away from playing reactionary characters. Cultural workers instructed amateur dramatists to remind their actors

---

[64] "Guanyu nongcun yeyu jutuan de jige wenti," 9.
[65] Ai Ke'en, *Zenyang ban nongcun yeyu jutuan* [How to create rural amateur drama troupes] (Beijing: Tongsu duwu chubanshe, 1956), 12–17.

that any reservations about playing roles were ideological problems; all roles were important and the purpose of acting was to enlighten, not to gain fame.[66]

After casting, came rehearsals. Here amateur troupes exhibited wide variations, with some shows needing as little as three days of preparations, while at other times a troupe might rehearse for weeks. At their most complex, amateur productions went through three stages of rehearsals, starting with "rough rehearsals" (cupai), when village actors would run through lines for the first time. During these initial rehearsals, directors were encouraged not interrupt or provide too many opinions, but instead allow actors to figure out movements on their own. Next came "fine rehearsals" (xipai), where actors refined movements and performances before the final "costumed rehearsals" (huazhuang paiyan), also known as "color rehearsals" (caipai). During rehearsals, directors often needed to help peasant amateur actors overcome stage fright. Directors, for example, might teach actors to think of themselves as the character they were portraying, not as an actor on stage. Actors were also to be warned against adlibbing or hamming it up to incite laughter.[67] In light of the bonds between political and cultural performances, unsanctioned improvisation could only be dangerous.

Only the extreme ingenuity of village troupes allowed the staging of amateur dramas in the countryside. Typical of the spirit behind the amateur drama troupe movement, Sun Lin encouraged troupes to use every possible resource on hand to bring their shows to life. Thus, in regards to stages, Sun Lin noted that many villages lacked the resources to even build a simple terrace or earthen stage (tutai). Instead of marshaling the manpower to construct a stage, Sun Lin encouraged amateur drama troupes to take advantage of local topography, using a cliff, ridge, or any plateau raised above its surrounding area. Noting that a "stage" only had to be higher than the audience, Sun Lin praised one troupe that had used a river bank for its stage, allowing its audience to enjoy the performance from the shore below.[68]

Balancing out this recognition of the material limitations placed on peasant drama troupes was a continued push for realism in productions, with handbooks providing detailed instructions for the use of props, costumes, make-up, lighting, and special effects. Cultural workers pushed amateur drama troupes towards the realism popularized by party affiliated professional drama troupes, but kept amateur troupes on shoestring budgets. Costumes did not present too great of a challenge for

---

[66] *Yeyu jutuan yanxi changshi wenda*, 16.   [67] Ibid., 23–36.
[68] Sun Lin, *Nongcun jutuan zenyang bianju he paiju*, 25.

amateur dramatists; staging dramas based on village life, peasant actors could wear their everyday outfits as costumes on stage. This was especially true when troupes created original works based on local events and local characters. Scenery setting (*bujing*), however, was considered "troublesome and complicated work." Troupes first had to obtain a curtain, although bed sheets could substitute if the troupe could not source a proper curtain. Troupes could also borrow simple props such as desks and chairs for indoor scenes, but exterior scenes (*waijing*) tested the creativity of amateur performers. Thus, for mountain scenes troupes might set up benches and other sturdy objects, covered with a hemp sack or cloth, to portray a mountainside. Amateur directors were advised to ensure the stability of their "mountains," lest the crowd break out in laughter when the "mountain" toppled under an actor's weight.[69]

Because the party frequently demanded that shows should never impede production, which naturally occurred during the day, lighting became a necessity for evening performances. For rural troupes, the most advanced form of lighting available were gas lights (*qideng*). Compared to professional troupes that might use changes in lighting and projected images as part of their shows, amateur troupes hoped to simply keep their stages lit without incident. All too often lights would break or run out of expensive gas. Cultural workers instructed troupes to train a peasant to oversee lighting; this light technician should regularly inspect the light and gas supplies, as well as keep on hand extra gauze covers and other needed supplies. For those drama troupes that could not afford gas lighting, alternate sources of light included homemade vegetable oil lamps (*zhiwuyou deng*).[70] This "do it yourself" ethos was also evident in special effects (*xiaoguo*), typically provided by villagers talented in the art of mimicry and simple noisemaking devices. For example, a swirling piece of bamboo served as a "wind machine," while empty oil barrels produced "thunder."

Makeup represented one of the few "professional" tools of the trade that amateurs used regularly on village stages. Along with lighting, makeup represented an unavoidable expense for underfunded amateur troupes. The essential starting point in a makeup artist's kit was greasepaint (*youcai*), which was especially important during nighttime shows under artificial lights; daytime performers could get away with simply using blush and lipstick. Troupes could purchase greasepaint, but it was much cheaper for amateurs to create their own by melting down petroleum jelly and adding various materials to create needed colors. Thus,

---

[69] *Yeyu jutuan yanxi changshi wenda*, 59.　　[70] Ibid., 60–61.

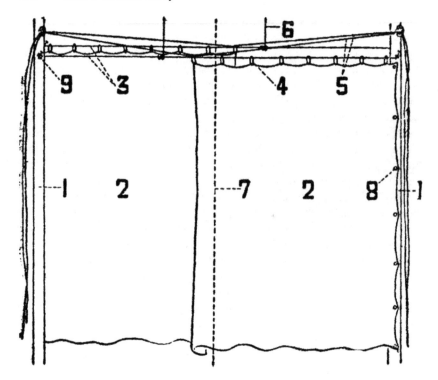

簡 單 的 前 幕 裝 置 圖

1.台口的木柱   6.吊住鉄絲，免得吃重
2.幕布   後向下彎軟的鉄絲
3.鉄絲   7.舞台的中線
4.窗帘上用的小銅圈   8.圖畫釘
5.細蔴繩   9.鉄釘

Figure 9 A cultural handbook explains how to create a curtain for
amateur drama productions

makeup artists could add vermillion (*yinzhu*) for red greasepaint, pine
soot (*songyan*) for black greasepaint, red clay (*hongtu*) for brown greasepaint, and zinc powder (*xinqifen*), found in Western medicine shops, for
white greasepaint. Handbooks advised makeup artists to first apply a
layer of foundation of petroleum jelly or lard before adding colored
greasepaint and then blush and lipstick.

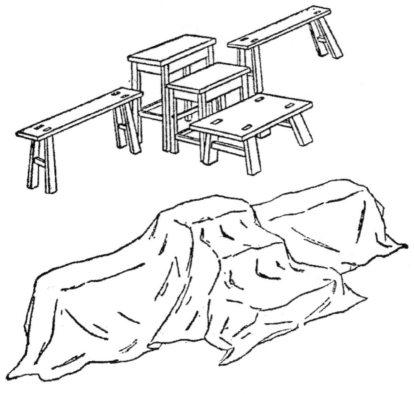

可以在上面走的近山坡或圩堤

Figure 10 Prop mountains for foreground placement

Skilled makeup artists helped peasant actors assume many different roles. Applying a bit of a gloomy (yin'an) color to actors' faces, for example, created aged, infirmed, or weak characters. Wrinkles, especially when drawn in the forehead region, quickly created the appearance of age. And because no part of the face could match the expressive power of eyebrows, makeup artists were advised to purchase an eyebrow pencil, although black greasepaint could be used in a pinch. Just as forehead wrinkles suggested age, downward angled eyebrows were the sure sign of reactionary characters.[71] A talented makeup artist, Sun Lin boasted, could create nearly any needed effect by sourcing alternative materials

---

[71] Ibid., 42–52.

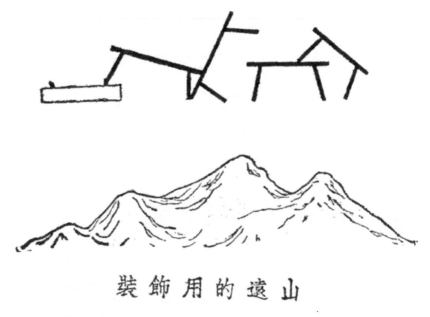

装 饰 用 的 远 山

Figure 11 Prop mountains for background placement

locally. Makeup artists, for example, could transform lamb's wool or dog fur into beards and moustaches. Boiling discarded rubber in oil created putty for "big noses," allowing peasant actors to perform as foreigners on village stages. Sprinkling white powder onto oil-slicked hair provided amateurs the needed effect to portray elderly characters, or perhaps a certain peasant girl living in the mountains. Bald-caps, manufactured from disinfected pig bladders, provide only the most visceral example of agricultural product turned theatrical prop.[72]

The emphasis on props, scenery, and makeup for rural amateurs reflects the importance of realism in the performance of revolutionary drama. Purporting to reflect village life, amateur performance demanded a realistic representation of rural life. Peasant actors, however, performed a "reality" that only made sense within the context of Communist ideology. In advising amateur drama troupes, Sun Lin pushed for a Maoist "realism," which presupposed class stratified villages as well as violent class conflict. As Sun Lin argued: "Peach blossoms do not bloom in winter, roosters do not lay eggs, and without being 'struggled' by the masses, landlords will certainly not voluntarily stop exploiting the

---

[72] Sun Lin, *Nongcun jutuan zenyang bianju he paiju*, 38–39.

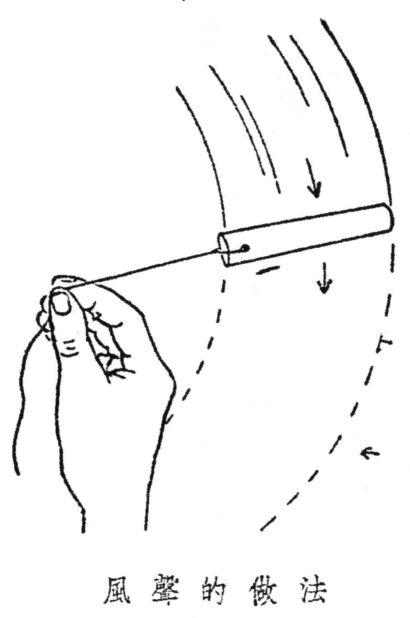

風 聲 的 做 法

Figure 12 A homemade wind machine

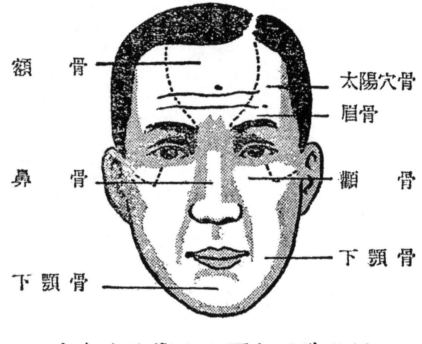

中年人的襯影和面部骨骼位置

Figure 13 Makeup instructions for making a middle-aged face

peasantry; nor will the poor peasants reverse themselves and side with the landlords in opposing land reform."[73] For Sun Lin, class struggle between upright peasants and evil landlords was as natural as the blooming of peach blossoms in the spring.

The "realism" expected from amateur performance was thus the Communists' sanctioned version of reality. In this discussion of wardrobes, Sun Lin noted how clothes expressed a character's identity (*shenfen*), which after the arrival of land reform meant class identity:

Pre-land reform landlords should be clothed in long gowns and jackets made of silk and satin, just like an old moneybags (*laocai*) that has gotten fat from drinking the blood of the poor. The hooligans, running dogs, traitors, and spies should be made to look crooked and improper, and thus make the expression of their shameful lives more obvious. When dressing our cadres, basic masses, or

[73] Ibid., 5–6.

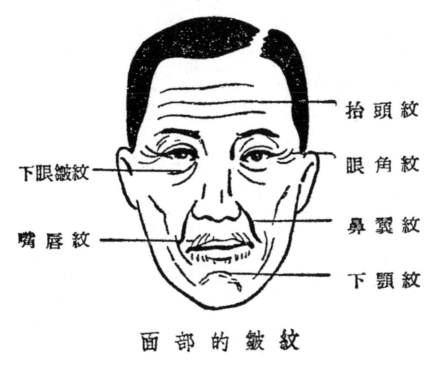

抬 頭 紋

眼 角 紋

鼻 翼 紋

下 頦 紋

下眼皺紋

嘴 唇 紋

面 部 的 皺 紋

Figure 14 Makeup instructions for applying wrinkles to amateur actors

activists, dress them simply and properly, so that they are clearly proper and will gain the respect and close affection of the people.[74]

This passage serves as a strong reminder that in drama, Communist education always came before entertainment. Amateur troupes might even have a lecturer (*baogao yuan*) explicitly state the message of the drama before it even began. Amateur drama troupes were thus instructed to mimic their professional counterparts and perform a Maoist reality, which villagers could re-perform during mass campaigns and everyday life in "New China."

Amateur finances in the PRC

The push for amateur "realism" also reflected the need to keep costs low, but village troupes could not avoid basic expenses, especially gas lighting

[74] Ibid., 42.

for evening performances. The official explanation for amateur troupe funding, published in *The People's Daily*, vaguely called for troupes to work with village governments instead of directly demanding money from fellow villagers.[75] Local governments, however, often gave the cultural realm short shrift, an issue some troupes vocalized as the "four don't cares" (*si bu guan*): prefecture, county, district, and village-level cadres all ignored cultural work.[76] At times, this was because of a disdain for cultural work, with one cadre going as far as to suggest the abolition of village troupes in the belief that their performances interfered with production. In other cases, it was simply a lack of cultural cadres, particularly at the county level and below. According to Su Yiping, furthermore, the much promoted model of troupe members performing extra labor to support performances was simply too great a burden to serve as a long-term solution. Su found other financing methods similarly unsuitable. Funds derived from village communal property, such as renting out village fields or selling local trees, proved unpopular. Asking for donations, finally, led to instances of corruption. According to Su Yiping, one troupe took advantage of the "Five Antis" Campaign to "collect" huge sums from local merchants. Another troupe sold off its village's land reform "struggle fruits," while yet another troupe embezzled funds collected to support the fight in Korea.[77]

Without proper fiscal backing, many talented amateurs moved towards professional status, leading *The People's Daily* to condemn the trend of "amateur" troupes touring, charging for shows, and leaving agricultural production.[78] For Su Yiping, the "contradiction between amateur drama troupes and professional drama troupes" represented one of the leading challenges facing rural drama troupes. Amateurs, already competing with professionals for rural audiences and often staging traditional numbers, might purchase expensive equipment in the hope of earning fame and fortune.[79] One 1955 handbook on rural drama troupes admitted the severity of the trend towards professionalization. Looking at four counties in Hebei province, the handbook counted 237 rural amateur drama troupes, 106 of which were "blindly developing towards professionalization" by frequently touring, charging for shows, performing during agricultural peak seasons, staging "big shows," and hiring professional teachers.[80] The Communists continuously railed against the trend towards

---

[75] "Guanyu nongcun yeyu jutuan de jige wenti," 10.
[76] Su Yiping, *Mingque nongcun yeyu jutuan de fangzhen bing jiaqiang lingdao*, 5.
[77] Ibid., 4.   [78] "Guanyu nongcun yeyu jutuan de jige wenti," 8.
[79] Su Yiping, *Mingque nongcun yeyu jutuan de fangzhen bing jiaqiang lingdao*, 2.
[80] Ai Ke'en, *Zenyang ban nongcun yeyu jutuan*, 6.

professionalism, but by demanding high-quality shows without providing proper funding, the party ensured that this problem would continue to plague their cultural army.

Conclusion: cultural workers in the early PRC

The Communists regarded rural cultural work, intimately connected to land reform and other state-building campaigns, as one of the lynchpins in their efforts to establish the new PRC order. Gathering in Beiping, top political leaders, including Mao Zedong and Zhou Enlai, stressed the centrality of drama and other cultural activities to the revolutionary enterprise. But by eliding the difficulties and setbacks that had characterized cultural work in the "old base areas," while simultaneously casting suspicion on urban artists, PRC cultural leaders had only complicated cultural work. At the regional level, cultural workers were given contradictory instructions, dispatched to the countryside to implement an orderly and peaceful land reform campaign, while also creating works that depicted confrontational and often violent class struggle. And at the village level, finally, cultural workers instructed amateur dramatists to create realistic revolutionary drama emulating their professional peers, despite the fact that the new PRC state consistently and systematically deprived amateurs of the funds needed to properly stage quality dramas that could please demanding village audiences. Many amateurs felt the draw of professional status, an illicit attraction that revealed the difficulties of amateur acting for the PRC state.

Contradictions plagued cultural work from capital to rural hamlet during the early years of the PRC. And the cultural workers overseeing the flawed and paradoxical cultural realm represented another volatile variable, often proving just as difficult to control as village artists. Cultural workers produced countless dramas, novels, songs, and stories concerning rural revolution and the coming of "New China" to the countryside, but these artists were not merely passive outlets for Communist propaganda. As talented artists, cultural workers typically had their own agenda which often challenged the party's idealized conception of cultural production. Wang Li, one of many cultural workers to emphasize the contention that characterized cultural creation in the countryside, spoke with the experience of carrying out land reform in Shandong. Discussing new cultural workers preparing to participate in the round of land reform following the 1950 harvest, Wang noted that "there were those who had a 'going to the countryside to take a bath' attitude"; the "bath" that Wang alluded to was the cleaning away of petty-bourgeoisie thinking.[81] While admitting the importance of this class "bath," Wang felt that superficial motives kept cultural workers from truly taking part in land reform.

For Wang, superficial motivations represented the least worrisome of the issues facing cultural workers in the countryside. Far more troubling, cultural workers tended to avoid contact with villagers and ignore the difficult work of land reform, opting instead to focus on gaining fame through cultural creation. Some obsessed over finding heroic model peasants, running "all over the place looking for characters like Li Youcai or Fugui [characters made famous by Zhao Shuli], but Li Youcai and Fugui are rare in the countryside."[82] Wang instead advised cultural workers to "do things" (ban shi) for the peasants, most importantly helping peasants navigate the complex process of land reform, including mundane steps such as filling out forms and measuring land. Cultural workers could also serve as accountants or primary schoolteachers. Wang further advised cultural workers to pay attention to their work style, join the local peasant associations, and respect village cadres. Turning to creation, Wang advised cultural workers to focus on common and ordinary peasants to craft typical and representative (dianxing) characters,[83] unwelcome advice for cultural workers hoping to create a famous work of art based on a powerful character like Xi'er or Liu Hulan.

Overall, Wang Li's exhortations to take part in the mundane details of land reform suggest that cultural workers cared more about cultural creation and their careers than measuring land or serving as village accountants. Landscape painter Ai Zhongxin further addressed this issue of cultural worker motivation through a study into the reasons that drove artists from the elite Central Arts Academy to participate in land reform. According to Ai, these elite artists did not join land reform to help villagers or to assist in the modernization of China. Instead, cultural workers primarily wanted to "experience life and reform their thinking, while the second reason was to gather materials for creative works and to see the spectacle."[84] Others, though few in number, went simply to appear revolutionary or because they felt they had no choice in the matter.

---

[81] Wang Li, "Wenyi gongzuozhe xiaxiang wenti" [Issues with cultural workers in the countryside], in *Tudi gaige yu wenyi chuangzuo* [Land reform and literature and arts creation], ed. Lin Dongbai (Shanghai: Xinhua shudian huadong zongfendian, 1950), 21.

[82] Ibid., 23.   [83] Ibid., 23–25.

[84] Ai Zhongxin, "Xian zuo hao gongzuo ne, xian tiyan shengyuo?" [First do good work, or first experience life?], in *Tudi gaige yu wenyi chuangzuo* [Land reform and literature and arts creation], ed. Lin Dongbai, (Shanghai: Xinhua shudian huadong zongfendian, 1950), 44.

Ai Zhongxin admitted the importance of elite artists transforming themselves through land reform, but insisted that cultural workers make the work of carrying out the campaign their top priority. The focus on creating a great work of art such as *The White-Haired Girl*, Ai argued, could actually impede land reform, especially if cultural workers arrived in the countryside with a preconceived narrative and attempted to force villagers to act out their plot. Wanting to capture the drama of earlier land reform creations, cultural workers might force a violent confrontation between peasants and landlords in a clear violation of PRC era land reform policy. Or cultural works might organize villagers to burn their deeds in order to use this dramatic moment in their land reform creations. But as Ai Zhongxin warned cultural workers, the burning of official land deeds, indicative of early land reform when the Communist burned deeds to show that the old order would not return, now contravened official policy. Ai praised self-reformation and the creation of new works, but insisted on the primacy of the complex and at times tedious business of conducting rural revolution.[85]

As Wang Li and Ai Zhongxin made clear, cultural workers faced many challenges in the countryside. Under orders to join with the masses and tell stories reflecting local affairs, many had difficulty in approaching, understanding, and living with peasants. Beyond this, however, cultural workers had personal goals and motives for joining a land reform team. Many wished to follow in the footsteps of Ruan Zhangjing and other artists who had gained national fame for depicting the dramatic transformation of rural China in land reform. This resulted in a tendency to avoid the less dramatic yet still essential aspects of the campaigns. Even more troubling, cultural workers might stage superfluous land reform rituals merely to later use them as a basis for their cultural creations. Cultural workers approached land reform not as pawns of the Communist Party, but as agents with their own motives that often ran counter to party goals.

While Wang Li and Ai Zhongxin directed their criticisms at newly enlisted cultural workers, even the much praised revolutionary artists of the "old liberated areas" refused to simply subordinate their personal careers to the Communist cause. Given the nature of political discourse in the PRC, such revelations were largely kept out of dramatist and actor memoirs, but one account of the Beiping Cultural Congress includes a revealing description of a meeting between Zhou Enlai and top PLA cultural workers. According to He Fang, a leading musician in the Third

---

[85] Ibid., 47.

Field Army's Second Cultural Work Team, around twenty cultural workers selected from the PLA's field armies were whisked to Zhongnanhai, where they drank tea while waiting for hours until Zhou Enlai joined them at around 10pm. During this meeting, cultural workers did not shy away from complaining about their shabby treatment and poor pay in the PLA, bluntly telling the Communist Party Vice Chairman that cultural workers had little chance of professional advancement within the army. One cultural worker, for example, complained bitterly that PLA artists were underappreciated by their superiors, who gave them much work but little support. These cultural workers had much "bitter water" to spill: their meeting with Zhou Enlai lasted until four in the morning.[86]

The practice of rural cultural work in the aftermath of the PRC's establishment was thus an incredibly messy affair. Top cultural leaders set high standards for mass work, eliding past difficulties while questioning the loyalty of those who would carry out party directives. Regional party leaders asked cultural workers to seek out "struggle" while implementing peaceful and non-violent land reform. Village artists were expected to serve the needs of land reform and other campaigns but were chastised for following the only viable drama troupe model available, that of the professional drama troupe. And cultural workers, finally, arrived in the countryside with their own set of concerns, which often clashed with the needs of the PRC state and its mass campaigns. How then, did mass cultural work ever aid the implementation of rural revolution and state-building projects during the PRC's formative years? The following chapter addresses this question through the exploration of Hubei Province, where land reform and rural drama campaigns ran in tandem.

---

[86] He Fang, "Zongsheng nanwang de Zhongnanhai zhi ye – ji Zhou Enlai fu zhuxi he jundui wenyi gongzuozhe daibiao zuotan" [An unforgettable night in Zhongnanhai: remembering vice chairman Zhou Enlai's forum with military cultural workers] JZSQ (1980s), 464–469.

6   Peasants on stage
Amateur actors in socialist China

In anticipation of its inaugural Peasant Association Representative Congress in the spring of 1950, Hubei's new government called together rural activists from across the province. These newly minted agents of the PRC state converged on Wuhan to prepare for upcoming mass campaigns, the most important of which was land reform.[1] While the focus of the Congress was primarily political, the prominent role of propaganda in these campaigns meant that cultural issues could scarcely be ignored. Hubei's cultural leaders thus took an active role in the Congress, organizing performances of *The White-Haired Girl* and other revolutionary operas before convening with over sixty peasant representatives to discuss cultural issues. This March 17 meeting proved a lively event, charged with an optimism that bubbled over as representatives arrived joyfully singing *The East Is Red*. Eager to discuss the revolutionary operas they had just seen, peasant activists voiced opinions and even criticized plotlines.

But when the topic turned to the arts in their home counties, the contrast with these expertly staged operas was stark. Representatives revealed that their fellow peasants anxiously awaited dramatic performances of any kind, with speaker after speaker expressing their hope that Hubei's new cultural leaders would dispatch troupes to the countryside to entertain and enlighten. One even requested operas that might influence his wife, who had threatened to stop cooking his meals in reaction to his political activism. But Jun County's Liu Shuying, one of only five women selected as a peasant representative, shared an altogether different experience. An upcoming political leader from Caodian Village, Liu Shuying had recently organized an amateur drama troupe to help her village "struggle" their newly labeled "local tyrant." Admitting that her troupe lacked the talent of the performers of *The White-Haired Girl*,

---

[1] For an overview of land reform in Hubei, see Vivienne Shue, *Peasant China in Transition: The Dynamics of Development toward Socialism, 1949–1956* (Berkeley, CA: University of California Press, 1980).

Liu Shuying detailed how peasant actors rehearsed and staged an original creation, a narrative reenactment of the crimes of the village's "local tyrant." The Caodian audience had wept and yelled while watching the show before using these emotions to successfully "struggle" their now hated class enemy. Liu Shuying concluded with a folk song that drew excited applause, but it was her tale of amateur performance inciting political action that truly caught the attention of Hubei's cultural leaders.[2] Inspired by Liu, before the year was out these leaders would launch a mass campaign to create thousands of amateur village drama troupes throughout the province

Liu Shuying enlisted herself into Mao's cultural army during a moment of profound transition for the dramatic realm. Early PRC state-building programs, while riddled with contradictions, insisted on the organization of the cultural world, including the systematization of revolutionary performances from capital to countryside. And with PLA propaganda teams now instructed to "perform for soldiers," professional and amateur drama troupes emerged as the most important performers of revolutionary drama. But these civilian troupes developed unevenly. In the "old liberated areas" of Shanxi, for example, cultural leaders focused on co-opting the many professional drama troupes roaming the countryside, a process explored in the following chapter. Rural Hubei, however, had few professional artists to speak of. In 1949, the start of a "recovery period" (*huifu shiqi*) for professional drama troupes, the province only counted twenty-seven professional opera troupes, twenty-one of which were crowded into the Wuhan market.[3] While the cessation of Civil War allowed the development of professional troupes, these performers were in critically short supply in the early 1950s. If Hubei was to have a cultural army to help implement rural revolution, it would have to be an amateur force.

In Hubei, political and cultural leaders, seeking to utilize the connections between cultural and political performances, launched a campaign to establish a provincial network of amateur village drama troupes in March 1950, just as the province started its first round of land reform. This was not a coincidence. Subsequent land reform campaigns provided the context for further development of amateur drama troupes in the countryside. As millions of Hubei villagers underwent land reform, so too would they have the opportunity to be educated and entertained

---

[2] "Nongmin daibiao tan wenyi," 6–9.
[3] Hubei sheng wenhuaju, "Hubei sheng wenhua shiye tongji ziliao, 1949–1959" [Hubei province cultural activities statistical materials, 1949–1959] HPA SJS-24 (1959), 38–40, 62–65.

by dramas staged by visiting troupes as well as their fellow villagers. Starting from a baseline of a few dozen recognized amateur rural troupes in 1950, by 1951 Hubei's cultural authorities could boast of over two thousand village troupes.[4]

The exploration of these troupes begins with an overview of Hubei's cultural infrastructure before examining in turn the local cultural scene, Hubei cultural workers, and the campaign to create amateur troupes. After a discussion of the development, composition, and creations of village drama troupes, this chapter closes with an investigation into the "deviations" the Communists found among village actors. The drama troupe movement developed through rural political campaigns, yet also played a critical role in promoting these very same campaigns. Dramatic performance served as one of the primary means of translating national politics for the local scene, giving immense power to those who would frame political issues on local stages. Despite the wishes of Hubei's cultural leaders, local art and local artists were never an easy fit with a state ideology that emphasized, above all, revolutionary politics and economic production. Local dramatists continually chafed against state efforts to control their activities and productions, resulting in constant disputes over the form, length, and especially content of their dramas. While some local actors privileged entertainment over education and propaganda, others went further and dared to use drama to question or subvert national politics. The deployment of village drama troupes in the Hubei countryside helped synchronize political and cultural perform-ances, but the tendency of amateur actors to focus on entertainment and even turn professional revealed deep contradictions within Mao's cultural army.

Cultural infrastructure in Hubei

The efforts of cultural workers greatly facilitated a series of mass cam-paigns carried out in the Hubei countryside during the first years of the PRC. While a number of organizations mobilized cultural workers, Hubei's provincial Wenlian took the lead in the development of rural culture through its many branches, typically established in conjunction with cultural centers at the county and district levels.[5] Hubei's Wenlian

---

[4] "Nongcun jutuan de gonggu yu fazhan" [The development and consolidation of rural drama troupes], in *Lun nongcun jutuan yundong* [Discussing the rural drama troupe campaign] (Wuhan: Hubei Wenlian, 1953), 4.

[5] Chen Meilan, ed., *Hubei wenyi 50 nian* [Fifty years of Hubei literature and art] (Wuhan: Changjiang wenyi chubanshe, 1999), 1–2.

was thus intimately involved in the transformation of village life, with many members personally taking part in land reform and other mass campaigns. During the summer of 1950, for example, a team of over one hundred Wenlian artists spent three months touring Mianyang prefecture, staging performances in support of mass political campaigns.[6] The Wenlian journal *Hubei Literature and Arts* (Hubei Wenyi), meanwhile, provided a forum for discussing the logistics of cultural campaigns at the local level, serving as an invaluable guide for Hubei cultural workers as they created the organizations and cultural works needed to support the revolutionary transformation of the countryside.

Hubei Literature and Arts was not the only arts journal unique to Hubei,[7] but the Wenlian journal was unmatched in its authority and ability to collect artistic works and opinions from the field. And while created by artists keen to present cultural activities in a positive light, the journal was quick to point out "deviations" and errors in local cultural practice, especially during "rectification" campaigns. The drive to present an idealized view of Hubei cultural work was also balanced by the relatively open nature of the journal, epitomized by its special "correspondents" section where cultural workers and amateur critics reported on arts organizations and activities. Local correspondents might comment on the development of rural drama troupes, or simply complain about a recent performance that failed to meet expectations. Significantly, the editors of *Hubei Literature and Arts* used this section to collect and spread information about campaigns at the village level, continually calling for new correspondents while asking for more information. When He Huo and Ke Ling wrote in to discuss cultural work in the Jingzhou area, for example, the editors asked these correspondents for more information about propaganda teams performing in the countryside.[8] Similarly, after a correspondent wrote in to detail the formation of a rural drama troupe in Panjiatai Village, the editors praised the account and asked other correspondents to contribute similar stories of troupe formation.[9] As this suggests, *Hubei Literature and Arts* provided Hubei's Wenlian a forum to gather information and promote models for emulation or criticism.

---

[6] Lin, "Hubei sheng wenhua gongzuotuan zai Xindi" [Hubei province's cultural work team in Xindi] HBWY 2.2 (1950), 40.

[7] The journal was sold alongside *Yangtze Literature and Art* (Changjiang wenyi), *Workers' Literature and Art* (Gongren wenyi), and *Hubei Culture Newsletter* (Hubei wenhua tongxun).

[8] He Huo and Ke Ling, "Jingzhou de wenyi huodong" [Jingzhou's arts and literature activities] HBWY 2.2 (1950), 37.

[9] "Panjiataicun de gaotaiqu huodong qingkuang" [The situation of Panjiatai Village's gaotaiqu activities] HBWY 2.4 (1950), 32–33.

With Wenlian providing leadership through its editorials and correspondent pages, cultural centers provided the infrastructure for carrying
out the rural drama troupe movement throughout the province. Quickly
established by building on the cultural infrastructure left by the Guomindang regime, PRC cultural centers hosted local Wenlian organizations
and served as publishing and distribution points.[10] Within a year of the
PLA's arrival in Hubei, the province had already established thirty-two
county cultural centers and was calling for the establishment of cultural
centers at the district level and seventy-three at the district level; by 1952,
these numbers had risen to 106 and 296 respectively. These cultural
centers averaged three workers at the county level, while district centers
generally had one full time worker.[11]

Compared to the People's Education Centers (Minzhong jiaoyu guan,
or Minjiaoguan) they replaced, PRC cultural centers not only had an
expanded infrastructural network, but also an increased reach into the
countryside. The Guomindang centers were little more than reading
rooms, which were not necessarily well stocked. The Xiaogan City
People's Education Center had over four thousand books on its shelves
when taken over by the Communists, yet the 1949 inventory from the
Xishui County People's Education Center was pathetic in comparison:
one table, two benches, two desks, one bookcase, one book rack, and just
over one hundred books. Reorganization by the Communists transformed
these reading rooms into important sites for reaching out to the countryside. By the end of 1952, the reorganized Xishui cultural center had
dispatched cultural workers to oversee the establishment of two district-
level cultural centers and fifty-four rural amateur drama troupes. The
center also organized the Xishui County Cultural Work Team, which
performed throughout the county during two stages of land reform.[12]

Hubei's Wenlian and its cultural center network provided the leadership and means for artists to use culture to help establish the regime's

---

[10] Li Renfu, "Jiangling Wenlian chou weihui chengli" [Jiangling's Wenlian preparatory
committee is established] HBWY 2.2 (1950) 39; Li Renfu, "Guanyu faxing gongzuo de
yijian," 36.

[11] *Hubei sheng zhi: shang, wenyi* [Hubei provincial gazetteer: Part one, literature and arts]
(Wuhan: Hubei renmin chubanshe, 1997), 435–436. One archival source claims that in
1952 the province was home to 112 centers at the county level and 306 at the district
level. See Hubei sheng wenhuaju, "Hubei sheng wenhuaju 1954 nian Hubei sheng
wenhua shiye jigou juchang qingkuang, dianyingyuan deng tongjibiao" [Hubei province
department of culture 1954 statistical chart for Hubei province cultural institutional
organizations, including theater situation and film houses] HPA SZ116-1-129 (1954), 5.

[12] This forty-five-member team performed a repertoire of 12 shows a total of 117 times for a
claimed audience of 327,000 *Xiaogan shi zhi: juan ershisan, wenhua* [Xiaogan city gazetteer:
Volume 23, culture] (Xiaogan, ca. 1980s), 13; *Xishui xian zhi: wenhua* [Xishui County
gazetteer: culture] (Xishui, ca. 1980s), 1–7.

power throughout the province, which was overwhelmingly agrarian in nature.[13] Wenlian leaders announced its first "rural campaign" in late 1949, signaling their intention to work in concert with land reform and other political campaigns and confirming that the countryside would indeed serve as their primary field of action. Thus, at the Conference on Arts and Literature Work in Rural Hubei, held in early 1950, cultural leaders promoted the slogan "popularization is number one, give priority to the countryside."[14] For Hubei cultural workers, this intense focus on the countryside translated into three interrelated responsibilities. First, artists would join regular land reform work teams and help villagers carry out the process of land reform. Second, Wenlian leaders organized cultural work teams to perform in support of mass campaigns. Finally, cultural workers were to establish amateur village drama troupes in order to create a continuous source of entertainment and propaganda at the local level following their departure. These troupes, told to "write it yourself, direct it yourself, act it yourself, and support it yourself,"[15] were to be fully self-sufficient. Once organized, amateur drama troupes could then aid the land reform campaign in neighboring villages, as well as continue to stage state-friendly performances following the completion of agrarian reform.

Traditional art and artists in Hubei

Decades of endemic warfare had devastated Hubei's professional drama troupes, but cultural workers venturing into the countryside found the province's operatic traditions alive and well. Home to a rich tradition of folk art, Hubei boasted twenty-two distinct opera styles, with rural audiences especially favoring Chu opera (Chuju).[16] The popularity of Chu opera in the countryside was not mirrored in cities, where urban audiences and the Guomindang held local opera and traditional artists in disdain and favored imported styles, most notably Peking opera and spoken dramas. During the Republican Era, for example, the Guomindang regime sought to use Peking opera and spoken dramas to promote patriotism and raise funds, while at the same time banning "vulgar" Chu opera works. In 1946, the Hankou city government forced hundreds of

---

[13] Hubei, like all Chinese provinces, was still an overwhelmingly rural society, with over 80% of the population living in the countryside. Shi Hu, "Zhunbei canjia tugai" [Prepare to participate in land reform] HBWY 2.4 (1950), 23.

[14] "Hubei nongcun wenyi gongzuo zuotan" [Conference on literature and arts work in rural Hubei] HBWY 1.4 (1950), 5.

[15] "Kuoda he gonggu nongcun jutuan yundong" [Enlarge and consolidate the rural drama troupe movement] HBWY 3.5 (1951), 11.

[16] Chen Meilan, *Hubei wenyi 50 nian*, 164.

Chu opera artists to report for ideological training, but did not make the same demands on Peking opera artists.[17] The following year the city government, working with the provincial Department of Education, again singled out local opera and artists as in need of reform.[18]

Peking opera, China's "national opera" and the most popular dramatic form in Hubei's cities, remained a curiosity in the countryside. During the inaugural Hubei Peasant Association Representative Congress, representatives revealed that their fellow peasants disliked Peking opera, which rarely found its way to rural Hubei. According to a representative from Nanzhang County, village audiences found Peking opera unintelligible and only watched these shows for their visual spectacle.[19] Peasants simply could not understand the northern dialect used by Peking opera actors, and Hubei actors attempting to mimic northern accents only made things worse.[20]

Representatives also expressed displeasure with *yangge* opera, which they found equally foreign, despite the fact that the Communist Party had heavily promoted this northern style as distinctly Chinese. One peasant representative suggested that this was a response to unfamiliar content, and pointed to an important scene in *The White-Haired Girl* that involved dumplings; the representative noted that in Hubei peasants did not eat dumplings and would thus misunderstand the significance of the moment. The real problem, of course, lay in the fact that *yangge* performances seemed foreign to Hubei audiences. Villagers in Huanggang County made their love of local styles clear during a drama festival that included a showdown between Chu opera and *yangge* performances. Voting with their feet, the audience showed a clear preference for Chu opera and criticized *yangge* as incomprehensible.[21] With the Communists' favored form of *yangge* openly rejected by Hubei audiences, cultural workers would need to perform local operas to attract rural audiences.

Cultural workers and cultural work teams

As the PLA turned Hubei's major cities over to Communist Party control in the summer of 1949, leaders of the newly created provincial Wenlian

[17] *Hubei sheng zhi*, 95–103.
[18] Hubei sheng jiaoyuting, "Hubei sheng jiaoyuting gailiang ben sheng difang xiju de baogao" [Report from the Hubei province department of education on improving local opera] HPA LS10–1–1122 (1947), 2–4.
[19] "Nongmin daibiao tan wenyi," 9.
[20] Li Feixiong, "Jingshan renmin jutuan" [Jingshan People's Drama Troupe] HBWY 2.5 (1950), 21.
[21] "Hubei nongcun wenyi gongzuo zuotan," 6–7.

had few cultural workers at their disposal, bluntly admitting that "Hubei cultural work lacks a foundation and only now is work getting started."[22] Despite this inauspicious beginning, the prospects for Hubei cultural work improved greatly with the influx of experienced cultural workers from North China.[23] And even though Hubei lacked a proper art academy, the province trained and mobilized cultural workers through newly created cadre schools.[24] Hubei Revolutionary University graduated the most prestigious cultural workers, but academies also sprouted up at lower administrative levels to help train cadres. The Jingzhou Propaganda Team, for example, had about thirty members, with nine trained at Hubei Revolutionary University and the rest graduating from the local Jingzhou Revolutionary Cadre Academy.[25]

Wenlian gave these newly minted cultural workers a complex set of tasks to carry out in rural Hubei. While dramatic creation and performance were always important concerns, cultural workers had to serve the dominant political campaigns of the day, which in the first years of the PRC meant, above all, land reform. Agrarian reform was in fact one of the "three major responsibilities" given to Hubei cultural workers in 1950, alongside disseminating propaganda and artistic creation.[26] The experiences of the Xishui County Cultural Work Team, however, reveal the difficulty of juggling artistic and political responsibilities. As the team traveled throughout the county, members made sure to balance their time between implementing land reform work and organizing amateur drama troupes, at times joining the two responsibilities by performing dramas during political meetings. But the heavy demands of political and cultural organization left no time for cultural creation.[27]

Hubei's cultural authorities organized its growing army of cultural workers into work groups at the provincial, county, and district levels. The units organized through Hubei's Wenlian and cultural centers were

---

[22] "Wei Hubei de wenyi goingzuo da hao jichu" [Create a strong foundation for Hubei's cultural work] HBWY 1.1 (1949), 2.

[23] *Hubei sheng zhi*, 151.

[24] The Hubei Mass Arts Academy (Qunzhong yishu xueyuan) was not founded until 1952. A second branch opened in 1953. In 1953, the province opened an actor training course (Yanyuan xunlian ban) and an Opera Academy (Xiqu xueyuan). Hubei sheng wenhuaju, "Hubei sheng wenhuaju 1954 nian Hubei sheng wenhua shiye jigou juchang qingkuang, dianyingyuan deng tongjibiao," 6.

[25] Zhang Jianchen, "Guanyu Jingzhou xuanchuan dui" [Regarding Jingzhou's propaganda team] HBWY 2.1 (1950), 37.

[26] Cheng Tan, "Hubei wenyi gongzuozhe dangqian san da renwu" [Hubei literature and arts workers current three big responsibilities] HBWY 2.6 (1950), 10–16.

[27] "Xishui wengongtuan fadong nongcun wenyu gongzuo chubu jiegou" [Summary of the Xishui Cultural Work Team's mobilization of rural cultural entertainment] HBTX #3 (1951), 11–13.

typically called "cultural work teams" (either *wengongtuan* or *wengongdui*), with "propaganda teams" (*xuanchuandui*) organized by the prefectural Communist Party branches. PLA drama troupes also performed for villagers, teaching *yangge* dancing and putting on large-scale revolutionary operas.[28] These PLA troupes, however, now focused on entertaining and motivating soldiers under the slogan "serve the soldiers" (*wei bing fuwu*), a play on Mao's call to "serve the people" (*wei renmin fuwu*).[29]

It was thus not military but civilian cultural work teams that took the lead in rural cultural campaigns. The most prestigious work teams were those directly organized by the provincial Wenlian. Provincial work teams drew on the talents of well-educated artists, with many team members having graduated from Hubei Revolutionary University.[30] These cultural work teams made several tours through the countryside in support of mass campaigns, performing operas, teaching artistic skills, and creating amateur drama troupes. Their activities, however, were unique in that they enjoyed the talent and resources to stage long and complex operas. They also possessed projectors to show movies in the countryside, an innovation village audiences greatly appreciated.[31] Despite their talents, these units were ultimately limited by their numbers, and the provincial Wenlian relied on lower-level organizations to fully promote mass campaigns and develop local amateur drama troupes.

In March 1950, Hubei's Wenlian thus called for the development of county and district-level cultural work teams, either by the prefectural Communist Party branch or the local Wenlian working through newly established cultural centers.[32] As archival documents from the following year demonstrate, the provincial Department of Education put much care into the creation and management of cultural work teams, which had to submit regular reports to cultural authorities at both the county and provincial levels. County-level cultural teams were instructed to use all methods of propaganda to promote state goals and develop rural culture. These teams, burdened with the problem of "few members but

---

[28] *Tianmen xian zhi* [Tianmen County gazetteer] (Wuhan: Hubei renmin chubanshe, 1989), 27.

[29] "Hubei junqu di er ci wengonghui bimu" [Hubei Military Region's second cultural work meeting closing ceremony] HBWY 2.6 (1950), 57.

[30] Li Xiannian, "Wenyi gongzuozhe ying zou de daolu" [The road that literature and arts workers should walk] HBWY 2.5 (1950), 16.

[31] Lin, "Hubei sheng wenhua gongzuotuan zai Xindi," 40. Film projection teams were in short supply at the outset of the PRC era. According to Paul Clark, there were only 100 such teams in 1949, although by 1955 there were 2,300 teams, roughly one per county. Clark, *Chinese Cinema*, 36

[32] Jiang Hantian, "Kaizhan yeyu de xiju huodong" [Promote amateur drama activities] HBWY 2.1 (1950), 9.

many tasks" (*ren shao shi duo*), had to ensure that every work team member was ready to serve in multiple capacities in order to carry out their prime directive of dissemination in the countryside, which meant staging short shows in local styles to reach rural audiences.[33]

Hubei's cultural authorities instructed work teams to devote a significant portion of their studies to learning local cultural forms. Work team leaders, furthermore, were explicitly instructed to reach out to and ally with local artists, with PRC officials noting that artists skilled in local opera might prove potentially powerful allies in the quest to make local culture serve political campaigns. These local artists proved difficult to work with, in part because of the many bad habits that cultural workers claimed to discover among such artists. Communist cultural authorities singled out overinflated self-worth, improper sexual relations, and above all opium use as endemic problems within the artistic community.[34] Cultural workers were instructed to take a tolerant approach to traditional artists, for example using persuasion to encourage artists to slowly give up opium. Wenlian leaders also took a lenient attitude towards old operas, announcing in the February 1950 Conference on Arts and Literature Work in Rural Hubei that given the paucity of new content works, old operas should be allowed to continue to flourish, at least for the time being.[35] But Communists distrusted the professional tendencies of traditional artists, and gave strict instructions to limit local artists to no more than one-third of any given work team. Old-style costumed performances, furthermore, had no place in work team repertoires.[36]

The need to quickly develop Hubei's cultural infrastructure elevated working with amateur performers to a top work team priority. The Department of Education thus directed teams to guide (*fudao*) amateur troupes, seen as the lynchpins of the rural culture movement. Cultural workers were to ensure amateurs mixed education and entertainment while at the same time raising the political and cultural levels of their charges. But work teams had to walk a fine line while developing these troupes, least amateurs seek to become professionals. Amateur performances, for example, were generally restricted to slack seasons.

---

[33] Hubei sheng renmin zhengfu wenjiaoting, "Hubei sheng renmin zhengfu wenjiaoting guanyu kaizhan xian ji wengong dui gongzuo de zhishi" [Directive from the Hubei province people's government Department of Education concerning developing cultural work team work at the county level] HPA SZ118-2-40 (1951), 1–2.

[34] Wang Keda, "Tianmen xian" [Tianmen County] HBWY 1.6 (1950), 38; Wang Keda, "Tianmen jiu yiren de gaizao" [Reforming Tianmen's old style artists] HBWY 2.5 (1950), 22.

[35] "Hubei nongcun wenyi gongzuo zuotan," 6.

[36] Hubei sheng renmin zhengfu wenjiaoting, "Hubei sheng renmin zhengfu wenjiaoting guanyu kaizhan xian ji wengong dui gongzuo de zhishi," 2.

And the Department of Education demanded that amateur troupes remain voluntary and firmly under the leadership (*lingdao*) of local governments and peasant associations. Work teams, finally, were encouraged to send artists to liaise with amateurs and create new dramas, thereby combing artistic creation with leadership of local artisits.[37]

A well-trained cultural work team was a potent force in the countryside, creating new works to promote mass campaigns, while at the same time organizing new cultural units to continue entertaining villagers with Communist approved messages. Indeed, while the initial call to organize county and district teams emphasized the use of short form shows, some of these units could match provincial work teams in staging long dramas, including the classic revolutionary operas *Wang Xiuluan* and *Red Leaf River*.[38] These teams, however, were not without faults. Some work teams had difficulty subordinating their artistic ideals to those of amateur dramatists and actors, an indication of the tension between elite urban artists and their rural counterparts. For example in late 1951, a provincial Wenlian team working in Honghu County encountered problems while staging *Majialing's Sky Clears*, a model opera created by an amateur village troupe. Work team members expressed their discontent with this opera, suggesting many ways to improve the show. Not until team leaders reminded these cultural workers that this opera had already been approved as a model by provincial cultural authorities did the show finally go on.[39] Another cultural work team, meanwhile, was criticized by a disgruntled audience member for its disrespectful staging of a new style Chu opera. Performing for a county cadre meeting, actors, especially those portraying villainous roles, hammed up their acting for laughs. This may have made for an enjoyable show for some, but for this critic the only result was lessening the impact of the villain's deeds and ruining the educational message of the performance.[40] This conflict between the demands of entertainment and education would prove to be one of the key tensions in the drama troupe movement.

The model drama troupe of Caodian Village

The provincial Wenlian had a mandate to use drama to advance Communist goals; its fortuitous meeting with Liu Shuying, discussed at the

---

[37] Ibid., 3.
[38] Wang Cangzhou, "Macheng wengongdui" [Macheng cultural work team] HBWY 2.2 (1950), 40.
[39] Jiang Peng and Jun Ming, "Zai tudi gaige xuanchuan gongzuo zhong" [Propaganda work in land reform] HBWY #6 (1952), 21–22.
[40] Chen Yi, "Hanchuan xian wengongdui yanxi taidu bu yansu" [The Hanchuan County cultural work team's performances are not serious] HBWY #2 (1952), 29.

outset of this chapter, provided a model to do so. Liu Shuying's troupe only developed after the botched struggling of Caodian's newly cast "local tyrant" Liu De'an during the campaign to "Oppose Local Tyrants." Accused of a number of truly heinous crimes, Liu De'an certainly seemed to fit the bill of a "local tyrant," yet the attempt to "struggle" him in January 1950 failed completely. Liu Shuying and her fellow activists then seized on the idea of dramatizing the crimes of Liu De'an in order to enlighten those who had been "tricked" into thinking he was a good man. The activists called together poor villagers to "speak bitterness" in order to collect information about his crimes, enlisting the village schoolteacher to take notes. The narratives of suffering spoken by Caodian villagers were quickly transformed into a simple script, complete with music and songs taken from the local repertoire.[41]

With *Caodian People's Bloody Hatred* (Caodian renmin xue chouhen) complete, Liu Shuying drew on newly established political organizations to mobilize over forty villagers to join what would eventually become the village drama troupe. Caodian's schoolteacher took charge of casting and directing the show, and after a few nights of rehearsals the troupe performed for an audience that numbered between four and five hundred, with some travelling over three miles to see the show. Reenacting the many crimes of Liu De'an, collected through "speaking bitterness," the show portrayed Liu collaborating with the Guomindang and exploiting the peasantry into extreme poverty. But as had been the case with *Red Leaf River* and other land reform operas, his sexual crimes truly drove the narrative. According to *Caodian People's Bloody Hatred*, Liu De'an had tricked a peasant into drunkenly gambling himself into utter poverty, leading the peasant to flee the village and eventually commit suicide. Liu De'an then forcibly took the dead man's wife as his concubine, and his continual mistreatment of his new concubine proved the emotional highlight of the narrative. By repackaging and representing the crimes of Liu De'an to his fellow villagers, this performance incited the audience to chant slogans and call for overthrow and execution of Liu De'an. The next day Caodian peasants successfully "struggled" Liu De'an and quickly did the same with other "local tyrants."[42]

Liu Shuying's drama troupe developed rapidly after Hubei promoted Caodian as a model for all provincial village troupes. The troupe, now under district-level direction, received funds from district leaders as well

---

[41] Lin Man, "Nongcun jutuan de daolu" [The path for rural drama troupes] HBTX #3 (1951), 5; Ding Tan, "Caodian cun cunjutuan shi zenyang chengli de" [How the Caodian Village Drama Troupe was established] HBWY 1.6 (1950), 20–21.

[42] Su Guangxi, "Caodian qu qunzhong jutuan" [Caodian District's Mass Drama Troupe] HBWY 2.5 (1950), 18; Ding Tan, "Caodian cun cunjutuan shi zenyang chengli de," 21–22.

as a share of the village's "struggle fruits." The troupe also worked together to open up wasteland to further fund its increasingly ambitious endeavors. Less than a year after its formation, the troupe boasted a repertoire of almost twenty operas, including the large-scale revolutionary operas *Liu Hulan*, *Wang Xiuluan*, and *Red Leaf River*. The troupe experimented with new forms of cultural production during the village's land reform, including all-female productions, and even began staging Peking operas.[43]

The troupe continued to create its own works, including *Tongzi ke*,[44] which the Communists published and promoted as a model opera throughout Hubei. Much like *Caodian People's Bloody Hatred*, this short opera presented the crimes of a "local tyrant landlord" in narrative form. In the opera, created for Caodian's land reform campaign, the landlord Li Ruian relies on his accounts manager Liu Quan and his "running dog" Xu Laoliu to terrorize the Zhou family and other poor peasants struggling to survive. As the opera opens, Li Ruian sings happily that he alone prospers, while peasants suffer through a prolonged drought. Breaking into spoken dialogue, he makes his evil nature clear: "I, Li Ruian, have both wealth and power, seeming to act for the good while I secretly harm people. Now the common people eat bark and grass roots, this is an excellent opportunity to make loans."[45] Li Ruian and his accounts manager devise a scheme to feed peasants substandard food in return for high payments. The narrative carefully depicts his exploitation of the peasantry, especially peasant women, until the arrival of the PLA marks a dramatic break in the plotline. As the opera ends, the landlord and his accomplice are tied up and carted off for "struggle," while peasants on stage celebrate the toppling of a "local tyrant."

Caodian served as a model for other villages throughout the campaign to create rural amateur drama troupes.[46] Its experiences, moreover, foreshadow important trends in the rapid development of rural drama troupes throughout Hubei. First, Caodian's amateur drama troupe owed its creation to a mass political campaign. Second, village political and educational organizations proved instrumental in staffing and leading Caodian's troupe. Third, as the troupe grew, Caodian peasants pushed for more shows and in more styles, while the troupe took advantage of opportunities to tour outside of the village. These three trends proved

---

[43] Su Guangxi, "Caodian qu qunzhong jutuan," 18–20.
[44] This title is a reference to the money-making scheme hatched by the opera's villainous characters.
[45] Junxian Caodian qunzhong jutuan, "Tongzi ke," HBWY 2.5 (1950), 54.
[46] *Hubei sheng zhi*, 465.

commonplace, but the last is particularly noteworthy. While Hubei's cultural leaders never addressed these issues, Caodian's model actors were moving towards professional status.

The Rural Amateur Drama Troupe Campaign, 1950–1951

The mobilization of amateur village drama troupes had a clear and necessary link to Hubei's land reform campaigns. As emphasized in November 1950 at the first Hubei Cultural Representative Congress, a provincial meeting following the national and regional models discussed in Chapter 5, this represented the strategy for all rural cultural work. In his report to the Congress, Xu Daoqi demanded cultural workers "take root" and disperse throughout the province during the land reform campaigns. Singling out Caodian's drama troupe as a model, Xu emphasized that the development of village troupes represented only one aspect of cultural work, which would require full commitment to taking part in land reform and using culture to advance the campaign.[47] The land reform and village drama troupe campaigns even used an identical organizational logic, trying out mobilization techniques in "test point" districts and villages before moving to full-scale implementation. Thus, in Pengxing, a "test point" district for both campaigns, cultural work teams organized by the Xiaogan County Wenlian helped villagers oppose "local tyrants" while at the same time organizing amateur drama troupes.[48] The Xishui County Cultural Work Team similarly implemented both campaigns in January 1951, using visits with poor villagers to seek out both political and cultural activists; political activists formed the core of Peasant Associations, while cultural activists headed *yangge* dance teams and drama troupes.[49]

Excepting the Caodian troupe's internal and spontaneous mobilization, two types of agents spurred the formation of village drama troupes: external work teams or inspired village activists. Examples abound of work teams organizing troupes in the campaign, but one of the finest comes from Huanggang County's Shahetu region, where a provincial Wenlian cultural work team organized seven drama troupes while also helping promote land reform through dramatic performances. By persuading skeptical village cadres that cultural work could in fact aid land

---

[47] Xu Daoqi, "Zai tugai zhong puji, zai tuigai zhong shenggen" [Spread through land reform, take root through land reform] HBWY 2.6 (1950), 21–29.

[48] "Fudao Huchenzhacun jutuan de jingyan" [Experiences from training the Huchenzha Village Drama Troupe] HBWY 3.4 (1951), 40–41.

[49] "Xishui wengongtuan fadong nongcun wenyu gongzuo chubu zongjie," 11.

reform, the work team developed local talent, organized troupes, and helped amateurs create and stage original operas. After establishing the Huilongshan Village Drama Troupe, for example, the provincial work team and the troupe collaboratively produced *Zhang Family Enmity* (Zhang jia yuanchou). This opera, describing the crimes and overthrow of a real-life "local tyrant," exemplifies the tight synchronization between cultural and political performances achieved during the latter stages of land reform.[50]

Despite the robust mobilization of cultural work teams, Hubei was simply too vast and too populous for teams to visit every village. But by creating drama troupes in select villages, cultural work teams dramatically enhanced their organizational reach. Drama troupes established by cultural work teams instantly became part of the amateur troupe campaign, inspiring activists in other villages. In this second organizational model, amateur drama troupes visited neighboring villages and staged local operas, promoting mass campaigns and providing a powerful example for their host villages. First, villagers living in rural areas, almost universally bereft of professional drama troupes, saw compelling shows staged in their beloved local styles, which helped meet a voracious demand for entertainment. Second, many dramas introduced audiences to revolutionary performances, which they could replicate during land reform and in everyday life in "New China." Third, seeing their neighbors' mastery of cultural and political performances, many host villages quickly imitated their guests and formed their own troupes.

The origins and development of the Minji Village Drama Troupe illustrate the draw of politics and entertainment. This Macheng County village was situated near a "test point" village, which had recently organized a drama troupe during its land reform. After this new troupe performed in Minji, local villagers pushed activists to emulate the touring actors, spurring a core group of cadres and members of village political organizations to come together and form a troupe of twenty members. The troupe created an original opera, successfully staging *The Big Tyrant Wu Jinkui* (Da eba Wu Jinkui), a twenty-three scene show that explicated the many crimes of the recently "struggled" Wu Jinkui. This performance provoked a passionate response from its audience, which angrily threw rocks at the stage; fearing for his life as rural revolution became reality, the actor portraying Wu Jinkui fled the scene. Later, some villagers expressed their disappointment in the drama, but only because their own sufferings had not been included in the narrative. As a result, the

---

[50] "Cun jutuan yundong zai Shahetu" [Village drama troupe movement in Shahetu] HBWY 3.4 (1951), 34–38.

drama troupe expanded its first opera into an epic forty-eight scene show. The troupe soon took their act on the road, inspiring the formation of more drama troupes.[51]

Three clear trends can be observed in the patterns of the rural drama troupe campaign. First, the most literate members of rural society, especially elementary schoolteachers, played an indispensable role in the campaigns. Wenlian leaders demanded that rural schoolteachers help in the campaign and from an early stage called on educators to take a leading role in the local cultural scene, reasoning that their literacy and understanding of village life made them essential at the local level.[52] Village schools thus served as a locus of cultural activity, a phenomenon evident in the formation of Huanggang County's Liujiaying Village Drama Troupe. Liujiaying's elementary schoolteacher had worked with a sub-county cultural center to organize this drama troupe; armed with six issues of *Hubei Literature and Arts* and directives to follow the Caodian model, the teacher first recruited actors and musicians. After rehearsing at the village school, the teacher's troupe successfully staged its first show in front of an enthusiastic crowd of over a thousand villagers. This opera was none other than *Tongzi ke*, Caodian's own model creation. Shortly after this show, the Liujiaying troupe also followed the Caodian example by touring the countryside.[53]

A second trend that emerged during the campaign was the importance of village political leaders in the cultural realm. Successful troupes overcame local opposition to cultural activities and brought village leadership into key positions of power within the troupe itself. Reports from Wenlian cultural work teams in the campaigns against local tyrants in Xiahe, an administrative village, provide an early case of local cadre opposition to the development of cultural organizations. In Xiahe, local leaders appreciated short performances before political meetings, but balked at allowing full operas, fearing these shows would negatively affect production. Despite several requests, the team did not perform a single opera, nor did it establish any amateur cultural organizations.[54] In April, 1951,

---

[51] "Macheng xian minjicun jutuan de chengzhang" [The growth of Macheng County's Minji Village Drama Troupe] HBWY 4.5 (1951), 29–30.

[52] Significantly, one of the main cultural projects given to elementary schoolteachers was leading the creation and staging of dramatic performances. Li Shi, "Wei zhankai nongcun wenyi xuanchuan yundong zhi nongcun xiaoxue jiaoshi yi feng gongkai de xin" [An open letter to rural elementary schoolteachers concerning developing the rural literature and arts campaign] HBWY 3.4 (1951), 11–12.

[53] Liu Sheng, "Liujiayingcun jutuan shi zenyang chengli de" [How the Liujiaying Village Drama Troupe was established] HBWY 3.5 (1951), 34–35.

[54] Deng Si, "Xiaxiang gongzuo zhong de ji dian renshi" [A few realizations from working in the countryside] HBWY 1.3 (1950), 39–42.

another Wenlian team encountered similar opposition in Huanggang's Shahetu region, where local cadres focused on production and ignored cultural work. Wenlian cultural workers, however, aimed to coordinate with the ongoing land reform campaign and emphasized increasing production, eventually founding seven village drama troupes, including the Majialing Village Drama Troupe, which would create the aforementioned model opera *Majialing's Sky Clears*. The performance of Majialing actors inspired their local cadre to proclaim: "Our village does not lose face. It doesn't matter if it is politics, economics, or culture. We have success in all areas."[55]

A final trend that characterized the organization of rural drama troupes was the reluctance of many villagers to perform on stage, either because of the traditional bias against actors or simple embarrassment. The Xishui County Cultural Work Team, for example, had difficulty finding amateur performers to join troupes. Male peasants feared losing face and refused to join; they also discouraged their wives from participating, fearing such freedoms would lead to divorce. Only patient work through the standard tools of mass campaigns, starting with sending activists to privately meet with reluctant villagers, persuaded peasants to join drama troupes. The work team also used simple propaganda techniques, including this slogan to encourage shy villagers: "Don't fear doing a bad job, just show up every day" (*bu pa gao bu hao, zhiyao tiantian dao*). The cultural work team found success with these techniques, organizing one drama troupe, and over twenty *yangge* dancing teams, which could be later converted into drama troupes.[56]

Amateur troupes and amateur performance in the countryside

Despite some initial reluctance, drama troupes found that the villagers needed to stage cultural performances in the countryside, and as might be expected given the connections between cultural and political performances, activists dominated troupe leadership positions. In Sui County's Dabeidian People's Drama Troupe, for example, the village peasant association chair led the troupe, with the village head and elementary schoolteacher serving as secondary leaders.[57] Bringing local leaders into village drama troupes emphasized that staging dramas was

---

[55] "Cun jutuan yundong zai Shahetu," 35.

[56] "Xishui wengongtuan fadong nongcun wenyu gongzuo chubu zongjie," 10–14.

[57] Deng Ganzhi, "Dabeidian remin jutuan de chengzhang" [Growth of the Dabeidian People's Drama Troupe] HBWY 3.5 (1951), 40–41.

now a political and revolutionary activity. These political activists, furthermore, could ensure that drama served mass campaigns, helping to coordinate cultural and political performances in the countryside. Finally, as discussed below, bringing village political actors into troupes often proved financially advantageous.

Besides local activists and teachers, rural artists formed a primary component of village amateur drama troupes. In stark contrast to the era of Red Drama, when the Communists shunned traditional artists, Wenlian leaders emphasized the need to work with whatever talent could be mobilized.[58] Cultural workers were instructed to seek out talented and politically progressive local artists, with the aim of turning these talented individuals into activists.[59] At the same time, however, Wenlian leaders warned against overreliance on local artists, as they could potentially leave the village to sell their performances during traditional festival seasons.[60] As this suggests, there was real tension between emerging amateur drama troupes and local artists who had traditionally earned an income through their performances. As the campaign kicked into high gear in mid-1951, Wenlian leaders warned cultural workers to heed special attention to local artists, least they withhold their talents out of fear that amateurs were "stealing their rice bowls."[61] The strong demand for talent made local artists an essential part of rural drama troupes, but their tendency to perform for profit helped push many village troupes away from amateur status.

Two other groups played a key role in troupe membership: children and women. Often the first to be mobilized because of their ties with village schools, children did not share their elders' concerns with public performance. In Baiyang Village, one young actor was quoted as declaring: "I joined the drama troupe, but I would not join the Youth League. Acting is fun."[62] Leaders of the aforementioned Xishui County Cultural Work Team, meanwhile, knew they would have difficulty with shy adults when only children dared join newly created *yangge* dancing teams.[63] While children made natural actors, the same could not be said of

---

[58] Shuo Ming, "Wei Hubei de wenyi gongzuo da hao jichu" [Create a strong foundation for Hubei's cultural work] HBWY 1.1 (1949), 2.
[59] Xie Feng, "Guanyu Hubei renmin wenyi de chuangzuo yu minjian wenyi de gaizao wenti" [On the problem of Hubei literature and art creation and folk art reform] HBWY 1.3 (1950) 4.
[60] "Cun jutuan yundong zai Shahetu," 37.
[61] "Kuoda he gonggu nongcun jutuan yundong," 11.
[62] Liu Ranying and Tian Jun, "Xishui Baiyang xiang jutuan zenyang jiehe fucha zhengdun zuzhi" [How Xishui Baiyang Village Drama Troupe coordinated with the reexamination campaign to rectify organization] HBWY #10 (1952), 33.
[63] "Xishui wengongtuan fadong nongcun wenyu gongzuo chubu zongjie," 12.

women, who had long been excluded from public cultural performances, especially in the countryside. Yet from the very start of the amateur drama troupe movement in Caodian, women actors played a starring role in rural campaigns. By the time the troupe was promoting anti-American propaganda in mid-1951, its repertoire included all-female numbers. Despite traditional mores, most drama troupes had a significant female presence: Tianmen County's Liuhe Village Drama Troupe, for example, reported that eighteen of its forty-one members were women.[64] Women dominated some troupes, as was the case with the Yuanquan Village Drama Troupe of Jingshan County. Organized through the local women's association, this troupe had such a preponderance of female actors that women initially performed male roles in drag.[65]

Provincial cultural leaders had little explanation of how to fund amateur performances, issuing only the vague instruction that they should be "self-supporting." A few fortunate troupes received publishing royalties, but the vast majority were not so lucky.[66] And while the Communists intended amateur drama troupes to operate with low overheads, some expenses, especially lighting oil, were simply unavoidable.[67] The Caodian model troupe had reclaimed wasteland for cultivation while also receiving funding from the Jun County government, a share of the "struggle fruits" from the village, and donations from "enlightened gentry."[68] Only the first of these methods of financing the troupe, reclaiming wasteland, was actively promoted by provincial cultural leaders, but this represented a significant if not impossible burden for most peasants.[69] Receiving a share of the property confiscated during land reform, meanwhile, meant that other villagers would receive less, in effect charging the entire village a fee for the activities of the troupe. Yet some villages, including Caodian, seemed to have used this gift as recognition of the role played by the troupe in the process of rural revolution. Some troupes also received funding from peasant associations or local governments, as seen in the

[64] "Tianmen xian Liuhecun jutuan zhengdun qianhou" [Before and after the rectification of Tianmen County's Liuhe Village Drama Troupe] HBWY #4 (1953), 31.
[65] "Jingshan xian Yuanquancun jutuan de chengzhang" [Growth of the Jingshan County Yuanquan Village Drama Troupe] HBWY 4.2 (1951), 27.
[66] *Huangshi shi Xishui xian wenyi huodong diaocha baodao*[Report on the investigation of arts and literature activities in Huangshi City and Xishui County] (Hankou: Zhongnan renmin wenxue yishu chubanshe, 1953), 28.
[67] Ma Liqun, "Huanggang xiangumiaocun jutuan qingkuang" [Situation of the Huanggang Xiangumiao Village Drama Troupe] HBWY 3.5 (1951), 38.
[68] Ding Tan, "Caodian cun cunjutuan shi zenyang chengli de," 22; Su Guangxi, "Caodian qu qunzhong jutuan," 18.
[69] As noted in Chapter 5, some cultural workers found this model of funding unsustainable. It is possible that the extra farming carried out by these "model" performers was overstated.

Jun County donation to the Caodian troupe. Such funding was much more likely when political leaders had a stake in the troupe, a point at least one Wenlian correspondent made explicit.[70] Overall, the Communists provided limited and irregular funding for drama troupes, but cultural authorities deemed this proper given their amateur status. Many troupes, however, harbored aspirations that transcended this purposefully limited vision.

Amateur performance formed another source of conflict between provincial leaders and village troupes. Village drama troupes proved capable of staging a full range of cultural performances, ranging from simple folk tunes to long-form operas both revolutionary and traditional. But Hubei's cultural leaders clearly preferred one type of work: short-form local operas narrating village life and true events. In their call to develop rural drama troupes, Wenlian leaders argued that long-form operas had no place in the repertoire of an amateur troupe, pointing to an unnamed drama troupe that wasted six months rehearsing *The White-Haired Girl*. Instead, Wenlian leaders suggested following the Caodian model of shorter works focused on local affairs,[71] which had the added benefit of simplifying the need for costumes and sets, always in short supply. The experiences of Wanhe Village's drama troupe suggest the limitations of amateur status; lacking costumes, makeup, and proper musical instruments, the troupe could barely perform short numbers.[72]

Village troupes also needed stages on which to perform, but Hubei's traditional stages, variously called opera stages (*xitai*), rain stages (*yutai*), opera towers (*xilou*), or ten-thousand year stages (*wannian tai*), were pavilion-style structures intended for elite audiences. These stages, furthermore, were extremely limited in number, with only sixteen surviving past 1949, all of which would be destroyed by 1958.[73] As these structures were clearly not suitable for staging the amateur drama troupe movement, rural dramatists adeptly found alternatives in improvised or cheaply constructed stages, colloquially known as "grass stages" (*caotai*). These venues came in two basic varieties. The first was the earth stage or terrace (*tutai*), which was simply a natural topographical feature that

---

[70] Song Genshui, "Kaizhan nongcun wenyi huodong de yijian" [Opinions on village literature and arts activities] HBWY 2.6 (1950), 59.

[71] "Kuoda he gonggu nongcun jutuan yundong," 11.

[72] Wanhe villagers focused their displeasure on the troupes' musical skills, and as the troupe produced better music, villagers were increasingly satisfied. Ding Qiang, "Cheng xiang jutuan chengli jingguo" [Town and country drama troupes' course to establishment] HBWY 2.5 (1951), 20–21.

[73] *Wenyizhi: ziliao xuanji liu* [Literature and arts gazetteer: compiled materials, Volume VI] (Hubei, 1984), 460–461.

could function as a stage. The second type of grass stage was a "built stage" (*datai*), a quickly constructed wooden stage.[74] While the simplistic nature of these "built stages" made them appropriate for village drama troupes, one special type of *datai* deserves mention for exemplifying the theatricality of rural revolution: the *fanshen* stage. This stage, used for struggling class enemies in land reform and other mass campaigns, was often built and torn down as needed. But as Wenlian cultural workers discovered, some villages "simply never tore down their *fanshen* stages, which village drama troupes used for putting on shows."[75]

Audiences flocked to these rural stages, traveling long distances and enduring long waits, with one frustrated correspondent complaining of having to wait for hours for a show to start.[76] The lack of ticket sales, the informal nature of many performances, and the tendency to inflate audience numbers all complicate attempts to gauge the actual size of village audiences. Thus, while many troupes estimated their audiences at around 1,000, Xiaogan cultural workers boasted that the three drama troupes they organized performing twenty-four shows for a total audience of 40,000, an average of 1,666 per show.[77] The aforementioned Yuanquan Village Drama Troupe was by far the most popular troupe, at least according to numbers advanced by the troupe and the Jingshan County Wenlian. This troupe claimed to perform twenty-one shows in support of the mass campaigns of 1951 for an audience of over 91,000, which would put average attendance for each show at well over 4,000.[78] But even at the far more reasonable average attendance figures put forth by the provincial Wenlian of about eight hundred per show,[79] it is clear that rural troupes promised the Communists an impressive cultural reach in the Hubei countryside.

In selecting works to stage, troupes had two basic options: perform a ready-made drama or an original creation. But rural correspondents spoke of a cultural plague that afflicted the countryside, a script famine (*juben huang*) that greatly vexed would-be dramatists.[80] Provincial cultural leaders had noted in late 1949 that despite a long history of revolutionary activism dating back to the 1920s, Hubei largely lacked progressive

---

[74] *Luotian xian zhi* [Luotian County gazetteer] (Beijing: Zhonghua shuju, 1998), 597–598.

[75] "Cun jutuan yundong zai Shahetu," 37.

[76] Li Ruzhou, "Dui difang wengongtuan de liang dian jianyi" [Two suggestions for local cultural work teams] HBWY 1.6 (1950), 23.

[77] "Zuzhi cun jutuan de ji dian tihui" [A few realizations from organizing village drama troupes] HBWY 3.5 (1951), 35.

[78] "Jingshan xian Yuanquan cun jutuan de chengzhang," 27.

[79] "Kuoda he gonggu nongcun jutuan yundong," 10–11.

[80] "Huangpi xian Zhangdian qu de nongcun jutuan" [Huangpi County Zhangdian District drama troupes] HBTX #6 (1951), 25.

folk art.[81] Thus, creating new works and providing scripts for drama troupes represented major responsibilities for cultural workers. Wenlian distributed scripts through *Hubei Literature and Arts* and other publications, including special collections of local operas. Cultural centers also published and distributed dramas, but the reach of Hubei's cultural infrastructure, while far beyond that of the deposed Guomindang regime, was still developing. Thus, while drama troupes had access to scripts penned by professional cultural workers and other amateur troupes, script supply never satisfied the voracious local demand, providing another impetus for amateurs to follow the Caodian model and try their hands at creation.

Explicitly directing amateurs to undertake cultural creation, cultural and political leaders demanded performances based on real-life village events and characters in the belief that such shows best suited the demands of mass political campaigns. Once again, the Caodian model proved instructive. The drama troupe's first creation provoked an outpouring of emotion and anger amongst its audience, leading directly to the successful struggling of the "local tyrant" Liu De'an. The Caodian troupe's next creation, *Tongzi ke*, was among a number of amateur produced scripts published and distributed throughout Hubei, so that the "real-life" events of some villages, captured in operas such as *Tongzi ke* and *Majialing's Sky Clears*, were reenacted on the grass stages of faraway villages.[82]

In creating "real-life" narrative dramas in the service of mass campaigns, amateurs had to balance the accurate recreation of village life with the demands of entertainment and especially politics. The same could be said for works created by professional cultural workers. Hubei Party Secretary Li Xiannian, for example, reminded cultural workers to always create art that served political ends. Yet Li also insisted that cultural workers never distort or misrepresent reality, lest they become the reincarnation of the Guomindang's Central News Agency, which he characterized as a conveyor of lies to trick the masses.[83] Despite Li Xiannian's call to "never tell a single lie," the Communists favored narratives that dogmatically followed the party line and promoted the synchronization of cultural and political performances in the countryside. Communist-influenced dramas, for example, promoted the Maoist view of village society as inherently cleaved by class lines and class struggle, with Communist-led "liberation" the only hope for exploited peasants living under an evil landlord class. But at the same time, these

[81] Xie Feng, "Guanyu Hubei renmin wenyi de chuangzuo yu minjian wenyi de gaizao wenti," 2–3.

[82] Su Guangxu, "Caodian qu qunzhong jutuan," 18–20.

[83] Li Xiannian, "Wenyi gongzuozhe ying zou de daolu," 14–15.

"real-life" dramas had to make sense to audiences, who were the subjects of the drama just as they were the objects of the performance. Thus, many local troupes took creating truthful dramas seriously. In Sui County's Wanhe Village, for example, a large amateur drama troupe with over one hundred members, unable to think of an appropriate "real-life" local villain, instead wrote a drama based on a popular local ditty concerning the crimes of "white bandit armies."[84] Audiences could also act to ensure truth in dramatic performances. The previously mentioned Minji Village Drama Troupe staged an opera detailing the crimes of its "local tyrant" Wu Jinkui. After the show's first performance, the audience demanded a rewrite to include their own tales of suffering, nearly doubling the length of the show.[85]

By focusing their creative energies on the production of short operas in local musical styles, many amateur drama troupes overcame the limitations of amateur status and developed a substantial repertoire of works. The Yuanquan Village Drama Troupe, initially forced by audiences to repeatedly stage their only show, was only one of many troupes to rapidly develop a diverse repertoire to meet the rapacious demand for entertainment in the countryside.[86] Despite the value Communist cultural authorities placed on original amateur creations, troupes needed scripts created by professional dramatists to fully satisfy audiences and their commitment to supporting mass campaigns. Wanhe Village's drama troupe, for example, would rehearse and stage almost twenty shows in its first year in existence. While original creations won them acclaim, most of these shows originated from outside of Wanhe.[87] But when faced with the difficulty of creation, many amateurs simply chose to stage traditional numbers, which continued to draw large audiences, despite the Communists' relentless promotion of modern works. As Hubei's amateur drama troupes performed ever-more shows for an ever-larger audience, the pull of traditional opera and professional status often proved too strong to resist. With a growing disparity between cultural and political performances, it was time for Hubei's cultural authorities to discipline the province's growing army of amateur drama troupes.

The rectification of rural drama troupes, 1951–1953

While cultural workers typically presented village troupes as well-organized and effective, many observers noted that the drama troupe

---

[84] Ding Qiang, "Cheng xiang jutuan chengli jingguo," 20.
[85] "Macheng xian Minji cun jutuan de chengzhang," 29–30.
[86] "Jingshan xian Yuanquan cun jutuan de chengzhang," 28.
[87] Ding Qiang, "Cheng xiang jutuan chengli jingguo," 20.

campaign suffered from recurring problems. Cultural workers detailed the difficulties of mobilizing actors. Troupe directors complained about the scarcity of quality scripts and their own struggles to create new works. Correspondents, finally, wrote in to criticize lackluster performances. This stream of complaints, however, increased dramatically with the "rectification" of amateur drama troupes. Once again, provincial leaders used political mass campaigns to carry out cultural work. Previously land reform had provided the context for the establishment of village drama troupes. Now a land reform "re-examination" campaign provided the context for an investigation into the membership and inner workings of the province's amateur drama troupes to ensure a tighter fit between cultural and political performances.

Where Caodian served as the model for a properly functioning drama troupe, Jintai Village of Huanggang County served as the model for the rectification of the many problems now afflicting Hubei's troupes. Founded in early 1951 after a visit from a neighboring village troupe, the Jintai troupe burst into the spotlight after its director attended a Huangguang County Congress for cultural representatives, where his questionable class background was exposed. According to Hubei's cultural authorities, this director, posing as a middle peasant, was in fact the son of a landlord. Deciding the Jintai troupe was in need of rectification, the county Wenlian launched an investigation that revealed that the troupe had been performing as an old-style *xibanzi* opera outfit. After an overhaul by visiting cultural workers, Jintai would reform its troupe, but the village would continue to provide a model for the rectification of all Hubei troupes.[88]

The rectification campaign uncovered many "class enemies" within the ranks of Hubei amateurs, but the issue of proper membership was not new. The problem of class emerged as early as October 1950 when Xiaogan cultural workers organized drama troupes in "test point" villages in Pengxing District. As these cultural workers later explained in their report to the provincial Wenlian, only those with proper political class backgrounds had been allowed to join the troupe. Yet Wenlian responded by warning against this practice, noting that such a "closed door" policy would limit the abilities of amateur troupes.[89] Even after the rectification campaign began, Wenlian continued to warn against setting the standard of membership too high. The issue was not always class: Wenlian chastised Minjiahe Village for not allowing a woman with a

[88] Huanggang Jintaicun jutuan de zhengdun jingyan" [Experiences from the rectification of the Huanggang Jintai Village Drama Troupe] HBWY 4.3 (1951), 25–27.
[89] "Zuzhi cun jutuan de ji dian tihui," 33.

questionable past to join its troupe.[90] But even as Wenlian pushed troupes to welcome new members, an investigation into one drama troupe in Xishui County revealed a membership process that confounded cultural workers: in order to join the troupe, one first needed the recommendation of a current troupe member. This recommendation would then be discussed and voted on by a small group before being brought to the entire troupe for another discussion and vote. If the lucky applicant was approved, he or she still had to endure a two-month probationary period. One village leader had undergone this application process, only to be ultimately rejected for a lack of enthusiasm.[91]

Yet shortly after publicizing the Jintai model, Wenlian leaders reversed course and railed against the many landlords and hooligans in drama troupes, a problem ascribed to emphasizing artistic talent and entertainment over education and political ideology. Jintai Village's mistake of entrusting its troupe to a landlord son was quickly trumped by a nearby village whose director had served the former puppet regime.[92] One of many troupes criticized for emphasizing talent and entertainment over class background and ideological purity, Jingshan County's Madian Village had made the mistake of giving starring roles to attractive young women from landlord families.[93] Statistics from the four counties and two towns under the jurisdiction of the Huanggang region demonstrate the scope of "rectification": investigating 449 drama troupes, cultural workers discovered and expelled 1,815 landlords, reactionaries, cult members, and hooligans. Many of these suspect individuals held positions of leadership and were charged with using their positions to work against land reform and other mass campaigns.[94] For comparison, the Sangdian village troupe's forty-seven members included six landlords, six rich peasants, two former Guomindang members, two former members of the Guomindang Youth League, and two hooligans, leaving only eleven poor peasants and twenty-four middle peasants.[95]

[90] Yang Baozhen, "Zai tudi gaige zhong jianli qi de cun jutuan" [The establishment of rural drama troupes in land reform] HBWY #12 (1952), 25.
[91] In response cultural workers suggested relaxing the requirements for joining the troupe. *Huangshi shi Xishui xian wenyi huodong diaocha baodao,* 29.
[92] Chen Yijin, Han Fengqi, and Ling Han, "Xiaogan pengxing qu cun jutan de yi xie pianxiang" [Some deviations in Xiaogan's Pengxing District village drama troupes] HBWY 4.9 (1951), 32.
[93] "Dajia ti yijian banhao cun jutuan" [Everyone raise opinions and create quality village drama troupes] HBWY #11 (1952), 5.
[94] "Nongcun jutuan yao xuanchuan Mao Zedong sixiang, jianjue fandui fengjian sixiang," 4.
[95] "Nongcun yeyu jutuan cunzai yanzhong wenti" [Serious problems exist in rural amateur drama troupes] HBWY #9 (1952), 32.

The rectification campaign also revealed that many drama troupes, increasingly focused on entertainment and profit, tended to develop the habits and styles of old-fashioned *xibanzi* opera troupes. This problem had emerged in Jintai, where the troupe hired expensive teachers to help them stage traditional operas, which could be performed for profit.[96] Cultural leaders, recognizing that the best village drama troupes tended to move towards professional status, frequently reminded troupes to remain amateur and never charge for shows. But the move to professional *xibanzi* status was prevalent throughout the countryside. An investigation into Anlu County drama troupes, for example, found extravagant spending on costumes and theatrical paraphernalia (*xingtou*), as well as improper funding methods. While these troupes did not directly charge for admission, they pressed peasants and local governments for payments. The Tongxing Village Drama Troupe, for example, forced all middle peasant households to give the troupe donations for its productions.[97]

Cultural leaders encouraged village drama troupes to perform hybrid dramas with political content, while still accepting that troupes would mix in folk songs and performances that drew on traditional operas. As some troupes moved toward professional status, however, they tended to abandon serious new-style shows for popular old operas, while other drama troupes inappropriately mixed the modern and the traditional. One critic, for example, wrote in to *Hubei Literature and Arts* to complain about the performance of *Marriage Law* (Hunyin fa) by the Sanzhou Village Drama Troupe. In this staging, the troupe narrated a supposedly contemporary story; but while the actors dressed in appropriately modern costumes, they acted like characters in traditional operas. Finding the plot unrealistic, the critic further noted that the female lead was dressed and made up to look like a seductress, "totally humiliating liberated laboring women." In sum, the critic charged that *Marriage Law* was nothing more than the traditional "lewd and corrupt" opera *The Street Peddler Sells Colored Thread* (Huolang mai huaxian) in a new and not at all convincing guise.[98]

Other drama troupes erred not by reverting to traditional operas but by actually promoting political messages that worked against the interests of the Communists. The investigation into Anlu County troupes, for

---

[96] "Huanggang Jintaicun jutuan de zhengdun jingyan," 25.
[97] "Nongcun yeyu jutuan cunzai yanzhong wenti," 33.
[98] The second show put on by the troupe that night, *Jiang Jieshi Takes Taiwan*, was equally worthy of complaint for portraying the Guomindang leader as a sad and tragic figure, causing some in the audience to take pity on him. Fan Ligong, "Dui Sanzhou xiang jutuan cuowu yanchu de piping" [Criticisms of the mistakes in the performances of the Sanzhou Village Drama Troupe] HBWY #12 (1952), 26–27.

example, found a host of issues with performances, including shows featuring contemporary characters speaking in classical styles, which audiences found amusing. But far more serious, some shows portrayed landlords as scholars and peasants as clowns. Actors performing as cadres wore green kerchiefs on their heads, suggesting that they had been cuckolded. Also just as bad was an opera concerning a soldier who volunteered to fight in Korea, staged by the drama troupe of the Sanhe administrative village. In this opera, based on a traditional number, the solider becomes corrupt and makes a fortune before returning home and taking multiple wives.[99] This performance directly contravened the new Marriage Law, as did the opera *Sending Fragrant Tea* (Song xiang cha), staged by the Shehe Village Drama Troupe. Detractors described this Chu opera as a haphazard mix of old and new, with an offensive plot concerning an incestuous brother–sister relationship.[100]

With the continuing presence of traditional operas, commonly regarded as "lewd and corrupt," it is little wonder that operas staged by village troupes often diverged from the PRC's new Marriage Law. Far more troubling for the state, some amateur dramas contradicted the land reform campaigns, a problem typically attributed to the mistake of letting landlords and other suspect elements into village drama troupes. This could lead to the reversal of expected village power relations. An investigation into Pengxing District troupes, for example, revealed a staging of *Beat the Horse Spirit* (Da ma shen) where a landlord actor played the peasant role and forced a poor peasant to play the horse spirit, whom he then beat on stage.[101] More seriously, one critic complained about *Rural Family Happiness* (Nong jia le), staged by the Zhaigang Village Drama Troupe, also from Pengxing. In this opera, a landlord scorns one of his daughters for marrying a peasant until land reform turned the landlord into a beggar. The once-scorned daughter takes pity on her father, supporting him and serving as a filial daughter. As the critic quickly noted, what kind of land reform opera would promote taking pity on landlords? Even if the story was true, he concluded, it should not be used as the basis for an opera.[102] Similarly, one Huanggang troupe, also said to be under the direction of landlords, created and staged *New People* (Xin ren), an opera that praised the lenient nature of the PLA and

---

[99] "Nongcun yeyu jutuan cunzai yanzhong wenti," 33.
[100] "Dajia ti yijian banhao cun jutuan," 6.
[101] Chen Yijin, Han Fengqi, and Ling Han, "Xiaogan pengxing qu cun jutan de yi xie pianxiang," 33.
[102] Shang Wen, "Dui Zhaigangcun jutuan shang yan *Nongjia le* de yijian" [Some opinions on the Zhaigang Village Drama Troupe's performance of *Rural Family Happiness*] HBWY 4.9 (1951), 33.

claimed that since the PLA had remade local tyrants and landlords, class struggle was no longer necessary. Hubei cultural leaders called *New People* and other operas deviating from proper Maoist performance as "sheer nonsense."[103]

Conclusion: mass culture, mass politics

Despite the serious "deviations" uncovered during the rectification campaign, Hubei's cultural workers had every right to be impressed by the results of the drive to establish amateur drama troupes throughout the province. Following the creation of the province's first recognized amateur drama troupe in Caodian Village in early 1950, cultural workers, rapidly deployed in the countryside for land reform, systematically developed an infrastructure of rural drama troupes. By the following summer, the province was home to at least 1,022 of these troupes, with Xishui, Macheng, and Huanggang counties each boasting over 100 troupes each.[104] Xishui went from three troupes to 106 troupes in just seven months; these troupes mobilized 3,465 actors, created 398 operas, and staged 1,260 performances for an estimated audience of 516,090.[105] By the time the campaign came to a close in late 1951, Hubei's cultural workers claimed to have created some 2,300 amateur rural drama troupes, a true provincial cultural army performing revolutionary drama throughout the countryside.[106] Archival documents from the provincial Department of Culture reveal that the number of troupes continued to grow in the aftermath of the campaign, rising to over six-thousand troupes by the mid-1950s.[107]

Hubei's cultural army, however, was not evenly distributed throughout the province. Counties near Wuhan and other urban spaces were far more likely to host cultural work teams and develop drama troupes. Isolated Enshi County, meanwhile, did not benefit from the campaign, even though the county had served as the temporary provincial capital

---

[103] "Nongcun jutuan yao xuanchuan Mao Zedong sixiang, jianjue fandui fengjian sixiang," 4.

[104] "Jiaqiang dui nongcun jutuan de lingdao" [Strengthen the leadership of rural drama troupes] HBWY 4.2 (1951), 6.

[105] "Xishui xian nongcun wenyi yundong de fazhan qingkuang he jinhou gongzuo jihua" [Summary of the development of the Xishui County rural literature and arts movement and future work plan] HBTX #7 (1951), 1.

[106] "Yingjie tudigaige kaizhan guangfan de wenyi xuanchuan yundong" [Welcoming the literature and arts propaganda campaign in the widespread development of land reform] HBWY 4.8 (1951), 6.

[107] Hubei sheng wenhuaju, "Hubei sheng wenhua shiye tongji ziliao, 1949–1959," 160–161.

during the era of Japanese occupation, when it hosted a flood of refugee artists and drama troupes.[108] This brief era of cultural prosperity ended alongside the war, causing the county's peasant representative to complain to the provincial Wenlian about a lack of operas in Enshi.[109] Enshi had land reform, but there was no concurrent move to establish amateur drama troupes in the county. The county cultural center's involvement in land reform, for example, was largely limited to collecting cultural artifacts.[110]

Luckily for entertainment-starved villagers, Hubei counties typically saw a firm connection between mass political campaigns and mass cultural campaigns, with the symbiotic nature of the cultural and political goals of the Communist Party most evident during the land reform era. Local cadres quickly realized that cultural performance offered the ideal way to promote land reform, as well as attract interest in meetings that many peasants found boring. Narratives proved effective at creating anger and disseminating Maoist conceptions of village society. Cultural cadres, meanwhile, realized that working with political campaigns gave them greater access to village leadership and increased legitimacy. The success of these political and cultural campaigns, however, was always contingent on the adoption of local styles and the co-opting of local artists. Hubei peasants had little interest in imported styles. Spoken dramas, northern *yangge*, and Peking operas found fans in cities, but rural audiences greeted these alien styles with indifference. Local artists, meanwhile, had little choice but to begin reforming old operas while learning new modern shows. But acceptance of Communist Party leadership was never easy, especially in light of the illicit attraction of professional status.

Hubei's cultural work teams mobilized amateur actors to stage Communist-friendly performances, with political leaders and local schoolteachers playing lead roles in the organization and development of amateur drama troupes. And while the importance of local political leaders underlines how the Communist Party hoped to use these troupes for political ends, Hubei's cultural authorities found controlling drama troupes inherently difficult. As a result of the tensions between the directives to educate and the desire to entertain, national politics played out on local stages in unexpected ways. Actors often played with stereotypes and acted broadly for laughs, and at times even dared to tell stories

---

[108] *Enshizhou zhi* [Enshizhou gazetteer] (Wuhan, Hubei renmin chubanshe, 1998), 919.
[109] "Nongmin daibiao tan wenyi," 7.
[110] *Enshizhou zhi*, 924.

that ran counter to party policies. Audiences were entertained, but political observers were not amused.

Amateurs, furthermore, found great joy in acting and felt the strong draw of professional performance, especially when their ranks included individuals talented in the traditional arts. As discussed in the following chapter, during the mid-1950s, Hubei's cultural authorities followed their Shanxi counterparts and intervened in the professional dramatic world by shifting their organizational focus to the "registration" of professional troupes. In pushing the Hubei government to increase its control over professional troupes, the national Ministry of Culture explicitly noted that one of the primary goals of the campaign was to halt the many amateur troupes then "blindly" moving towards professional status and to force "amateur" actors to return to production.[111] Hubei's army of amateur drama troupes, despite "rectification" in the aftermath of land reform, remained an unruly force. In its "registration" drive, Hubei's cultural authorities moved to limit performance opportunities for amateurs and demanded that amateurs no longer perform for money, revealing the false distinction between amateurs and professionals in the countryside. The great effort put forth by the Communists to maintain control over amateur village troupes serves as reminder of both their importance as well as their volatility. The following chapter, however, reveals that the young PRC state found professional actors even more difficult to discipline.

---

[111] Hubei sheng wenhuaju, "Bixu jiji er wenbu de jinxing quan sheng minjian zhiye jutuan de dengji gongzuo" [Must actively and steadily implement all province folk professional drama troupe registration work] HPA SZ34-2-0635 (1955), 25–27.

7 Tradition in conflict
Professional drama troupes and the PRC state

The completion of land reform in the early 1950s signaled the victory of Mao's rural revolution and the true arrival of the PRC state in the Chinese countryside. The ensuing shift from military and agrarian revolutions to regime consolidation and state-building, however, did not lessen the importance of Mao's cultural warriors. Prosperity in the pacified countryside created an ever-growing demand for entertainment, while the Communists continued to view drama as the surest method of reaching their own rural audiences. But with PLA propaganda teams and drama troupes focused on "serving soldiers," civilian drama troupes now took over the performance of revolutionary drama in the countryside. And while amateurs accounted for the majority of the drama troupes in the PRC cultural army, its most talented and popular performers worked professionally. In the 1950s, recognizing the necessity of controlling these professionals, the young PRC state sought to systematize the dramatic realm, part of a larger reorganization of China's artistic world. The Communists' takeover of the arts proved a decidedly messy and uneven process, with the state ultimately emerging as the dominant patron of the arts.[1] Among the many artists resisting state control, however, few had more backing than professional actors.

This chapter returns to rural Shanxi, spotlighting the Changzhi region to explore the evolution of the tenuous relationship between the PRC state and professional drama troupes. Because this relationship first developed in urban centers, the initial push to control Shanxi's dramatic world was largely confined to the Taiyuan, the provincial capital. After its "liberation" in April 1949, party cadres flooded into Taiyuan, putting the world of the dramatic arts into upheaval.[2] In early 1951, when over

---

[1] As Richard Kraus has argued, the Communists reorganized the artistic realm "in a series of only partially coordinated economic and administrative measures implemented between 1949 and 1957." Richard Curt Kraus, *The Party and the Arts in China: The New Politics of Culture* (Lanham, MD: Rowman & Littlefield Publishers, 2004), 37.

[2] As breathlessly reported in Shanxi's newly created arts journal, Taiyuan dramatists were studying modern works with contemporary themes, engaging in creation, and organizing for further mobilization. See Li Hong, "Ge di wenyi huodong jianxun" [Literature and

ninety cultural organizations paraded through Taiyuan's streets in a massive New Year's celebration, onlookers may have seen the new cultural order as vigorous and complete.[3] While the Communists celebrated the arrival of "New China" in Shanxi's capital, however, peasants inhabited an entirely different cultural world in the countryside. In Hubei, concurrent campaigns to develop state power and cultural infrastructure had resulted in an explosion of amateur drama troupes. But Shanxi peasants had completed land reform and other essential rural campaigns during the height of the Civil War, well before the founding of the PRC. Without a sustained drive to organize amateur actors at the village level, Shanxi audiences would rely heavily on professionals in private drama troupes (*siying jutuan*) for their entertainment.

Home to eight major regional styles and as many as fifty-two distinct local forms, Shanxi opera (Jinju) is perhaps best known for its *bangzi* "wooden clapper" styles.[4] Recognizing the popularity of these operatic performances, provincial cultural authorities moved to bring traditional artists under state control through a series of state interventions into Shanxi's dramatic world over the course of the early 1950s. These interventions often respected and protected local opera traditions. Shanxi's Department of Culture, for example, announced its intention to follow the reconciliatory artistic policies foreshadowed by the 1952 First All-China Opera Trial Performance Convention.[5] Unlike the later drama conventions that produced Cultural Revolution model works, the lineup for this Beijing drama festival overwhelmingly favored traditional numbers.[6] The Department of Culture also publicized the national Ministry of Culture's 1953 directive against "chaotic revision" (*luan gai*), banning works without cause, and other "bad" practices.[7]

arts activity news in brief from all parts]. SXWY 1.3 (1950), 40. Also Xiu Zhen, "Ge di wenyi huodong jianxun" [Literature and arts activity news in brief from all parts] SXWY 1.4 (1950), 29.

[3] Li Qun, "Shenru kangmei yuanchao jiaqiang aiguozhuyi sixiang jiaoyu" [Deepen ideological education to resist America aid Korea and strengthen patriotism] SXWY 1.7 (1951), 4.

[4] "Clapper" operas are not unique to Shanxi, and can be found in Shaanxi, Hebei, and Shandong provinces, but those *bangzi* operas are distinct from those found inside of Shanxi. *Shanxi wenhua yishu zhi* [Shanxi culture and art gazetteer] (Taiyuan: Shanxi sheng difangzhi bianzuan weiyuanhui bangongshi, 1989), 38.

[5] Shanxi sheng renmin zhengfu wenhua shiye guanli ju, "1953 niandu tuanjie sheng neiwai ge juzhong zhengce de zhixing qingkuang de zhuanti baogao" [1953 special report on the situation of implementing the policy of uniting all provincial and non-provincial drama troupes] SPA C76.6.12 (November 1953), 83

[6] As Paul Clark has noted, only eight out of eighty-two performances during this first convention focused on contemporary subjects. Clark, *The Chinese Cultural Revolution*, 12.

[7] Shanxi sheng renmin zhengfu wenhua shiye guanli ju, "1953 niandu tuanjie sheng neiwai ge juzhong zhengce de zhixing qingkuang de zhuanti baogao," 84.

But because respecting traditional opera did not mean leaving artists to their own devices, the early years of the PRC witnessed aggressive state intervention into Shanxi's dramatic world. The Department of Culture hosted over a dozen of its own "trial performance" (*guanmo yanchu*) conventions in the hope of steering creation.[8] Following directives from the Ministry of Culture and the All-China Union, the department also pushed drama troupes to visit and perform for workers.[9] Most importantly, Shanxi's cultural authorities policed the province's many private drama troupes through a strict policy of "rectification and strengthening." While only a handful of troupes became state-run outfits, all performers found themselves supervised by their local governments. Round after round of "rectification," cresting during the "Three Antis" and "Five Antis" campaigns of 1951 and 1952, ensured the Communist influence within rural Shanxi's most popular drama troupes. The first half of this chapter explores Shanxi's cultural infrastructure at the provincial, regional,[10] and county levels, emphasizing the decidedly limited ability of the state to perform revolutionary dramas or even properly organize amateur performance, which elevated private drama troupes to the lead role in Shanxi's cultural army. The second part of this chapter recreates the world of Shanxi's private drama troupes, tracing the ever-increasing role of the state in the cultural realm, evidenced in the creation of state-run and state-subsidized troupes, the rectification of private troupes, and the policing of the boundaries between professional and amateur performers.

Local opera offered the state an established and popular medium for disseminating policies and ideology throughout rural China. The revolution had ended in victory for the Communists, but revolutionary performance continued in the countryside, with villagers continuing in their roles as Maoist peasants. Policing performance was an important task for the Communists, but controlling drama troupes proved difficult. The provincial Department of Culture successfully intervened in

---

[8] Ibid., 87.

[9] Shanxi sheng renmin zhengfu wenhua shiye guanli ju, "Jiedai Zhongguo jingjutuan wei changkuang gongdi wei wen yanchu gongzuo de zongjie baogao" [Summary report of receiving the China Peking Opera Troupe to perform in appreciation at factory and mine workplaces] SPA C76.6.17 (1953), 8.

[10] Seven regional administrative governments (*zhuanshu*) governed regions (*zhuanqu*) in 1950: Yuci, Changzhi, Xinxian, Yuncheng, Linfen, Fenyang, and Xingxian. Shanxi had ninety-two counties and only one provincial city, Taiyuan. As was so often the case, this administrative system was in flux, and by 1952 there were six regions, including the new Yanbei region; the remaining regions were Xinxian, Yuci, Changzhi, Linfen, and Yuncheng. In 1953, finally, Shanxi laid claim to four provincial cities (Taiyuan, Datong, Yangquan, and Changzhi) and 103 counties.

professional drama troupes, but two interrelated trends ensured that the PRC cultural world remained a highly contested realm. First, while the Department of Culture was intent on halting the expansion of drama troupes, at least until these organizations could be molded into a proper cultural army, popular demand for entertainment provided ample opportunity for talented amateurs to turn professional. Second, rural audiences in Shanxi continued to demand traditional operas at the expense of modern works. Just as had been the case with the Lucheng County Popular Drama Troupe in 1948, opera troupes ignored the autonomous power of peasant audiences at their professional and even personal peril. And as seen in the drive to "register" professional drama troupes in Hubei, discussed at the close of this chapter, these trends towards professionalism and traditionalism were by no means limited to Shanxi. With official policy in opposition to popular culture, state intervention only guaranteed conflict throughout the PRC's cultural world.

Cultural organization in Shanxi at the dawn of the PRC

While the Ministry of Culture (Wenhuabu) directed cultural policies on the national level, Richard Kraus has argued that it did so ineffectively, claiming that despite its size and scale of its activities "China's great ministry failed to exercise cultural leadership during the 1950s."[11] The investigation into drama troupes during this era, however, shows that the Ministry of Culture slowly but surely ramped up its control over local cultural production. At the outset of the PRC era, to be sure, the Ministry had little say as to what happened in the Shanxi countryside. Within Shanxi, provincial-level administrations, most importantly the Department of Culture (Wenhuaju),[12] oversaw actual implementation of cultural work. In the early years of the PRC, Shanxi's cultural leaders only controlled two work teams. The first team, typically busy with

---

[11] Kraus, *The Party and the Arty in China*, 49.

[12] Here the Department of Culture is used as shorthand for string of cultural administrations that saw continual reorganization in the years following the founding of the PRC. At the start of the PRC era in Shanxi, the key cultural organ was the Education Department (Jiaoyu ting). In the spring of 1950, this body changed its name to the more inclusive and appropriate Culture and Education Department (Wenjiao Ting). Within the department, a Cultural Department (Wenhua chu) was established, which oversaw a Theater Reform Office (Xiju gaijin ke). Further administrative changes occurred in November 1952, when a trend towards specialization returned the Culture and Education Department to its roots as the Education Department (Jiaoyu ting); it was at this time that Shanxi province formed its Cultural Affairs Management Department (Wenhua shiye guanli ju). In 1955, this organ's name was simplified to the Department of Culture (Wenhuaju).

artistic creation, crafted new shows on a diverse set of contemporary topics, including marriage reform, increasing production, and exposing superstition.[13] The second team was largely staffed by former members of the Xiangyuan Rural Drama Troupe.[14] As detailed in previous chapters, members of this professional troupe had struggled to overcome drug addiction before helping party intellectual Ruan Zhangjing develop *Red Leaf River*. Now transferred into a state-run cultural work team, the former Xiangyuan players continued to perform *Red Leaf River* as one of their signature shows.[15]

With only a handful of provincial-level drama troupes and organizations in Shanxi,[16] the burden of staging revolutionary dramas fell to lower-level administrations. Taiyuan and the province's seven administrative regions each directed its own cultural work team, staffed with talented intellectuals and artists drafted out of professional drama troupes.[17] Typically focused on artistic creation and staging didactic dramas, these teams proved of limited use in Shanxi's massive and populous regions. In August 1950, for example, the work team for the Yuncheng region toured three counties, performing nine different shows, including *Liu Hulan*. Other dramas concerned the conflict in Korea, raising production, challenging superstition, and the importance of winter schools. The Yuncheng work team, much like its Yuci and Linfeng region counterparts, created new works, toured the countryside, and performed in celebration of holidays and special events.[18] While these tours brought teams into the countryside, the challenges of serving an entire region proved overwhelming: the Yuncheng team only visited three of the region's seventeen counties.

County cultural centers and work teams

As had been the case in Hubei, the PRC state established a network of cultural centers in Shanxi in the hope of influencing all aspects of provincial culture, with a strong focus on the dramatic realm. Shanxi

---

[13] Xiu Zhen, "Ge di wenyi huodong jianxun," 29.

[14] Changzhi shi wenhua ju, *Changzhi shi yishu biaoyan tuanti shigao*, 183–184.

[15] Xiu Zhen, "Ben sheng wenyi huodong jianxun" [Provincial literature and arts activity news in brief] SXWY 1.2 (1950), 4.

[16] The Shanxi Province Drama Association (Shanxi sheng juxie), composed of Shanxi's elites dramatists, was a final important provincial-level drama organization. Formed during the initial meeting of Shanxi cultural representatives in December 1949, in July 1950 the association sent several of its members to the countryside to investigate the Yiguandao in order to create new shows against superstition. Xiu Zhen, "Ge di wenyi huodong jianxun," 29.

[17] For example, see Changzhi shi wenhua ju, *Changzhi shi yishu biaoyan tuanti shigao*, 107

[18] Xiu Zhen, "Ge di wenyi huodong jianxun," 29.

cultural centers, much like their Hubei counterparts, housed reading rooms, published creative works, promoted cultural events, and directed cultural organizations. Yet a comparison with Hubei reveals the wildly uneven development of cultural infrastructures in Mao's "New China." Shanxi's network of county-level cultural centers rapidly expanded in the aftermath of the PRC's founding, with 117 cultural centers formed by 1952.[19] Archival documents concerning the Lucheng County Cultural Center, however, reveal the impossibility of effective cultural center work at the dawn of the PRC era. Initially founded as a People's Education Center, the Lucheng center consistently lacked personnel and funds. As a result, the center simply could not influence local culture in a meaningful manner. The Communists often transferred the county's tiny staff, leaving one person in charge of the entire county's cultural affairs. The center's regular distribution of grain and banknotes, meanwhile, often ran short.[20]

The Lucheng center lacked a cultural work team and was only able to exert direct control over eight traditional artists, seven of whom were blind. Organized into two "blind person propaganda teams" (*mangren xuanchuandui*), these local artists represented the extent of the cultural center's involvement with folk arts. After creating new ditties to promote increasing production, the two "blind person propaganda teams" toured the countryside, visiting over forty villages in six months.[21] Most cultural center work, however, was limited to the Lucheng County seat. And despite plans for public blackboards and radio stations, little had been done. Recalling the early propaganda workers of the Long March, the pasting of slogans around the county seat provided the rare tangible proof of cultural work.[22]

Directed to focus on rural propaganda and educational work, the center largely relied on exhibits and slide shows to promote the Communists' message. While occasional temple fairs (*miaohui*) provided an opportunity to overcome its limited resources and reach a wider audience, the

---

[19] These centers divided their duties among a number of small groups (*zu*). An average county-level cultural center would have a literature and arts instruction team (*wenyi fudao zu*), a literature and arts creation team, a library team, and a general affairs team (*zongwu zu*). *Shanxi wenhua yishu zhi*, 220.

[20] Lucheng xian renmin wenhuaguan, "Lucheng xian renmin wenhuaguan bannian lai gongzuo gaishu" [General description of past half year work by the Lucheng County people's cultural center] LCA A1–1–1378 (August, 1949), 4.

[21] Ibid., 5.

[22] In the summer of 1949, for example, 192 old slogans had been washed off to make room for 144 new slogans. But this was only possible because the cultural center farmed out the labor of sloganeering: owners of the walls in question were mobilized to wash off the old slogans, while schoolteachers painted the new slogans. Ibid., 6–7.

center typically relied on schools and representative meetings to host its exhibits and slide shows. The center's slide show included a wide range of topics; current events, the importance of increasing production, child care, the story of a Lucheng female hero, and party history were all projected for Lucheng audiences. Even cultural center workers, however, had to acknowledge that Lucheng audiences found the history of the Communist Party boring.[23]

Lucheng cultural workers claimed slide shows were a "powerful propaganda weapon,"[24] yet also admitted that they were in fact failing to reach out to the countryside. In late 1949, even their ideal vision of cultural work was limited: the center hoped to expand its staff to at least three cadres, including specialists in painting and cultural theory. The cultural center also planned to expand its slide shows and exhibits, organize temple fair propaganda, and further promote education and hygiene. The center's resources, then consisting of only three hundred books and magazines in addition to subscriptions to four newspapers, also needed funds for development. The county had great plans, including a cultural club for the county seat, the purchase of loudspeakers, and artistic creation to promote the fight against locusts. But even their most ambitious proposal, to develop a proper literature and arts work team (*wenyi gongzuodui*), would only create a small five-person unit to bring slide shows into the countryside, accompanied with additional *kuaiban* "wooden clapper" numbers and other small-scale performances based on local music and tastes.[25]

As seen in Lucheng, Shanxi's county cultural centers were understaffed and underfunded, but the failure to organize sub-county cultural centers (*wenhua zhan*) revealed the true limitations of the province's cultural infrastructure. In stark contrast to Hubei, where a dense network of cultural centers brought cultural workers down to the district level in the years immediately following the establishment of the PRC, Shanxi did not establish sub-county cultural centers until well after the close of the Cultural Revolution.[26] As readers will recall from Chapter 6, by the end of 1950 Hubei had seventy-eight cultural centers at the county level and seventy-three at the district level; by 1952, these numbers had risen to 106 and 296 respectively.[27] So while Shanxi and Hubei had nearly

---

[23] According to the center's own calculations, its exhibits and slideshows were able to reach an audience of 57,693, or nearly 48% of the county's population of 120,000. Ibid., 2–6.
[24] Ibid., 7.   [25] Ibid., 8–12.
[26] By the 1980s, of course, the increasing availability of alternate forms of mass media entertainment, most notably radio and television, made the belated arrival of these sub-county cultural stations anticlimactic.
[27] *Hubei sheng zhi*, 435–436.

identical numbers of county-level cultural centers, Shanxi simply had no match for Hubei's sub-county cultural infrastructural reach.

Hampered by this weak cultural infrastructure, Shanxi's cultural centers failed to play a meaningful role in the staging of drama in the countryside. In 1952, for example, Shanxi cultural center work teams staged 305 shows for an estimated audience of 207,030.[28] Claiming a very reasonable average of nearly 680 viewers per show, cultural work teams performed for sizeable audiences. Yet from the perspective of Shanxi's massive population, estimated in 1952 at nearly fourteen million,[29] these audience numbers fail to impress. Ninety-nine percent of Shanxi residents never saw these cultural center work team performances, and those that did typically lived in cities or county seats.

A provincial cultural conference in 1951 explicitly addressed the failure to implement cultural work throughout Shanxi's ninety-two counties. As one speaker noted, the primary propaganda units at the county level were slide projector teams; and, as had been the case in Lucheng, counties typically had only one team. But slide shows like *The Victory of the Chinese People* (Zhongguo renmin de shengli), lauded for their ability to convey a large amount of information in just two hours, proved a poor substitute for live dramas. And while cultural workers had succeeded in getting new dramas on to Shanxi stages, old shows (*jiuju*) remained far more popular and influential throughout the countryside. Some cadres attempted to address the obvious imbalance between old and new dramas by banning old shows outright. The Communists condemned this misguided policy and instead instructed cultural workers to preserve and revise traditional operas while creating new works with broad appeal such as *Liu Hulan*.[30] With Shanxi's anemic cultural infrastructure, however, this would require collaboration with private drama troupes.

Caught between audiences and the state: private drama troupes in Shanxi

Determined to direct dramatic performance in the countryside, Shanxi's cultural authorities moved to intervene in the province's rapidly expanding corps of professional drama troupes. One of the centerpieces of this state intervention into the dramatic world was the 1953 creation of one state-run (*guoying*) and seven subsidized private (*minying gongzhu*)

---

[28] *Shanxi wenhua yishu zhi*, 232–232.   [29] *All China Data Center*, Online Database.
[30] Pei Dai, "Zai xianyou de puji de jichu zhi shang tigao yi bu" [Raise the current dissemination level] SXWY 1.8 (1951), 2–4.

opera troupes. As approved by the cultural authorities in the North China regional administration,[31] the state-run troupe was to perform *zhonglu bangzi* operas, considered the most common and influential of the eight major regional styles grouped under the umbrella term Shanxi opera. The seven subsidized private troupes, meanwhile, would specialize in the Shanxi opera styles most popular in their respective home bases: Taiyuan and Shanxi's six administrative regions.[32]

After the decision to form the state-run Shanxi Opera Troupe was made in February 1953, the provincial Department of Culture turned to the private sector to staff the troupe – as would become standard practice – and selected four talented Taiyuan troupes specializing in *zhonglu bangzi* opera. But archival documents reveal that despite going through "democratic reform" under the state's tutelage, many performers in the four troupes wanted nothing to do with this state-run troupe. At the outset of the attempt to create the new troupe, Shanxi's cultural leaders admitted that many actors longed to remain in the private sector, where they could rely on their popularity (*renyuan*) to prosper. But the Department of Culture, believing that actors would eventually "voluntarily" convert to a state-run troupe, pressed on.[33] Subsequent communication with the North China cultural authorities reiterated the importance of not forcing the private troupes to turn into a state-run troupe. However, reminders to pay attention to ideological concerns and to "educate" artists to help them cast aside "individualism" demonstrate that actors ultimately had little choice in the matter.[34] The writing was on the wall, and even Ding Guoxian, recognized as a national "First-Grade Performer" in 1952 and the first female to perform leading male roles (*xusheng*) in Shanxi opera, joined the troupe.[35]

[31] The regional administration system was abolished in June, 1954.

[32] The province planned for the eventual establishment of ten subsidized troupes. See Shanxi sheng renmin zhengfu wenhua shiye guanli ju, "1953 niandu tuanjie sheng neiwai ge juzhong zhengce de zhixing qingkuang de zhuanti baogao," 84. On the various styles of Shanxi opera, see Shanxi sheng renmin zhengfu wenhua shiye guanli ju, "Guanyu xiqu jutuan jiben qingkuang de zhuanti baogao" [Special report regarding the general situation of opera troupes] SPA C76.6.12 (December, 1953), 55.

[33] Shanxi sheng renmin zhengfu wenhua shiye guanli ju, "Jianli guoying jutuan jihua cao'an" [Draft plan for the establishment of a state-run Shanxi opera troupe] SPA C76.6.12 (1953), 53

[34] Shanxi sheng renmin zhengfu wenhua shiye guanli ju, "Pifu jianli guoying jutuan wenti" [Response to problems in establishing the state-run drama troupe] SPA C76.6.12 (1953), 12.

[35] Shanxi sheng renmin zhengfu wenhua shiye guanli ju, "Jianli guoying jutuan jihua cao'an," 53.

Even with this aggressive intervention into the cultural world, high-lighted by the creation of the elite Shanxi Opera Troupe,[36] Shanxi's cultural leaders had very little power to manage the staging of public performances, especially at the village level. The formation of state-run and subsidized private troupes in 1953, while of great significance for a few drama troupes, only gave the Shanxi government control over a small fraction of the dramatic realm. As cultural leaders were well aware, professional drama troupes, already numbering seventy-seven in 1952,[37] remained the most important performers in rural Shanxi. But as seen in the Changzhi region, the Communists faced great challenges in recruit-ing private troupes into its cultural army.

Located in the southeastern corner of Shanxi Province, Changzhi boasts a particularly rich tradition of local opera. In the early twentieth century, nearly forty troupes toured the region until the ravages of war made travel dangerous and put Changzhi's professional troupes out of business. *Bangzi* "wooden clapper" operas and other local styles, how-ever, found new life in Communist base areas after local cadres started using traditional culture for revolutionary purposes. As discussed in previous chapters, the Taihang Mountains Drama Troupe performed regularly in the Changzhi countryside, while the Xiangyuan Rural Drama Troupe and the Lucheng County Popular Drama Troupe both called the region home; few localities outside of the Yan'an wartime capital could boast of a more significant heritage of revolutionary drama troupes. Yet the connections between revolutionary struggle and drama troupes complicated the local cultural scene. After Japan's surrender in 1945, for example, the Communists systematically disassembled the Taihang Mountains Drama Troupe, transferring actors to new performance units as the Eighth Route Army moved into new territories. The experiences of the Xiangyuan and Lucheng troupes, meanwhile, demonstrated the difficulty in keeping entertainers focused on politics, especially when audiences demanded traditional shows.

With increased prosperity following the end of decades of warfare, performances of local operas steadily increased, with traditional and modern works both finding their way to Changzhi stages. Anxious to get modern representations of nationalistic, class-conscious, and hard-working peasants on stage, the Communists recognized the powerful

---

[36] The Shanxi Opera Troupe was the province's most prestigious unit, but their failure to impress Shanghai audiences during a 1959 tour would bring great shame to Shanxi natives Peng Zheng and Bo Yibo. Kraus, *The Party and the Art in China*, 51.

[37] Shanxi sheng renmin zhengfu wenhua shiye guanli ju, "Guanyu xiqu jutuan jiben qingkuang de zhuanti baogao," 55.

draw of traditional opera and moved to capitalize on its popularity. As experienced cultural workers long understood, old favorites drew in rural audiences, who would stay to watch modern shows. The fact that many modern shows drew on traditional musical styles made the transition between old and new shows relatively seamless, helping maintain fickle rural audiences. This balance between traditional and modern shows, while successful, did not come about naturally. Only the sustained effort from local governments ensured modern and overtly political performances a place on stage.

Archival sources, however, demonstrate that government supervision of private drama troupes in Changzhi was difficult to enforce. Li Yuxing, a cultural cadre dispatched to Changzhi in 1953 to investigate the region's private troupes, uncovered a host of problems among performers nominally under party leadership. Some troupes, attempting to implement perceived government policy, had shunned old artists and abandoned established traditions. Other troupes, ignoring propaganda and focused on drawing large audiences, fixated on flashy lighting and special effects.[38] Li Yuxing's investigation reveals the real but limited scope of state control within Changzhi's dramatic realm. The state, largely represented by the provincial Department of Culture and the Changzhi regional government, had significant power over performers, including the ability to curtail the steady increase in the number of professional troupes. And while audiences strongly preferred traditional shows, through "rectification" Shanxi's cultural authorities ensured that professional troupes undertook reform and staged modern shows featuring state-friendly performances that peasants were expected to reenact in their everyday lives. State power was perhaps most evident in the ability to disband troupes and transfer troupe members seemingly at will. But the continued autonomy of Shanxi audiences vexed cultural workers attempting to bring performances of hard-working Maoist peasants to Changzhi stages. Demanding traditional shows and technological innovation at the expense of modern works and didactic messages, peasant audiences guaranteed that the PRC cultural realm remained a contested arena.

Producing and policing a professional cultural army

The "rectification and strengthening" (*zhengdun gonggu*) policy of freezing the number of professional troupes was a response to the rapid

---

[38] Li visited thirteen troupes in eleven counties over fifty-one days; some visits were as short as a day, while others stretched out to over ten days. Shanxi sheng renmin zhengfu wenhua shiye guanli ju, "1953 niandu tuanjie sheng neiwai ge juzhong zhengce de zhixing qingkuang de zhuanti baogao," 85.

creation of new troupes in the aftermath of the Civil War. In the Changzhi region, new troupes were forming right up to the announcement of the "rectification and strengthening" policy in 1953. The Lucheng County Common People's Drama Troupe, for example, originally an amateur village drama troupe, turned professional in 1950 with the full support of the Lucheng party branch. Under the leadership of the county, the troupe performed a mixture of traditional and modern shows.[39] As this suggests, local governments in Changzhi were actively involved in creating professional drama troupes, and despite the state's role these troupes staged traditional operas. In 1952, the Licheng County government transformed an "amateur propaganda unit" into the Dawn Winds Drama Troupe, which quickly hired an opera teacher to help actors rehearse and stage traditional shows. With expensive costumes and a strong focus on traditional shows, the troupe had no trouble winning over demanding peasant audiences, despite lacking female actors at a time when most Changzhi troupes had already integrated female actors into their ranks.[40]

Shanxi's Department of Culture drafted its policy of "rectification and strengthening" to halt this explosive growth in the province's private cultural army, least the rank and file grow too numerous for effective discipline. But archival documents show that many local governments attempted to circumvent the ban against new troupes. In Pinglu, for example, the county government proposed expanding and then splitting an existing professional drama troupe, with one half of the divided troupe becoming a subsidized private drama troupe. Citing the policy of "rectification and strengthening," the Department of Culture denied this request.[41] As the department made clear in its official instructions to the Linfen regional government when it made a similar request, the formation of a subsidized private troupe was not an excuse for training additional artists and covertly forming new outfits; only extant private troupes and troupe members could be used as the basis of a "new" troupe.[42] Drama troupes that attempted to get around the policy of "rectification and strengthening" drew official rebuke.[43]

[39] Changzhi shi wenhua ju, *Changzhi shi yishu biaoyan tuanti shigao*, 110–111.

[40] Ibid., 80.

[41] Shanxi sheng renmin zhengfu wenhua shiye guanli ju, "Pifu bu ying fazhan xin de zhiye jutuan" [Official reply to not allow the development of new professional drama troupes] SPA C76.6.24 (November, 1953), 21.

[42] Shanxi sheng renmin zhengfu wenhua shiye guanli ju, "Hanfu zhuanqu bu chengli xin de gejutuan" [Response to districts on not establishing new opera troupes] SPA C76–6–24 (May 1953), 53–55.

[43] Shanxi sheng renmin zhengfu wenhua shiye guanli ju, "Guanyu xiqu jutuan jiben qingkuang de zhuanti baogao," 69.

But popular demand for new troupes threatened to overwhelm Shanxi's cultural authorities. As the Department of Culture made clear in its correspondence with the Ministry of Culture in late 1953, requests for new professional troupes were pouring in from all over Shanxi ever since the ban went into place. Counties bereft of drama troupes used any possible chance to demand the ability to organize performers. Formal government requests flowed up to Taiyuan, while representative meetings and commerce associations became forums to press for the expansion of Shanxi's cultural ranks, with many arguing for a professional troupe to help "liven things up" (*zhuxing*) at markets. Local governments tried to get around the directive of "rectification and strengthening" by expanding and splitting existing troupes or by adopting troupes from outside their jurisdiction. Besides threatening the authority of the Department of Culture, the continued push for new drama troupes, especially the poaching of outside drama troupes, promised to create tensions among different administrative bodies. Changzhi city, for example, campaigned to formally adopt the New Era Drama Troupe, a Henan troupe. Jiang County proposed splitting off the Henan *bangzi* "wooden clapper" performers from a drama troupe from Shaanxi's Tongzhou County, despite a lack of agreement from the entire troupe, let alone its Shaanxi patrons.[44]

The ban against new troupes, however, found its strongest resistance from amateur actors longing to turn professional. While Shanxi never organized amateur troupes on the scale that marked cultural infrastructure building in Hubei, many talented amateur performers and troupes naturally populated the countryside. With minimal ties to local governments and driven by professional ambition, many amateurs tended towards professionalism, even after the announcement of the "rectification and strengthening" policy in 1953. Leaders of one Changzhi County amateur troupe, after repeatedly failing to gain official status because of the new policy, decided to simply pass their troupe off as a professional outfit. Now heading a "professional troupe" complete with dummy party organizations, the conspirators swore allegiance to a "killer small group" (*da si ren xiaozu*) within the troupe that promised to murder anyone who threatened their shared secret. This "professional troupe" left Changzhi County and found wild success until its troupe leader absconded with its profits, leaving actors and musicians destitute.

---

[44] Shanxi sheng renmin zhengfu wenhua shiye guanli ju, "Qingshi guanli siying jutuan wenti" [Request for instructions for managing private drama troupes] SPA C76.6.12 (November 1953), 42.

Taking the name of an established private professional troupe offered another method to claim legitimacy and circumvent state control, but sophisticated peasant audiences made this a dangerous gambit. One amateur troupe in Pingshun County, for example, forged an official seal and went on tour in nearby Wu'an County as the well-known Fenghe Drama Troupe. Irate audiences, seeing that the phony troupe obviously lacked the real troupe's famous actors, sent the imposters packing without pay, forcing the would-be professionals to sell their equipment to cover their return costs. The Department of Culture received multiple complaints of villages hiring "amateur" drama troupes,[45] revealing that audiences, dramatists, and even local governments continued to push for more drama despite the policy of "rectification and strengthening."

Rectification in the early 1950s

For private troupes, the 1953 policy of "rectification and strengthening" represented just another signpost along the long road of negotiations with an intrusive state presence. These troupes had already undergone repeated "rectifications," coinciding with the "Three Antis" and "Five Antis" campaigns of 1951 and 1952. During these rectifications (either called *zhengfeng* or *zhengdun*), the Communists forced professional troupes to accept the leadership of their local government, welcome cadres into their ranks as instructors or even troupe leaders, and undergo "democratic reform." At times, rectification threatened to become a permanent condition, even for troupes that regularly staged modern shows.[46]

Unlike the rectification of amateur actors in Hubei, the rectification of Shanxi's professional drama troupes did not center on the investigation into class status. A few troupe members, charged with being landlords or reactionaries, were expelled from private troupes during the Campaign to Suppress Counterrevolutionaries. But investigations into drama troupe ranks revealed, unsurprisingly, that the vast majority of Shanxi's actors

---

[45] Shanxi sheng renmin zhengfu wenhua shiye guanli ju, "Guanyu xiqu jutuan jiben qingkuang de zhuanti baogao," 69.

[46] This was the case with the Establish the Nation Drama Troupe. Staging modern shows at night and using a variety of local styles to spread party propaganda, this was a seemingly model troupe. Yet the Changzhi government accused the troupe of organizational, artistic, and ideological problems. This first led to a 1951 rectification with two other Changzhi troupes, when gambling and drug use were singled out as particularly vexing "traditional" problems. But other issues, most importantly the troupe's preference for traditional operas, meant that the troupe was subject to frequent rectifications in the following years. Changzhi shi wenhua ju, *Changzhi shi yishu biaoyan tuanti shigao*, 38.

hailed from the poorest levels of society. Because of the traditional bias against acting, aptly captured in the local aphorism "if your family has a bit of chaff, don't go into opera," only the poorest families sent their children to join drama troupes. Actors thus generally came from poor and thus "good" family backgrounds, but the Communists believed that the difficult and oppressive nature of opera apprenticing had turned many actors into drug-using hooligans. As seen in earlier eras, party persistence tamed actors of their most egregious behaviors, at least as far as the Communists were concerned. According to archival sources, by 1953 drug use and improper sexual relations were essentially things of the past, leading to rising respect for the acting tradition. Most troupes, especially in the "old liberated areas" around Changzhi, also boasted strong party organizations. But while "democratic reform" had eliminated the old "gang master" (batou) apprenticing system, troupes still tended to divide into factions,[47] with the divide between traditionally trained actors and their younger counterparts the most troublesome rift, especially during moments of state intervention.

Working with the state: benefits and pitfalls

Rectification was never truly optional, but troupes had reasons to welcome state intrusion. As Paul Clark has argued, state supervision offered drama troupes "more stability, with regular salaries, subsidies for performances, and guaranteed access to performance spaces."[48] Shanxi's private drama troupes had long received grain and other forms of material support from local governments. As seen in the Lucheng County Popular Drama Troupe, during wartime such backing helped troupes survive and provided a strong incentive to stage propaganda-heavy shows, including Red Leaf River. While private troupes generally prospered after 1949, government support continued and diversified. In addition to material support, for example, local governments regularly dispatched cadres to help troupes organize political and cultural education.[49]

The experiences of the Qin County Zhang River Drama Troupe suggest the real material benefits in coming under state leadership. As a new troupe, actors had initially been paid through a simplistic and egalitarian "subsidy system" (butie zhi), with all members getting three

---

[47] Shanxi sheng renmin zhengfu wenhua shiye guanli ju, "Guanyu xiqu jutuan jiben qingkuang de zhuanti baogao," 66.
[48] Clark, The Chinese Cultural Revolution, 13.
[49] Shanxi sheng renmin zhengfu wenhua shiye guanli ju, "Guanyu xiqu jutuan jiben qingkuang de zhuanti baogao," 69.

sets of clothes a year in addition to a set monthly wage. Developing during the early PRC, the troupe moved to the more professional "bonus system" (*fenhong zhi*), a graded pay scale that heavily favored lead actors and musicians. But the unproven troupe lacked the popularity needed to demand high booking fees, so while some performers prospered others found difficulty in making ends meet. A government subsidy, however, helped keep the troupe afloat until it could improve its reputation and draw larger audiences and revenues. In return, the Zhang River players, like their fellow Changzhi actors, performed a mixed repertoire with nights reserved for modern shows such as *Wang Xiuluan* and *Liu Hulan*.[50]

Archival sources, however, reveal the difficulties that characterized the relationship between professional troupes and local governments. While some cadres enjoyed the arts too much and took advantage of their positions of power to watch shows at half price,[51] cadres more commonly displayed a continued hostility towards the traditional arts. One county, for example, banned shadow puppet shows (*piyingxi*), drawing a rebuke from the Department of Culture.[52] Another county barred a village from hosting a drama troupe without cause, a decision that launched a series of investigations before finally resulting in a formal apology to the village. Even in cities, cadres mistreated actors. Dispatched to rectify the New Sounds Drama Troupe during the "Three Antis" Campaign, cultural cadres in Yangquan forced one drama troupe to construct a basketball court. Further reports of cadres abusing actors in the provincial capital only underline the doubts many cadres had about the value of cultural work.[53] Uneven treatment from cadres complicated the real benefits of rectification, but drama troupes ultimately had no choice but to work with the Communists.

Modern dramas, traditional dramas

Rectification explicitly aimed to reform dramatic performance, putting local traditions in peril. In the early PRC, the Ministry of Culture was perfectly willing to ban individual shows. In 1952, for example, the ministry suppressed the Peking opera *Inviting a Wolf into the Room* (Ying lang ru shi) for expressing reactionary ideology.[54] But as seen in the

---

[50] Changzhi shi wenhua ju, *Changzhi shi yishu biaoyan tuanti shigao*, 30–31.

[51] Shanxi sheng renmin zhengfu wenhua shiye guanli ju, "1953 niandu tuanjie sheng neiwai ge juzhong zhengce de zhixing qingkuang de zhuanti baogao," 83.

[52] Ibid., 84.   [53] Ibid., 83.

[54] Zhongyang renmin zhengfu wenhuabu, "Wei chajin Jingju ben 'Yin lang ru shi' zhishi zunjiao ban liyou" [Method and rational for abiding the directive to ban the Peking opera "Inviting a wolf into the room"] SPA C76.6.10 (June 1952), 66.

ministry's 1953 directive concerning opera reform, which demanded an end to "chaotic revision" and the banning of traditional forms, national cultural leaders generally tolerated traditional drama,[55] giving Shanxi's Department of Culture a mandate to protect the legacy of local opera. In 1953, for example, the department instructed Shanxi's regional governments to mobilize local drama troupes to transcribe their scripts for preservation, even distributing funds to help coordinate and ensure the completion of this directive. A desire to control local culture, of course, also motivated this interest in local styles and scripts. Through its script examination and approval group (*shending zu*), the Department of Culture gave official sanction to revised scripts. Regular conferences, furthermore, disseminated models and pushed back against unwelcome trends.[56]

Rectification effectively reformed many aspects of Shanxi opera. Troupes learned to keep their most "lewd and obscene" (*yindang weixie*) performances off stage, and eliminated unflattering portrayals of laborers and other model groups. No longer did directors dare to place fierce masks (*xiong'e lianpu*) on peasant rebel characters. Shanxi troupes also undertook music reform, forging a tighter connection between music and acting. This often simply meant weakening (*xueruo*) the musical accompaniment to ensure that audiences could actually hear a show's dialogue. Besides putting more effort into costumes and scenery, rectification pushed troupes to rehearse new shows and revise traditional numbers.[57] The long-running hostility towards popular folk art traditions, however, complicated the rectification of Changzhi troupes. Despite calls to preserve local opera, the push for modern dramas inevitably created conflict with artistic traditions.

State intervention into Shanxi's dramatic world resulted in at least one clear victory for the Communists: private drama troupes were in fact staging revolutionary dramas. Most drama troupes, moreover, finally gave their highly prized evening performance times to modern shows. The speed with which some professionals adapted revolutionary classics for their own stages was impressive. For example, the Red Light Drama Troupe, after welcoming female actors into its ranks in 1951, quickly staged the land reform opera trifecta of *The White-Haired Girl*, *Liu Hulan*,

---

[55] Shanxi sheng renmin zhengfu wenhua shiye guanli ju, "1953 niandu tuanjie sheng neiwai ge juzhong zhengce de zhixing qingkuang de zhuanti baogao," 84.

[56] Ibid., 86.

[57] In the past cadres had banned shows outright, but by 1953 "chaotic revision" emerged as the primary problem. Shanxi sheng renmin zhengfu wenhua shiye guanli ju, "Guanyu xiqu jutuan jiben qingkuang de zhuanti baogao," 67.

and *Red Leaf River*.[58] Other troupes, however, struggled with the transition. The Establish the Nation Drama Troupe initially performed revolutionary dramas in old-style costumes, an odd mixture of the modern and the traditional that must have confused village audiences. In response, the county government dispatched a "cultural instructor" (*wenhua jiaoguan*) to teach the troupe how to properly stage modern shows.[59]

In her study of painters during the early decades of the PRC, Julia Andrews portrayed the tensions between tradition and propaganda among elite artists as largely a question of individualism versus politics.[60] But drama troupes performing in the field had to negotiate first-hand with audience expectations, profoundly complicating any move away from local culture. Despite the wishes of Shanxi's cultural authorities, market preference for traditional opera largely dictated private drama troupe repertoires, heightening the tensions between modern and traditional shows. Take, for example, the Huguan County People's Drama Troupe. Founded by party activists during the Sino-Japanese War, these Huguan actors initially specialized in modern shows. But by 1947, popular demand for traditional costumed shows forced the troupe to expand its membership and engage in a period of intensive artistic study. With a new policy of "walking on two legs," the troupe attempted to balance old and new shows, but deficiencies in personnel, costumes, and props hampered their traditional shows and left audiences dissatisfied. Absorbing a local opera troupe in early 1949 solved all of these problems, providing an influx of talented actors and valuable theatrical equipment.[61]

By demanding traditional dramas over their modern counterparts, audiences could wreak havoc on the functioning of a professional troupe. Actors tended to specialize in either modern or traditional roles, and because roles in old and new dramas were far from interchangeable,[62] a sudden shift in repertoire would push some actors off stage. In 1951, for example, a Wuxiang County village demanded a visiting Tunliu County drama troupe change its scheduled nighttime performance from a modern to a traditional show, explicitly rejecting the state's preferred schedule. Emboldened by the audience's demands, traditionally trained actors attacked modern shows and their state-friendly performances as inherently unpopular. Racked by factionalism, the troupe was called back

---

[58] The troupe's production of *Liu Hulan* was said to be particularly powerful. Changzhi shi wenhua ju, *Changzhi shi yishu biaoyan tuanti shigao*, 17–18

[59] Changzhi shi wenhua ju, *Changzhi shi yishu biaoyan tuanti shigao*, 37.

[60] Andrews, *Painters and Politics in the People's Republic of China*, 12.

[61] Changzhi shi wenhua ju, *Changzhi shi yishu biaoyan tuanti shigao*, 117–118.

[62] Clark, *The Chinese Cultural Revolution*, 13.

to its home county for eleven months of rectification.[63] In 1950, after a village audience heavily criticized the Tunliu County Jianghe Drama Troupe for staging too many modern shows, popular senior actors led a revolt against modern shows. The ranks of the disaffected included the troupe's second-in-command, a party member who led an exodus of actors from the troupe. The depleted troupe continued to perform a mixed repertoire of modern and traditional shows, but the low quality of their traditional shows prompted ever-greater audience criticism. Some villages even withheld payment in protest of their low-quality operas. Recognizing the importance of pleasing demanding peasant audiences, the troupe purchased quality traditional costumes in Changzhi City and experimented with lighted backgrounds (*diandeng bujing*). By investing in quality traditional costumes and the latest in modern special effects, the troupe finally found itself on the path to success, making its first trip to Taiyuan in 1952 and soon becoming a model for the Changzhi region.[64]

Changzhi troupe histories demonstrate that audience expectations shaped performance choices and empowered traditionally trained artists. Archival documents further reveal that audiences were willing to take violent action to ensure their expectations were met. In July 1953, a drama troupe performing in Quzhen, a town in the Yuncheng region, left its audience dissatisfied. The audience, led by the Quzhen town head (*zhenzhang*), demanded an additional performance, which the troupe refused. The situation came to an unexpected climax when the town militia commenced hurling bricks at the troupe, destroying the troupe's theatrical equipment. To add insult to injury, the troupe's complaint to the regional government was met with indifference. A similar incident of brick throwing and damaged equipment after demands for further performances occurred elsewhere in the same region. This time, however, it was a district head in the audience. But the end result was the same, as the district head had also sided with the crowd and against the troupe. Ignoring the troupe's explanation that the performance was over, the district head insisted that actors continue to perform until the audience was satisfied, even if it took three shows.[65] As these incidents made clear, the Communists could not simply legislate away audience expectations.

---

[63] While the inner workings of those eleven months are unknown, the result of the lengthy ordeal was a mixed repertoire of old and new shows. Changzhi shi wenhua ju, *Changzhi shi yishu biaoyan tuanti shigao*, 8.

[64] Ibid., 89–90.

[65] Shanxi sheng renmin zhengfu wenhua shiye guanli ju, "Guanyu xiqu jutuan jiben qingkuang de zhuanti baogao," 70.

Taikou and ticket sales

While professional drama troupes in Shanxi looked to local governments for financial support, the bulk of troupe income still came from booking shows. A handful of urban troupes sold individual tickets for shows in theaters, but this was the exception in Shanxi. Troupes performing in the countryside typically sold contracts called "stage mouths" (*taikou*), a term that emphasized the intimate relationship between booking shows and economic survival. A *taikou* contract required a troupe to perform two to three shows per day in a given village for a three- to five-day engagement. In return, the troupe received a set performance fee from the village, as well as complementary room and board; with no individual ticket sales, audience members were free to come and go as they pleased.

While *taikou* had a long precedent and had proven popular with actors and villagers alike, Shanxi's cultural leaders found this contract system increasingly worrisome. First, because *taikou* emphasized the rural audience as a collective, the system encouraged villages to demand traditional shows with famous actors, blocking the development of modern dramas, and of the younger actors specializing in these shows. Second, *taikou* placed a great deal of power in the hands of the village cadres drawing up these contracts, creating fears of waste and extravagance. Hoping to promote modern operas and gain firmer control over village finances, the Department of Culture moved to end the *taikou* system in favor of individual ticket sales. Many private drama troupes, fearing that ticket sales would bring about financial ruin, objected to this change. A Department of Culture investigation into ticket sales in Changzhi, however, argued that troupes could prosper under the new system. Cadres visiting the Changzhi Victory Drama Troupe in May 1953, for example, found that the troupe was in fact making more money after switching to individual ticket sales.[66]

For drama troupes such as the Establish the Nation Drama troupe, however, the move to ticket sales created years of financial difficulty.[67] Most troupes did prosper in the 1950s, but their prosperity was largely the result of the "rectification and strengthening" policy, which put established professional troupes in high demand. The ability to perform operas in a peaceful countryside with limited competition ensured large audiences, especially for drama troupes that specialized in traditional shows.[68] The Department of Culture, finally, admitted that in response

[66] Ibid., 65.
[67] Shanxi sheng renmin zhengfu wenhua shiye guanli ju, "1953 niandu tuanjie sheng neiwai ge juzhong zhengce de zhixing qingkuang de zhuanti baogao," 85.
[68] See, for example, Changzhi shi wenhua ju, *Changzhi shi yishu biaoyan tuanti shigao*, 97–98.

to improving material conditions and the opportunity for profits, some troupes quickly abandoned individual ticket sales.[69] The traditional preference for *taikou* style booking would remain a constant source of tension for Shanxi's cultural authorities. As was the case with local opera, state control over the dramatic realm was particularly weak when rural audiences backed traditional drama troupe practices.

Control and autonomy: transferring troupes, actors for hire, and factional divides

As repeated rounds of rectification demonstrated, the young PRC state wielded considerable influence over private drama troupes. Perhaps the clearest example of the Communists' control over the dramatic realm was the state's ability to transfer troupe members and even eliminate entire troupes. The Red Light Drama Troupe, for example, inherited members from two drama troupes that had been disbanded during the rectification waves of the early 1950s.[70] The Establish the Nation Drama Troupe gained a future troupe leader in the same fashion.[71] Some troupes were simply eliminated, their members dispersed to other units.[72]

When looking for potential state-run or state-subsidized troupes, provincial and local governments targeted the best private troupes, as had been the case when the Xiangyuan Rural Drama Troupe was transformed into a provincial-level cultural work team. A similar fate awaited the Victory Drama Troupe, one of the older and more influential troupes in the Changzhi region; one of its leaders, Wang Congwen, had even attended the Beiping Cultural Congress. The troupe was also notable for being one of the first to have female actors, and had also taken the lead in bringing *The White-Haired Girl* to Changzhi after learning the opera from a PLA drama troupe. As the top troupe in the region, rectification meant becoming a private subsidized troupe directly under the control of the Changzhi regional government.[73]

The state had the power to transfer actors and disband troupes, but performers, powered by Shanxi audiences, possessed their own mobility. Troupes constantly toured, with larger urban communities, especially Taiyuan, providing a draw for troupes throughout Shanxi. Some visiting troupes never left: one drama troupe, after visiting for two years, simply

---

[69] Shanxi sheng renmin zhengfu wenhua shiye guanli ju, "Guanyu xiqu jutuan jiben qingkuang de zhuanti baogao," 70.
[70] Changzhi shi wenhua ju, *Changzhi shi yishu biaoyan tuanti shigao*, 17–18.
[71] Ibid., 38–39.　　[72] Ibid., 161.
[73] Changzhi shi wenhua ju, *Changzhi shi yishu biaoyan tuanti shigao*, 52–54.

become a Taiyuan troupe.[74] And even in the countryside, touring troupes might seek a new patron in their host county.[75] But drama troupes struggled with a different type of movement. With quality traditional opera in high demand, the power of leading actors grew. The state pushed back against this unwelcome trend, but as Paul Clark has noted, the individual power of actors in traditional opera was one of the primary reasons that the art form proved so resistant to change.[76] Demanding high pay and exemptions from political study, elite actors jumped from troupe to troupe in search of better treatment, resulting in the widespread adoption of the "bonus system." In this system, in addition to room and board, troupe members were paid on a sliding scale based on skill level and popularity, allowing the best actors to draw large salaries for performing traditional operas.[77] The power and popularity of leading actors, of course, made the shift to modern dramas particularly difficult.

"Formalism": spectacle and special effects in private productions

While state intervention drove most of the rapid changes in Shanxi's dramatic realm during the early years of the PRC, market forces were also bringing changes to local stages. Drama troupes, for example, increasingly obsessed over costumes, scenery, and lighting. Much like their Hollywood counterparts, Shanxi's professional dramatists sought to awe their audiences with spectacle and special effects. Eager to follow the latest trends and gain an advantage in the competitive dramatic world, troupes promoted their "scientific lighting" (*kexue dengguang*) to emphasize the spectacle of performances and draw large audiences. But, for the state, this focus on costumes and effects, which cultural authorities disparaged as formalism (*xingshi zhuyi*), overshadowed the didactic performances embedded in drama, making spectacle a source of tension between the propaganda demands of the state and the professional concerns of drama troupes.[78]

Troupe histories from the Changzhi region reveal the importance of costumes, props, and lighting for drawing audiences. The fortunes of the aforementioned Huguan County People's Drama Troupe, for example,

---

[74] Shanxi sheng renmin zhengfu wenhua shiye guanli ju, "1953 niandu tuanjie sheng neiwai ge juzhong zhengce de zhixing qingkuang de zhuanti baogao," 85.

[75] Shanxi sheng renmin zhengfu wenhua shiye guanli ju, "Guanyu xiqu jutuan jiben qingkuang de zhuanti baogao," 69.

[76] Clark, *The Chinese Cultural Revolution*, 11.

[77] Shanxi sheng renmin zhengfu wenhua shiye guanli ju, "Guanyu xiqu jutuan jiben qingkuang de zhuanti baogao," 68–70.

[78] Ibid., 67.

took a dramatic turn for the better after the troupe merged with a traditional opera troupe. Part of their newfound success resulted from the influx of traditionally skilled actors, but these actors also brought along curtains and props, as well as gaslights to replace the troupe's old lard lamps. With the addition of a generator to project lighted backgrounds, the troupe staged traditional shows with the latest in special effects, drawing large audiences even after the troupe increased its booking fees.[79] By moving away from propaganda-heavy modern shows and towards traditional shows featuring expensive costumes and flashy effects, the troupe found the secret to success, and other troupes followed its lead in using projected backgrounds to please rural audiences.[80]

Peasants flocked to spectacular shows laden with special effects, filling the coffers of private drama troupes. But archival documents reveal the extent of government's disdain for "formalism." As the Department of Culture repeatedly charged, obsessive emphasis on awing audiences ruined local opera. One Yangquan troupe marred its staging of *Legend of the White Snake* (Bai she zhuan), the department claimed, by using too many over-the-top effects and props, including a huge prop boat that overtook the stage. The most common complaint, however, concerned the use of modern lighting to project images on stage. Troupes using "scientific lighting" may have thrilled audiences, but cultural critics looking for didactic performances and serious shows were not impressed. The department thus criticized a Changzhi troupe for continually projecting flying animals on stage, noting that this special effect added nothing to the opera's story. Another troupe came under official scrutiny for a fifteen-minute special effects scene that projected a wide variety of images unrelated to the story, including a rabbit giving birth. One troupe, finally, was sanctioned for insisting on visualizing all of its lyrics, so that a song about mandarin ducks would necessitate projecting ducks on stage.[81] Yet while Shanxi's cultural authorities criticized such spectacle, audience demand pushed professional troupes to embrace special effects and other "formalistic" methods that stole the spotlight from the didactic performances the Communists ceaselessly promoted.

The limits of professional resistance

As the constant sanctions and complaints flowing from Taiyuan to the Shanxi countryside attest, private drama troupes proved unruly soldiers

---

[79] Changzhi shi wenhua ju, *Changzhi shi yishu biaoyan tuanti shigao*, 117–119.
[80] See, for example, Ibid., 107–109, 127.
[81] Shanxi sheng renmin zhengfu wenhua shiye guanli ju, "Guanyu xiqu jutuan jiben qingkuang de zhuanti baogao," 68.

in the cultural army patrolling Mao's "New China." The autonomy of professionals ultimately stemmed from the love of local opera that profoundly characterized Shanxi audiences. Their persistent preference for traditional operas performed with professional flourish could not be legislated away. Fueled by audience support, Shanxi opera troupes found ways to resist the state's attempt to bring the dramatic realm under full bureaucratic control. As seen above, troupes drew most of their income from selling their performances, and thus could not favor education and propaganda over entertainment. Troupes continued to favor traditional operas and even sought out new patrons when necessary. This resistance was real, but had equally real limits.

The tensions between professional actors and the state are well encapsulated in the conflict between the Shanxi provincial government and Wang Xiulan's opera troupe.[82] One of Shanxi's most renowned female actors, Wang had represented the province in the First All-China Opera Trial Performance Convention. Wang's eponymous troupe had been touring Henan during the 1953 New Year's celebration when Shanxi's Department of Culture informed the troupe that it was slated to "voluntarily" become a subsidized private troupe under the Yuncheng regional administration. The troupe's subsequent actions, however, provide ample evidence as to how its members felt about this "voluntary" shift. Despite repeated requests for the troupe to return to its home province, Wang Xiulan's players remained in Henan throughout the spring and summer of 1953. Eventually the Department of Culture called on Lu Ruifan, the troupe's party representative, to come back to Taiyuan to explain the troupe's recalcitrance. As Lu explained, most actors firmly opposed state control, and some had even objected to Lu's return to Shanxi. The department instructed Lu to return to the troupe and press actors to make the "voluntary" choice to become a subsidized private troupe. This resulted in open conflict between Lu and the troupe, with Lu pleading the department to send an official letter to force the troupe to return to Shanxi and accept its fate.[83]

The Department of Culture, keen to keep the pretense of "voluntarism" alive, refused to send Lu such a letter. And when political pressure from Shanxi made it difficult for Wang and her players to remain in Henan, the popular troupe opted not to return to Shanxi but instead

---

[82] This was the Wang Xiulan Pu Opera Troupe, named after its famous female actor. Pu opera is a local opera popular in southern Shanxi, Henan, Shaanxi, Gansu, Ningxia, and Qinghai provinces.

[83] Shanxi sheng renmin zhengfu wenhua shiye guanli ju, "1953 niandu tuanjie sheng neiwai ge juzhong zhengce de zhixing qingkuang de zhuanti baogao," 85.

moved on to Xi'an in neighboring Shaanxi province. In the end, however, the growing power and reach of the PRC state made the troupe's Shanxi homecoming inevitable. By reaching out to the Shaanxi Department of Culture in Xi'an, Lu was finally able to create enough pressure on the troupe to force a return to Shanxi in early October, and soon the troupe indeed became the official Yuncheng regional troupe.[84] After successfully resisting the demands of Shanxi's cultural authorities for months, Wang Xiulan's troupe discovered that, in the end, there was no safe haven from the ever-increasing reach of the PRC state.

Conclusion: professional drama troupes in the PRC

Shanxi intervened into the dramatic world at a relatively early date, foreshadowing a national push to bring China's private drama troupes under state control. Other provinces moved slowly, drawing rebuke from the Ministry of Culture. Hubei's Department of Culture, influenced by the tolerant policy of allowing the artistic world to "let a hundred flowers bloom, weed through the old to let the new emerge" (*bai hua qi fang, tui chen chu xin*),[85] largely left private troupes to their own devices. But by the mid-1950s, the cultural authorities in the Ministry of Culture, calling for cultural workers to take full leadership of private drama troupes and place artists firmly under state control, pushed Hubei to intervene into the province's private cultural realm. In 1955, for example, local cultural authorities were directed to bring greater oversight to Hubei theaters and ensure that favored drama troupes received the longest contracts. Shows were to start on time and conclude at a reasonable hour, while late-arriving patrons would be forced to wait until intermission to be seated. The theater experience, finally, was to become more civilized. Not only did the ministry demand an end to the selling of food and drink, it even attempted to ban smoking and spitting.[86]

The growing number of professional drama troupes roaming the province, however, proved the greatest challenge for Hubei's cultural leaders. As previously noted, in 1949 Hubei had a limited professional dramatic corps, with most troupes bunched into the Wuhan market.

---

[84] Ibid., 86.
[85] This tolerant approach was heavily promoted by Zhou Yang in the September 1953 meeting of PRC cultural leaders, a follow up to the Beiping Cultural Congress. Zhou, repeatedly quoting Mao Zedong, stressed the importance of using traditional forms to carry new content, especially socialist realism. See Andrews, *Painters and Politics in the People's Republic of China*, 119.
[86] Zhongyang renmin zhengfu wenhuabu, "Zhongyang wenhuabu guanyu jiaqiang juchang guanli gongzuo de zhishi," 33–34.

But by 1955, the province already had sixty-six "folk professional drama troupes" (*minjian zhiye jutuan*) boasting some four thousand members.[87] With these local opera troupes increasingly numerous and ever-more popular, the Ministry of Culture directed Hubei to take control of its dramatic realm. While eschewing the term "rectification" in favor of the more neutral "registration" (*dengji*), Hubei followed the pattern of increased state supervision laid down in Shanxi. As revealed in archival documents, this Hubei registration mimicked the previous rectifications of Shanxi's private drama troupes. The Ministry of Culture first promoted the registration of Hubei troupes in late 1953, suggesting that Hubei's cultural authorities only allow troupes with proper personnel and equipment to register. After registration, furthermore, troupes were to regularly report to local governments and submit all tour plans ahead of time for approval; troupes that did not fully submit to these demands could be disciplined or even dissolved.[88]

After a year of inaction in Hubei, the Ministry of Culture formally called for the registration of Hubei's professional drama troupes in an October 14, 1954 directive. Noting that while performers ran most of the province's troupes in new-style "republic troupes" (*gonghe ban*), the ministry argued that Hubei's dramatic realm needed increased state leadership.[89] Compared to Shanxi's drama troupe "rectification," the "registration" of Hubei's private troupes moved in an orderly and systemic fashion. Following the tried-and-tested pattern established in Hubei's land reform campaigns, the Department of Culture carried out "test point" registration with three Xiaogan and two Wuhan troupes before launching two massive registration drives in 1955 and 1956. Working with cultural authorities from Xiaogan and Wuhan, the Department of Culture organized cultural workers and selected cadres into two work teams, which first engaged in a month of study.[90] Eventually, these teams divided into small work groups to carry out registration of the "test

---

[87] Hubei sheng wenhuaju, "Bixu jiji er wenbu de jinxing quan sheng minjian zhiye jutuan de dengji gongzuo" [Must actively and steadily implement all province folk professional drama troupe registration work] HBA SZ 34–2–0635 (1955), 25.

[88] Zhongyang renmin zhengfu wenhuabu, "Zhongyang wenhuabu guanyu minjian zhiye jutuan de dengji gongzuo de zhishi" [Central Ministry of Culture directive concerning registration work of folk professional drama troupes] HBA SZ 34–2–0635 (October 1954), 29–31.

[89] Hubei sheng wenhuaju, "Bixu jiji er wenbu de jinxing quan sheng minjian zhiye jutuan de dengji gongzuo," 24–26.

[90] During this education period, work team members learned policy, discussed the importance of drama reform, and learned about drama troupes. Hubei sheng wenhuaju, "Minjian zhiye jutuan shidian dengji gongzuo zongjie (chugao)" [Summary report of test point registration work of folk professional drama troupes (initial draft)] HPA SZ 34–2–0635 (November 1955), 16.

point" troupes, investigating their target troupes before carrying out educational work, explaining, for example, the significance of registration and the meaning of temporary performance permits. Registration mainly consisted of educating troupe members, coupled with gathering data concerning troupe members and performances.[91]

After "test point" registration, the Hubei Department of Culture understood private drama troupes as an important but troubled division of the PRC cultural army. Cultural workers, for example, found that not all drama troupes welcomed registration. Work groups dispatched to "test point" troupes in Xiaogan and Wuhan discovered varying degrees of reform and political awareness. According to cultural workers, politically aware artists mindful of the party's artistic wishes ran the Xiaogan Qingguang Chu Opera Troupe. For such troupes, registration meant little more than reaffirming their current practices. Other troupes, however, remained old-style *xibanzi* opera outfits with a single-minded focus on popularity.[92] Here cultural workers had to first win over artists by explaining party policies and the benefits of doing "good" shows. Visiting these "test point" troupes, cultural workers discovered that many actors resisted registration, fearing that registration represented the first step in becoming a state-owned troupe. As had been the case in Shanxi, few actors favored state control of any kind. Those actors that did look forward to registration did so in the mistaken belief that registration provided an opportunity to "struggle" their more successful peers, giving them not only revenge but leading roles as well. The tendency for some troupes, finally, to do anything for larger audiences, proved a difficult habit to break.[93] For opera actors, fame proved far more addictive than opium.

In the end, the registration drives succeeded in forcing the state into Hubei's professional dramatic realm. As directed by the Department of Culture in late 1955, cities and counties gave local troupes strict timelines for applying for registration, issuing temporary performance permits while applications were processed. Troupes provided information about members, productions, and even study habits. Successful registration required a demonstration of a sufficient number of skilled actors and musicians, as well as all the needed costumes and props. Once approved, troupes were expected to keep banned shows off their stages and report

---

[91] Hubei sheng wenhuaju, "Minjian zhiye jutuan shidian dengji gongzuo jihua" [Registration work plan for test point folk professional drama troupes] HBA SZ 34-2-0635 (October 1955), 23–24.

[92] Hubei sheng wenhuaju, "Minjian zhiye jutuan shidian dengji gongzuo zongjie (chugao)," 15.

[93] Ibid., 16

regularly to their local governments on their shows, audiences, members, and future plans. Tours, finally, were to come under close scrutiny to keep performers from using distance to escape the yoke of the state. Troupes had to submit detailed tour plans for approval and to make contact with local cultural authorities after their arrival; these local cultural authorities had to approve any changes to a troupe's original tour plan.[94]

After the process of registration came to a close, Hubei's cultural authorities, typical of the PRC state's carrot-and-stick approach to enforce dominance over the cultural realm,[95] used a system of benefits and punishments to keep professional artists under control. Troupes that performed "beneficial" shows, displayed a high level of skill, or worked with political campaigns were all eligible for rewards, including material assistance and plum bookings for large joint performances. But the Department of Culture also had the power to discipline troupes for not reporting on troupe activities for over one year, staging banned shows, contravening government policies, staging poor-quality shows, or not performing for three months without approval.[96] Just as had been the case in Shanxi, troupes were closely bound to the PRC state.

Hubei troupes ultimately followed the lead of their Shanxi counterparts and accepted the new role of the state within the dramatic realm. Richard Kraus has warned against the standard narrative depicting the PRC as an all-powerful state that easily controls powerless artists. Instead, he proposed that scholars see the story of PRC artists "as a protracted struggle for professional status and security."[97] The experiences of professional drama troupes in the 1950s reveal this to be an intense struggle with profound implications for artists. But while the state had the upper hand, artists had a powerful ally in their audiences. Despite the best efforts of cultural authorities, audiences ensured that traditional opera continued to dominate China's stages, especially in the countryside. In 1963, over a decade after PRC cultural authorities first intervened into the private dramatic realm, a frustrated Mao Zedong complained that dramatic performances still featured "emperors, kings, generals, chancellors, maidens, and beauties" instead of proper revolutionary

---

[94] Hubei sheng weiyuanhui wenjiao bangongshi, "Hubei sheng minjian zhiye jutuan dengji guanli banfa" [Hubei province folk professional drama troupe method of registration and management] HBA SZ 34–2–0635 (December 1955), 12–13.

[95] Andrews, *Painters and Politics in the People's Republic of China*, 7.

[96] The provincial Department of Culture had final say on the disbanding of a troupe, with their report forwarded to the national Ministry of Culture. And while troupes could appeal, if their infractions were serious, the banned troupe could not perform during the appeal process. Ibid., 14.

[97] Kraus, *The Party and the Arty in China*, 59.

characters.[98] His cultural army had provided the performances that informed political culture in rural China during the revolution, but audiences ultimately wanted entertainment, not education, from their operas. With political and cultural performances fused in Mao's revolution, popular disdain for his peasant characters on stage was intolerable to radical cultural leaders. The eventual attempt to overcome audience expectations, the Cultural Revolution, proved costly and ultimately ineffective.

[98] Quoted in Mittler, *A Continuous Revolution*, 79.

Conclusion

The Chinese revolution was a profoundly theatrical event. With Mao Zedong determined to use revolutionary drama to promote the Communist cause, performances by propaganda teams and drama troupes became embedded within the core of his revolutionary enterprise. Following the breakdown of the First United Front, Mao and his comrades retreated to the countryside, where "Red Drama" educated and motivated soldiers, a role they continued to play even as the Communist cause seemed doomed on the Long March. During the long fight against Japanese invasion, propaganda teams and drama troupes brought international warfare onto village stages, stoking anger against enemy forces until the Guomindang and landlords resumed their villainous roles with the start of Civil War and land reform in the mid-1940s. After the successful establishment of the People's Republic, Mao's "New China," the Communists called for a massive expansion of his cultural army, enlisting thousands of civilian troupes, both amateur and professional. Overseen by a growing state apparatus dedicated to controlling the cultural sphere, these troupes performed throughout the countryside as rural revolution came to a close and the PRC state took root.

Revolutionary dramas did not remain confined to their stages. Instead, these shows transgressed the boundaries separating cultural performance from rural and military revolution. PLA soldiers, seeing an enemy soldier execute a young female activist or a landlord rape a helpless peasant girl, attacked at these scoundrels with murderous intent, even though the "enemy soldier" and "landlord" were all actors performing for the Communist cause. Villagers watched their neighbors take to the stage to perform dramas depicting how "landlords" abused "peasants" until the arrival of Communist power allowed the struggling of these villains. The next day, audiences took to the very same stages as "peasants," taking turns hurling insults and ritualistically abusing their newly cast "landlords," reenacting last night's show. In this real-life drama, villagers acted as class-conscious Maoist peasants fighting the evils of feudal society and its nefarious forces. It was a long show. The rhetoric and ritual embedded in revolutionary dramas were essential for the complex implementation of rural revolution, but they permeated the countryside, both on and off stage, until long after Mao's death. The revolutionary culture expressed in shows like *Red Leaf River*, chockfull of class-based rhetoric and rituals of "struggle," did not die out until the Communists started to relax their grip on what was left of Mao's cultural army in the late 1970s.

In using cultural performance to inform military and political action, the Communists relied heavily on the precedents of Chinese traditions. In the nineteenth century, the Taiping rebels foreshadowed Red Drama by using music and drama to entertain soldiers.[1] During the Boxer Uprising, meanwhile, "possessed" villagers, performing as the martial gods of local operas, attacked Christian and Western targets.[2] Chinese audiences had a long history of watching operas and using operatic performances as a guide for offstage action. But for the Communists, utilizing audience traditions for revolutionary goals proved a long and difficult process. For the practitioners of Red Drama, the constant pressures of Guomindang encirclements and the horrors of the Long March skewed propaganda in increasingly desperate directions. Some Red Drama innovations, such as *gudongpeng* agitation sheds, helped motivate Red Army soldiers during the low point of the Communists' revolution. Other attempts at propaganda, such as shouting slogans at entrenched enemy forces, reveal the limitations of a cultural army in the field. That Mao Zedong, He Long, Zhang Guotao, and other patrons of Red Drama never lost faith in the power of culture testifies to how quickly the ideal of Communist-directed cultural performance became firmly embedded into revolutionary practice.

Historians have long pointed to the Sino-Japanese War as the key moment for Communist drama, arguing that the "national forms" debates in Yan'an, by pushing party artists to abandon petit bourgeois artistic forms in favor of hybrid folk styles, allowed the Communists to find the right formula to reach rural audiences. While the artistic changes within Yan'an eventually proved highly influential, propaganda teams and drama troupes outside of the Yan'an capital were too busy fighting off imperialist aggressors to follow these debates. Yet drama troupes in the field, interacting with rural audiences, could not ignore demands for local opera. One year before Mao's "Talks at the Yan'an Forum," the Taihang Mountains Drama Troupe had already formed its Shanxi Opera Team to raise funds for the Eighth Route Army. As the portly comedic

[1] Mackerras, "Theater and the Taipings," 484.
[2] Joseph Esherick, *The Origins of the Boxer Uprising* (Berkeley, CA: University of California Press, 1987).

actor Zhao Ziyue correctly predicted, these for-profit shows drew massive crowds, proving that even during wartime audiences were willing to pay for entertainment.

The hybrid styles created in Yan'an were a mishmash of local opera, folk ditties, and Western spoken drama, often scored with Western musical instruments. While Yan'an era artists pioneered this form, not until the Civil War and land reform did the hybrid forms of *yangge* and *geju* operas come into their own. Only then, with advancing PLA armies and the implementation of land reform, did propaganda teams and drama troupes actually visit the countryside in significant numbers, playing a number of important roles in the Communists' dual-front war against the Guomindang and "feudal" forces. When not conducting rear-line support, performers staged shows for their war-weary comrades and even took the surrender of Guomindang soldiers. Acting for the enemy, propaganda teams and drama troupes showed prisoners of war how to perform the ritual of "speaking bitterness," which the PLA expected its captive audience to reenact offstage in order to prove their break with the Guomindang. And when not mobilizing villagers to take part in land reform, propaganda teams and drama troupes staged shows heavy in the Maoist political culture that informed the novel and confrontational process of rural revolution.

In the ubiquitous land reform opera, constantly performed within the growing realm of Communist power, Mao's cultural army found its most powerful weapon to direct political action. Built around powerful narratives featuring evil landlords abusing helpless young peasant women, land reform operas generated immense anger in rural audiences. By watching land reform operas, soldiers and villagers learned to "speak bitterness" using new terms and concepts skillfully introduced in these revolutionary dramas. Alongside this rhetoric, new ritual forms were enacted on stage as models to emulate in political campaigns and everyday life. But while the popularity of these shows was predicated on their successful adaptation of local operatic styles, archival sources reveal that land reform operas failed to truly win over rural audiences. While the lack of entertainment options and the heightened relevancy of modern dramas during rural revolution ensured that land reform operas played to huge crowds, audiences still preferred their local operas. Only through constant intervention into the cultural realm did the Communists keep their politically charged performances on stage.

After the founding of the PRC, newly established cultural authorities attempted to bring order to China's dramatic realm. But while revolutionary drama played an even larger role in the latter half of land reform, inconsistencies and contradictions marked the emerging cultural order. Cultural leaders issued confusing directives regarding the performance of "struggle" on rural stages. The Communists instructed amateur troupes to perform high-quality shows but failed to provide troupes the necessary funding to bring Maoist drama to life. Talented amateurs naturally moved towards professional status, a move the Communists relentlessly opposed. State intervention into private professional drama troupes, meanwhile, ensured revolutionary dramas a place in the repertories of China's most talented performers. But just as had been the case at the height of rural revolution during land reform and the Civil War, audiences refused to abandon local opera, pushing back at every occasion to demand more traditional shows. Mao may have been successful in taming his cultural army, but he was powerless in the face of rural audiences.

The contradictions that marked the PRC cultural realm, especially the enduring popularity of traditional opera, set the stage for the Cultural Revolution, when Jiang Qing and her radical allies attempted to decisively alter China's dramatic landscape. But the legacy of revolutionary drama also pervaded everyday life in Mao's "New China." Taking on roles informed by Communist-directed dramas during land reform and other early mass campaigns, Chinese citizens discovered acting to be a daily routine, with the theatricality of the Chinese revolution peaking during the Cultural Revolution. Discussing the model works, omnipresent slogans, and other hallmarks of that era, Ban Wang proclaimed life in the Cultural Revolution to be "aesthetically driven, ritualistic, and theatrical."[3] Paul Clark has similarly noted that performance was one of the hallmarks of Chinese youth throughout the PRC era; during the Cultural Revolution this meant performing Maoist loyalty dances or interpreting the "official cultural canon."[4]

Steven Mosher, one of the first anthropologists to conduct research in rural China following the Cultural Revolution, was one of the earliest commenters to stress the theatricality of political life in the PRC. Writing about a rural cadre surnamed Jian, Mosher wrote: "Yet Jian was an actor of sorts. Like everyone in China with the exception of the peasants, Jian wore a mask of political orthodoxy in public, carefully projecting the image sanctioned by the state."[5] Mosher, no doubt influenced by his sympathy for Chinese villagers, need not have exempted "peasants" from the long list of Chinese actors. Sigrid Schamlzer has proposed scholars

---

[3] Ban Wang, *The Sublime Figure of History: Aesthetics and Politics in Twentieth-century China* (Standford, CA: Stanford University Press, 1997), 209.

[4] Later PRC youth performance, expressed through activities, including dancing and body building, tended to be decidedly non-political. Paul Clark, *Youth Culture in China: From Red Guards to Netizens* (Cambridge University Press, 2012), 192.

[5] Steven W. Mosher, *Broken Earth: The Rural Chinese* (New York: The Free Press, 1983), 6.

accept "peasant" as an "actor category" that became real over the course of Maoist revolution.[6] Tracing the activities of Mao's cultural army and their performances in rural China confirms that peasants and landlords were indeed roles to be performed both on stage and off. The theatrical nature of rural revolution helps explain the success of the Communists in the countryside, but on-stage portrayals of landlords as over-the-top villains was not without consequence. Those in the audience unlucky enough to classed as landlords would quickly learn that this class category was assumed to be both morally corrupt and without hope of redemption. Ultimately, however, the theatricality of Mao's China also explains how the Chinese people were able to rapidly and successfully recover from his revolution. Today's Chinese leaders may still call for party propagandists to build "a strong army" to seize the battleground of popular culture,[7] but Maoist performance is a relic of the past. Left to their own devices, the troupes that once formed the core of Mao's civilian cultural army abandoned revolutionary dramas and once again drew audiences with their traditional operas. Citizens, no longer required to act out Mao's drama, were also quick to discard their class-based identities for a multiplicity of new roles. The drama of Chinese political life continues today, but the ever-increasing cultural diversity of post-Mao China has effectively disarmed any would-be cultural army.

---

[6] Sigrid Schmalzer, *The People's Peking Man: Popular Science and Human Identity in Twentieth-Century China* (Chicago: University of Chicago Press, 2008), xvii.

[7] Huang, Cary and Keith Zhai, "Xi Rallies Party for Propaganda War on Internet," *South China Morning Post*, September 4, 2013, A1.

Select bibliography

Ai Ke'en. *Zenyang ban nongcun yeyu jutuan* [How to create rural amateur drama troupes]. Beijing: Tongsu duwu chubanshe, 1956.

Ai Zhongxin. "Xian zuo hao gongzuo ne, xian tiyan shengyuo?" [First do good work, or rirst experience life?]. In *Tudi gaige yu wenyi chuangzuo* [Land reform and literature and arts creation], edited by Lin Dongbai. Shanghai: Xinhua shudian huadong zongfendian, 1950.

Anagnost, Ann. *National Past-Times: Narrative, Representation, and Power in Modern China*. Durham, NC: Duke University Press, 1997.

Andrews, Julia Frances. *Painters and Politics in the People's Republic of China, 1949–1979*. Berkeley, CA: University of California Press, 1994.

Apter, David E. and Tony Saich. *Revolutionary Discourse in Mao's Republic*. Cambridge, MA: Harvard University Press, 1998.

Ban Wang. *The Sublime Figure of History: Aesthetics and Politics in Twentieth-century China*. Stanford, CA: Stanford University Press, 1997.

Belden, Jack. *China Shakes the World*. New York: Monthly Review Press, 1970.

Brown, Jeremy. *City Versus Countryside in Mao's China: Negotiating the Divide*. New York: Cambridge University Press, 2012.

Brown, Jeremy and Paul G. Pickowicz, eds. *Dilemmas of Victory: The Early Years of the People's Republic of China*. Cambridge, MA: Harvard University Press, 2010.

Changzhi jiaoqu zhi [Changzhi suburban gazetteer]. Beijing, Zhonghua shuju chubanshe: 2002.

Changzhi shi wenhua ju, *Changzhi shi yishu biaoyan tuanti shigao* [Draft history of Changzhi City's performing organizations]. Changzhi shi wenhua jubian, 1993.

Chen Baichen and Dong Jian, eds. *Zhongguo xiandai xiju shigao: 1899–1949*. [Chinese modern drama draft history: 1899–1949]. Beijing: Zhongguo xiju chubanshe, 2008.

Chen Houyu and Xing Shaosi, eds. *Balujun zongbu zai Zuoquan* [The Eighth Route Army in Zuoquan]. Beijing: Zhongyang wenxian chubanshe, 2008.

Chen Meilan, ed. *Hubei wenyi 50 nian* [Fifty years of Hubei Literature and Art]. Wuhan: Changjiang wenxue chubanshe, 1999.

Chen, Xiaomei. *Acting the Right Part: Political Theater and Popular Drama in Contemporary China*. Honolulu: University of Hawaii Press, 2002.

Clark, Paul. *Chinese Cinema: Culture and Politics Since 1949*. Cambridge: Cambridge University Press, 1988.

The Chinese Cultural Revolution: A History. Cambridge: Cambridge University Press, 2008.

Youth Culture in China: From Red Guards to Netizens. Cambridge: Cambridge University Press, 2012.

Cohen, Myron. "Cultural and Political Inventions in Modern China: The Case of the Chinese Peasant." *Daedalus* 122, no. 2 (1993).

DeMare, Brian James. "Casting (Off) Their Stinking Airs: Chinese Intellectuals and Land Reform, 1946–52." *The China Journal*, No. 67 (January 2012).

Deng Bangyu, ed. *Jiefangjun xiju shi* [A history of PLA drama]. Beijing: Zhongguo xiju chubanshe, 2004.

Deng Xiaoping. "129 shi wenhua gongzuo de fangzhen renwu ji qi shili fangxiang" [Policies and direction for cultural work in the 129th division]. In *Deng Xiapoing wenxuan di yi juan* [Selected works of Deng Xiaoping: Volume I]. Beijing: Renmin chubanshe, 2005.

Diamant, Neil J. *Embattled Glory: Veterans, Military Families, and the Politics of Patriotism in China, 1949–2007*. Lanham, MD: Rowman & Littlefield Publishers, 2009.

Du Runsheng, ed. *Zhongguo de tudigaige [China's land reform]*. Beijing: Dangdai zhongguo chubanshe, 1996.

Enshizhou zhi [Enshizhou gazetteer]. Wuhan: Hubei renmin chubanshe, 1998.

Esherick, Joseph. *The Origins of the Boxer Uprising*. Berkeley, CA: University of California Press, 1987.

Esherick, Joseph and Jeffery Wasserstrom, "Acting out Democracy: Political Theater in Modern China," *The Journal of Asian Studies*, Vol. 49, No. 4 (November 1990).

Fei, Faye Chunfang. *Chinese Theories of Theater and Performance from Confucius to the Present*. Ann Arbor, MI: The University of Michigan Press, 1999.

Gao, James Z. *The Communist Takeover of Hangzhou: The Transformation of City and Cadre, 1949–1954*. Honolulu: University of Hawaii Press, 2004.

Gao Jieyun. "Guanyu yinyue chuangzuo de jingguo" [Regarding the process of the musical creation] (1949). In *Chi ye he* [Red-Leaf River] by Ruan Zhangjing. Beijing: Xinhua shudian, 1950.

Geertz, Clifford. "Religion as a Cultural Symbol." In *The Interpretation of Cultures*. New York: Basic Books, 1973.

Goodman, David S.G. "JinJiLuYu in the Sino-Japanese War: The Border Region and the Border Region Government." *The China Quarterly*, No. 140 (December, 1994).

Social and Political Change in Revolutionary China: The Taihang Base Area in the War of Resistance to Japan. New York: Rowman & Littlefield Publishers, 2000.

Goldstein, Josh. *Drama Kings: Players and Publics in the Re-creation of Peking Opera, 1870–1937*. Berkeley, CA: University of California Press, 2007.

"Guanyu nongcun yeyu jutuan de jige wenti" [A Few Questions Concerning Amateur Rural Drama Troupes]. *Renmin ribao* [The People's Daily] July 17, 1953.

Guizhou shengzhi: wenhua zhi [Guizhou provincial gazetteer: Culture gazetteer]. Guiyang: Guizhou renmin chubanshe, 1999.

Guo Bing, ed. *Hongse Ruijin* [Red Ruijin]. Beijing: Zhongyang wenxian chubanshe, 2010.

Guo Tongzai, ed. *Changzhi geming laoqu* [Changzhi's old revolutionary base areas]. Taiyuan: Shanxi renmin chubanshe, 2007.

Hartford, Kathleen. "Repression and Communist Success: The Case of Jin-Cha-Ji, 1938–1943." In *Single Sparks: China's Rural Revolutions*, edited by Hartford, Kathleen J. and Steven M. Goldstein. New York: M.E. Sharpe Inc, 1987.

He Jingzhi and Ding Yi. *Baimao nü* [The White Haired Girl]. Beijing: Renmin wenxue chubanshe, 1952.

Hinton, William. *Fanshen: A Documentary of Revolution in a Chinese Village*. Berkeley, CA: University of California Press, 1997.

Holm, David. *Art and Ideology in Revolutionary China*. New York: Oxford University Press, 1991.

"Hua Guofeng and the Village Drama Movement in the North-West Shanxi Base Area, 1943–45." *The China Quarterly*, No. 84 (December, 1980).

Houn, Franklin W. *To Change A Nation: Propaganda and Indoctrination in Communist China*. New York: Crowell-Collier Publishing Co., 1961.

Huang, Philip C.C. "Rural Class Struggle in the Chinese Revolution," *Modern China*, Vol. 21, No. 1 (January, 1995).

Huang Renke. *Luyi ren: hongse yishujiamen* [Luyi people: Red artists]. Beijing: Zhonggong zhongyang dangxiao chubanshe: 2001.

Huangshi shi Xishui xian wenyi huodong diaocha baodao [Report on the investigation of arts and literature activities in Huangshi City and Xishui County]. Hankou: Zhongnan renmin wenxue yishu chubanshe, 1953.

Hubei sheng zhi: shang, wenyi [Hubei provincial gazetteer: Part one, literature and arts]. Wuhan: Hubei renmin chubanshe, 1997.

Hung, Chang-tai. *Mao's New World: Political Culture in the Early People's Republic*. Ithaca, NY: Cornell University Press, 2010.

War and Popular Culture: Resistance in Modern China, 1937–1945. Berkeley, CA: University of California Press, 1994.

Hunt, Lynn. *Politics, Culture, and Class in the French Revolution*. Berkeley, CA: University of California Press, 1984.

Judd, Ellen R. "Prelude to the 'Yan'an Talks': Problems in Transforming a Literary Intelligentsia." *Modern China*, Vol. 11, No. 3 (July, 1985).

"Revolutionary Drama and Song in the Jiangxi Soviet." *Modern China*, Vol. 9, No. 1 (January, 1983).

Kraus, Richard Curt. *Brushes with Power: Modern Politics and the Chinese Art of Calligraphy*. Berkeley, CA: University of California Press, 1991.

The Party and the Arty in China: The New Politics of Culture. Lanham, MD: Rowman & Littlefield Publishers, 2004.

Lee, Hong Yung. *From Revolutionary Cadres to Party Technocrats in Socialist China*. Berkeley, CA: University of California Press, 1990.

Lee, Lily Xiao Hong, ed. *Biographical Dictionary of Chinese Women: The Twentieth Century 1912–2000*. New York: M. E. Sharpe Inc., 2003.

Leese, Daniel. *Mao Cult: Rhetoric and Ritual in China's Cultural Revolution.* New York: Cambridge University Press, 2011.

Levine, Steven. *The Anvil of Victory: The Communist Revolution in Manchuria, 1945–1948.* New York: Columbia University Press, 1987.

Liaoning shengzhi: wenhua zhi [Liaoning provincial gazetteer: Cultural gazetteer]. Shenyang: Liaoning kexue jishu chubanshe, 1999.

Lieberthal, Kenneth. *Revolution and Tradition in Tientsin, 1949–1952.* Stanford, CA: Stanford University Press, 1980.

Lin Yinpin, ed. *Zenyang banhao nongcun heibanbao* [How to run the village blackboard-news]. Jinan: Xinhua shudian Shandong zong fendian, 1950.

Link, Perry. *The Uses of Literature: Life in the Socialist Chinese Literary System.* Princeton, NJ: Princeton University Press, 2000.

Luo Pinghan. *Tudi gaige yundong shi* [A history of the land reform movement]. Fuzhou: Fujian renmin chubanshe, 2005.

Luotian xian zhi [Luotian County gazetteer]. Beijing: Zhonghua shudian, 1988.

Mao Zedong. *Selected Works of Mao Zedong*, Volume I. Beijing: Foreign Languages Press, 1965.

Mackerras, Colin. *The Chinese Theatre in Modern Times: From 1840 to the Present Day.* Amherst, MA: University of Massachusetts Press, 1975.

"The Drama of the Qing Dynasty." In *Chinese Theater: From its Origins to the Present Day*, edited by Colin Mackerras. Honolulu: University of Hawaii Press, 1983.

"Theater and the Masses." In *Chinese Theater: From its Origins to the Present Day*, edited by Colin Mackerras. Honolulu, University of Hawaii Press, 1983.

"What about Those at the Margins?: A Lacuna in Chinese Theatre Research." *Asian Theatre Journal*, Vol. 11, No. 1 (1994).

McDougall, Bonnie. *Mao Zedong's "Talks at the Yan'an Conference on Literature and Art": A Translation of the 1943 Text with Commentary.* Ann Arbor, MI: Center for Chinese Studies, University of Michigan, 1980.

Mittler, Barbara. *A Continuous Revolution: Making Sense of Cultural Revolution Culture.* Cambridge, MA: Harvard University Asia Center, 2013.

Mosher, Steven W. *Broken Earth: The Rural Chinese.* New York: The Free Press, 1983.

"Nongcun jutuan de gonggu yu fazhan" [The development and consolidation of rural drama troupes]. In *Lun nongcun jutuan yundong* [Discussing the rural drama troupe campaign]. Wuhan: Hubei Wenlian, 1953.

Pepper, Suzanne. *Civil War in China: the Political Struggle 1945–1949*, 2nd edn. Lanham, MD: Rowman and Littlefield Publishers, Inc., 1999.

Perry, Elizabeth J. *Anyuan: Mining China's Revolutionary Tradition.* Berkeley, CA: University of California Press, 2012.

Ruan Zhangjing. *Chi ye he* [Red-Leaf River]. Revised Edition. Beijing: Xinhua Shudian, 1950.

Schoenhals, Michael. "Consuming Fragments of Mao Zedong: The Chairman's Final Two Decades at the Helm." In *A Critical Introduction to Mao*, edited by Timothy Cheek. New York: Cambridge University Press, 2010.

Schmalzer, Sigrid. *The People's Peking Man: Popular Science and Human Identity in Twentieth-Century China*. Chicago: University of Chicago Press, 2008.

Shaanxi sheng xiju zhi: shengzhi juan [Shaanxi provincial drama gazeetter: provincial edition]. Xian: Sanqin chubanshe, 2003.

Shandong shengzhi: wenhua zhi [Shandong provincial gazetteer: cultural gazetteer]. Shandong: Shandong renmin chubanshe, 1995.

Shanxi wenhua yishu zhi [Shanxi culture and art gazetteer]. Taiyuan: Shanxi sheng difangzhi bianzuan weiyuanhui bangongshi, 1989.

Shanxi tongzhi di sishi juan: wenhua yishu zhi [Shanxi general gazetteer #40: Culture and art gazetteer]. Beijing: Zhonghua shuju, 1996

Shi Man, Tian Benxiang, and Zhang Zhiqiang. *Kangzhan xiju [War of Resistance drama]*. Kaifeng: Henan daxue chubanshe, 2005.

Shue, Vivienne. *Peasant China in Transition: The Dynamics of Development toward Socialism, 1949–1956*. Berkeley, CA: University of California Press, 1980.

Su Yiping. *Mingque nongcun yeyu jutuan de fangzhen bing jiaqiang lingdao* [Clarify the direction and strengthen the leadership of rural amateur drama troupes]. Xi'an: Xibei xingzheng weiyuanhui wenhuaju, 1953.

Sun Lin. *Nongcun jutuan zenyang bianju he bianpaiju* [Playwriting and production for village drama troupes]. Shandong: Shandong renmin chubanshe, 1951.

Tianmen xian zhi [Tianmen County gazetteer]. Wuhan: Hubei Renmin Chubanshe, 1988.

Tung, Constintine and Colin Mackerras, eds. *Drama in the People's Republic of China*. Albany: State University of New York Press, 1987.

Vogel, Ezra F. *Canton under Communism: Programs and Politics in a Provincial Capital, 1949–1968*. Cambridge, MA: Harvard University Press, 1980.

Wang Li. "Wenyi gongzuozhe xiaxiang wenti" [Issues with Cultural Workers in the Countryside]. In *Tudi gaige yu wenyi chuangzuo* [Land reform and literature and arts creation], edited by Lin Dongbai. Shanghai: Xinhua shudian huadong zongfendian, 1950.

Wenyizhi: ziliao xuanji liu [Literature and arts gazetteer: compiled materials, Volume VI]. Hubei, 1984.

Westad, Odd. *Decisive Encounters: The Chinese Civil War, 1946–1950*. Stanford, CA: Stanford University Press, 2003.

Wong, John. *Land Reform in the People's Republic of China: Institutional Transformation in Agriculture*. New York: Praeger Publishers, 1973

Xibei zhandou jushe [Northwest Combat Dramatic Society]. *Liu Hulan*. Beijing: Renmin wenxue chubanshe: 1952.

Xiao Ben and Qi Shun. *Li Fengmei*. In *Tugai xuanchuanju* [Land reform propaganda plays]. Hangzhou: Zhongguo ertong shudian: 1950.

Xiao Gan, "Cong Li Aijie de yi sheng kan Hunan nongmin de fanshen" [Viewing the fanshen of Hunan peasants from the life of Li Aisheng]. *Renmin ribao* [The People's Daily], March 20, 1951.

Xiaogan shi zhi: juan ershiyi, wenhua [Xiaogan city gazetteer: Volume 23, culture]. Xiaogan, ca. 1980s.

Xishui xian zhi: wenhua [Xishui County gazetteer: culture]. Xishui, ca. 1980s.

Yang, Benjamin. *From Revolution to Politics: Chinese Communists on the Long March*. Boulder, CO: Westview, 1990.

Yeyu jutuan yanxi changshi wenda [Questions and answers concerning general knowledge of amateur drama troupe performance]. Nanjing: Jiangsu renmin chubanshe, 1955.

Young, Helen Praeger. *Choosing Revolution: Chinese Women Soldiers on the Long March*. Urbana and Chicago: University of Illinois Press, 2007.

Yuan Chenglong. "'Shuangjian' gongzuotuan zai Linshu" ["Double reduction" work team in Linshu]. *Hongse Jiyi* [Red recollections]. Beijing: Zhonggong dangshi chubanshe, 2009.

Zhou Gangwu. *Lun qunzhong wenyi yundong* [On the mass culture movement]. Guangzhou: Xinhua shudian huanan zongfen dian, 1951.

Zhou Zhiqiang. *Zhongguo gongchandang yu zhongguo nongye fazhan daolu* [The Chinese Communist Party and the path of Chinese agricultural development]. Beijing: Zhonggongdang shi chubanshe, 2003

Index

In this index, the titles of dramas appear in italics.

Advanced Position Drama Troupe, 89, 103
agitation stations, 41, 51
agrarian reform. *See* land reform
Ai Qing, 152
Ai Zhongxin, 176–177
All-China Federation of Literary and Art Circles (Wenlian), 147
All-China Literary and Art Circles Resistance Association, 148, 150
All-China Literature and Arts Worker Representative Congress. *See* Beiping Cultural Congress
All-China National Cultural Worker Congress, 112, 122
All-China Opera Trial Performance Convention, 210
amateur rural drama troupes: pre-1949
   attraction of professional status, 55, 78
   balancing entertainment and propaganda, 181, 188
   as challenge to village norms, 79–80
   competition from *xibanzi* troupes, 81
   in Jin-Cha-Ji Border Region, 73–80
   Mao's visions for, 69
   mobilization campaigns, 55, 77, 153, 179–181, 206
   rectification of, 66
   in Sino-Japanese War, 73–80
amateur rural drama troupes: post-1949
   audience reach, 199
   casting and rehearsals, 165–166
   class status of performers, 202–206
   funding problems, 197–198
   importance of Maoist realism, 166, 170–173
   local cadres and, 195
   mobilization campaigns, 5, 179–181, 188–195, 206

performance of traditional opera, 165, 201, 204, 236
performances, 179–180, 189–192, 195–201
rectification of, 201–206
reluctance of villagers to perform, 195
script creation, 157–159, 163–165, 176–177, 191, 199–201
staging amateur performances, 161–163, 166
subversive activities, 204–206
tendencies towards professionalization, 164, 174, 221
women and children in, 196
Anagnost, Ann, 13
Andrews, Julia, 146–147, 226
Apter, David, 13
audiences
   attitudes to Peking opera, 184–185
   audience reach, 60, 86–87, 199
   autonomous power of, 137–140, 142–143, 219
   effect of performances on, 2, 60, 85, 113, 117, 142–143, 179–180, 193
   effect on repertoires, 226–227
   preference for entertainment not education, 230–231
   preference for traditional opera, 4–5, 81, 137–140, 142–143, 153, 165, 219, 226–227, 231–233
August 1 Drama Troupe, 33–34
August 12 Song and Dance, 107

Ba Jin, 150
Beat the Local Tyrant, 29
Beiping Cultural Congress
   on class issues among cultural workers, 151–153
   divisive themes, 150–151
   glorification of pre-1949 cultural work, 152–154

249

CPSIA information can be obtained
at www.ICGtesting.com
Printed in the USA
LVHW082028200720
661090LV00008B/81